# Stephen:
# From the Inside Out

## By Susie Stead

IMPRESS
BOOKS

Stephen: From the Inside Out

Copyright © 2021 by Susie Stead

Printed by Impress Books, March 2021

Cover design by Lawston Design

Illustrations by e.k.mosley

ISBN 13: 978-1-911293-68-2

www.impress-books.co.uk

*For Tim, my beloved, my home*
*For Peter, Aidan and Lara*
*For Stephen*

*'In our love,*
*However little,*
*We create a web*
*Which breaks a person's fall.'*

# Preface

It is 2018 and I'm sitting in a small room attached to a public library. I'm here to register Stephen's death. It is strangely and repeatedly painful to have to keep telling people that he has died. Two days after it happened, I found myself sobbing in the changing room at a swimming pool. Grief surprised me.

The woman registrar facing me is kind and friendly as she asks me questions and fills in the death certificate. Date of birth? 3rd April 1955. Occupation?

In his whole life Stephen had only one paid job, as a road sweeper, and he lost that after a couple of weeks because he fell asleep. I refuse the description, 'unemployed'. I consider Stephen for a moment, and then I know what to say.

'Poet.'

'Retired poet?'

'No, just poet'

She writes 'poet' and then 'widower' and we carry on filling in the form, but a warm wave of pride, happiness and grief rises inside me. How I wish Stephen could see that title. He would chuckle with pleasure, or perhaps look at me solemnly and say 'Susie, I *am* a poet!'

I've kept a copy of that certificate and every time I remember

'Occupation: Poet', a feeling of gladness fills me. 'Poet' affirms what was central and precious to Stephen, his love of words, the free spirit that would not be silenced.

When I first met Stephen, this was not what I thought. When I first met Stephen, he was a 'poor soul with mental illness' who just needed a little help. And I was going to help him.

# Introduction

## Characters, Stage and Set-Up

*February 2014*

Recently Stephen watched 'One Flew Over The Cuckoo's Nest' again on TV. He tells me: 'It was good, but it disturbed me. Much worse things happened to me, Susie, much worse.'

I'm interested. I'm perched on a wooden chair facing Stephen. He is folded into his ancient armchair, wearing an equally ancient jumper, his cigarette alight, ash about to fall, and I'm taking notes while a February sky squints at me through the smoke-stained bay window of his front room. In the background, Classic FM gently hums and Charlie's claws clack up and down the hallway of the flat (Charlie is Stephen's dog). I remember 'One Flew Over The Cuckoo's Nest', set and filmed in a mental hospital in Oregon. It won five Oscars. Jack Nicholson with his arched eyebrows, wicked smile and black, wild hair, played the charismatic rogue trying to avoid prison by feigning mental illness. I look at Stephen with his untidy black hair, serious eyebrows and intense dark eyes and an image rises in my mind; Jack Nicholson's face contorted in pain as he is given electric shock treatment. It had never occurred to me before that this might have been visited on Stephen. 'Did you ever have that electro whatsit?'

Stephen drops his voice. 'I did.'

'What's it called?' I don't catch what he says. 'Sorry?' Still no good. 'What?'

He spits each word out loudly, carefully, with repulsion: 'E.C.T. – Electro Convulsive Therapy… look, it doesn't matter. You're obviously hard of hearing.'

I am not hard of hearing. He hasn't got his teeth in. I grind mine: 'No I'm not. I just couldn't hear what you said.'

'You are hard of hearing, Susie, you are hard of hearing.'

Grind. 'Ok, I'm hard of hearing, but if you could speak up that would help me. Did it help you, the ECT?'

'Most people are hard of hearing.'

'Fancy that.'

My irony and his disappointment with the human race hang in the smoky air between us.

*When I read this part back to him, he still asserts emphatically that I am hard of hearing.*

I get back on subject: 'Was the ECT helpful?'

'It didn't help me.'

'Was it painful?'

'Very painful.'

'I'm sorry. Did you agree to it, or was it forced on you?'

'Forced on me.'

'Could you give me some dates when you had it?'

'76. I don't want to talk about it anymore.'

~

In this manner, Stephen and I recorded his life, meeting every few weeks for five years, settling ourselves in the front room of his one-bed flat, or in the garden. He lived on the ground floor of a two-storey building, sharing a hallway with the occupant of the other flat. On entering Stephen's home, you either turned a slight right into the front room with bay windows facing the road, or left down the narrow corridor, passing his bedroom and bathroom before arriving in the kitchen which opened onto a small, enclosed garden, separated by a dropped narrow path.

In good weather we'd sit in the garden but our main recording took place in the front room, high ceilinged and squarish, with Classic FM in the background and Charlie the dog wandering in and out. The walls were cream, damp-stained stucco, decorated with a few framed prints plus photos, postcards and large handwritten signs fixed in place with Blu-Tack. The bay windows were covered by faded net curtains and framed by old brown curtains, which trailed in twin heaps on a floor of stained bare boards covered by a threadbare mat.

The door to this room was permanently held back against the wall by a fire extinguisher, and the door handle was used to hang the aprons that Stephen wore to protect his clothes while eating his meals. When you entered the room and faced the windows, the round wooden table where Stephen sat to eat was on your left. One space was held clear by an elderly placemat, while the rest of the surface was taken up by his radio, boxes of medication, cigarette packets, cards and photos, all of which were encrusted with bits of old food.

The table was pushed against the wall and had a pair of simple wooden chairs tucked under it. Between there and the window resided the TV, opposite which were Stephen's comfy chair and coffee table. This, too, was heavily populated: cigarette packets, lighters, two large ash trays, magazines, rotas for Stephen's carers, letters, pieces of paper, boxes of earplugs, nasal inhalers and various medications. The two heavily-laden tables were kept apart just far enough to allow a narrow passageway from Stephen's chair to the doorway.

He smoked 30 to 40 cigarettes a day, so the room was ingrained with the stagnant smell. In the ten years he lived there, the flat received one full clean.

The above is a fairly objective, observational take on Stephen's flat, written after his death. From outside-in, so to speak. He would not have liked this depiction. While he was alive, I would read Chapters back to him and either edit them or make additions based on his comments, but when I came to write this, it was too late. How would he have described it, from the inside out?

Stephen would have said his flat was 'special, very special' because he loved this flat. It was his precious home, and his front room was his safe place. The prints on the wall were ones he'd chosen and the postcards all came from long-standing friends. The pictures carefully blu-tacked on beside them had been cut out from the *Country Life* calendars that he asked me to buy him each year; prancing lambs and foxes, eagles in flight. Carers had sellotaped encouraging notes on the wall, like 'Smile Stephen – Think happy ☺', and the photos balanced on the tables and in front of the TV were of loved ones, his dog and snaps I'd taken of him on outings with my family. The radio and TV were essential: sources of information, humour and sublime beauty. What would he have done without music? As for the garden, I can tell you what he thought of that: 'a great and truly special garden', with the 'enchanting song of those ever-captivating birds, so very special indeed.'

From the outside in, this flat was in desperate need of cleaning and repair, but from the inside out it was a haven, it was home. This was the setting I entered each month, complete with my notepad and voice recorder, not just an external biographer writing about a man diagnosed with mental illness but a member of the cast, inextricably caught up in his story. Susie, the 'normal' one, unimpaired by labels of mental illness but with her own array of historical baggage, internal voices, and sets of beliefs. In this book, I keep my own name, unlike most members of the cast. Stephen wanted to remain anonymous when he was alive, and while naming and shaming certain individuals might cool my rage and offer some justice, it is probably best that all identities and most places have been altered.

It was here, in this flat, that we went back to two different beginnings; the day Stephen was born and the day we met. Each chapter in Part 1 of this book is divided into two parts, following the flow from each of those beginnings, 1955 and 2000. In Part 2, like a river with two tributaries, these stories meet and the one story carries forward.

So, let us begin at the beginnings.

# Part 1

Two Rivers

# Chapter 1

## The Importance of Dates

*'My life has been a complete and total waste of time'.*

Stephen 2013

*1955 – A beginning*

A traditional English rhyme from Devonshire declares that our fortunes are determined by the day upon which we are born:

Monday's child is fair of face,

Tuesday's child is full of grace,

Wednesday's child is full of woe,

Thursday's child has far to go,

Friday's child is loving and giving,

Saturday's child works hard for his living,

And the child that is born on the Sabbath day

Is bonny and blithe, and good and gay.

Both Stephen and I were born on a Sunday. His was even more auspicious: Easter Sunday, April 3rd 1955. Mine was seven years later, February 25th 1962. We were both healthy babies, but he was born in England and I was born in the Philippines. My mother likes to recall that my father was on the golf course at the time, and the duty doctor looked about 15 years old. The additional piece of information Stephen chooses to give me is that his birth occurred the day after Ruth Ellis was hanged, the last woman to be executed in England.

Stephen often links moments in his life with wider political and social events. He has an exceptional memory and will give me precise dates and sometimes the day of the week that something occurred. For instance, on November 9th 2013, he replied to a question I asked without pausing: 'I moved to

[Beech] house on Wednesday May 9th 2001. Twelve and half years ago today.' I had to count the months on my fingers to check. With regard to the abuse he's suffered he will add the precise time of day.

When he told me about the events surrounding his birthday, I did some research and I was stunned. He was wrong on two counts. Firstly, in 1955, Easter Sunday was on April 10th, a week after Stephen's birth. Secondly, April 10th 1955 was the day Ruth Ellis killed her lover, David Blakely; she would not actually be hanged until July 13th.

It turned out that David Blakely had regularly beaten Ruth and ten days before she shot him, she had suffered a miscarriage as a direct result of him punching her in the stomach. The jury never received this information, and even if they had, it might well have changed nothing. The defence of 'diminished responsibility' did not exist at the time. Ellis' son, aged ten at the time of her execution, was later diagnosed with schizophrenia and committed suicide in 1982.

After reading this I found myself wondering why someone with a precision memory would have chosen to align his birth with this particular story. When I brought it up on my next visit, though, Stephen told me to cut it. He didn't want it in the book. I couldn't see why, as it didn't seem to be exposing anything sensitive or awkward. I challenged him – he looked abashed and said it was because he'd got the date wrong. 'Stephen, you have the best memory of anyone I know – so you must have chosen this story. Why did you choose this story to link with your birth?'

At first, he said he didn't know, it was a spur of the moment thing, but I pushed him, asking when he'd found this information out and how he'd felt about it at the time. He recalled seeing it on TV many years afterwards and he said it had upset him a great deal.

I led the witness. I suggested that, at some sub-conscious level, Stephen had made a link between himself and Ruth Ellis. She was someone who had done wrong, and to whom a great wrong had been done, in the name of the law. He considered this, agreed and then muttered, 'I think it should be written. Hurrah!'

As an afterthought he then added that Anthony Eden came into power soon after he was born; Thursday May 5th, to be precise. I suggested Eden was a good man, but Stephen snorted with derision. 'He bungled Suez. What an idiot!' So, I asked, was Stephen linking himself with a man who bungled everything? Stephen laughed out loud. 'Yes! Bungled everything.'

Stephen was born an ordinary baby on an ordinary Sunday on 3rd April 1955, a month before the 'idiot' Anthony Eden became Prime Minister. Fortunately for Eden, no-one thought to have him categorized as an idiot and put away under the then effective 1913 Mental Deficiency Act (which repealed the earlier Idiots Act of 1886).

The 1913 Act provided separate institutional provision for people deemed to be *defective* from birth or an early age, and classed them very precisely as follows: *idiots, imbeciles, feeble-minded persons* or *moral imbeciles* (It feels indecent even writing these words). At one end of the scale were *idiots*, considered *unable to guard themselves against common physical dangers*, at the other were *moral imbeciles* displaying *a permanent mental defect coupled with strong vicious criminal propensities on which punishment has had little or no deterrent effect.*

The Mental Deficiency Act had the power to put such people away for life.

If baby Stephen was found to be *defective* then it would be a legal requirement for him to be institutionalised and his parents would have no say. At the time, Cyril Burt, a child psychologist, was appointed to ensure that all defectives were correctly identified.

I see him now, appearing out of the London smog in his silk top hat and black cloak knocking on the door of prospective victims with his bone-handled stick. He was no slacker. By 1915, over 14,000 defective children had been dispatched to residential institutions/special schools in England and Wales and this rose to over 17,000 by 1927.

If however, a child was mentally ill rather than defective, they were not recognised under British law and technically received no special welfare entitlements or provisions. The choice was either nothing or having a child put away, yet diagnosis was not simple. In 1923 London's Maudsley Hospital became the site for the UK's first state-funded mental health facility but when faced with a child who was mute and/or extremely disturbed, doctors there were often at a loss as to which diagnosis to give them.

Fortunately for Stephen, by 1955, the relatively more liberal 1959 Mental Health Act was on its way. Stephen, however, does not consider himself fortunate. As far as he is concerned, the 1959 Mental Health Act was 'a gross intrusion into ordinary civil liberties.' Specifically, his.

*The Year 2000*
*Another Beginning*

*'I've had precious little sleep – I've been up several times in the night, the rhinitis was extremely bad, Susie. You people all sleep very well.'*

Stephen is tired and grumpy. I'm reading this section back to him as we sit in the garden in July 2014. We agree that I will stop reading when it becomes too much.

~

Stephen and I met for the first time on Friday 5th May 2000. At the time I was living in a medium sized town located in the Home Counties. A group from my local Anglican church, the 'social action' group, had decided to visit 'The Yews,' a nearby drop-in-centre for people with mental health problems. There were three or four of us do-gooders/befrienders/nosy buggers (choose your epithet). I was 38 years old, new to the town and to the church. We had moved less than a year before: Tim my vicar husband, three young kids, no pets. As political and social action have always been 'my thing', I joined in enthusiastically with this project.

I remember a big old building in the centre of town. The drop-in centre was on the second floor – a long corridor with rooms off it – high ceilings, dark wood and the heavy smell of cigarettes. On a metal trolley was cheap coffee and that repulsive, but requisite, institutional milky weak tea. There were various rooms including one with a full-sized snooker table but only one room was designated for smoking, so of course, it was full. It was at the far end of the corridor down some steps.

I separated from our group and entered the smokers' room, partly for the chance to inhale. I was never able to become a fully paid-up smoker due to its tendency to give me throat problems, but I've always loved the smell.

The room was crowded and I looked around for someone to talk to. Stephen seemed interesting and sparky so I introduced myself. He was in his mid-forties, slightly taller than me with glossy black hair, alert brown eyes and a disarming chuckle. He was also articulate, and we got off to a roaring start with politics, discovering our shared disappointment with the Labour Party. Having successfully shredded Tony Blair, we stuttered at religion. Stephen held strong views and attended the local URC (United Reformed Church). I needed to be vetted. He did NOT like the evangelicals. Was I evangelical? No. 'The evangelicals' had told him that if he smoked, he'd go to hell. He'd go to hell. He blew smoke over my shoulder. What did I think of that? Hmm? What did I think of that? Did I think he was going to hell? I was outraged. I passed the test.

Moving from future to present hell, he informed me of his current incarceration at the local mental hospital.

'You wouldn't like it Susie, you wouldn't like it, you wouldn't like it.' He often speaks to me in this manner, as if I'm constantly demanding he should be grateful and outlining the wonders of three meals a day, a bed and all the drugs he could want. I found myself repeating like a parrot: 'No, I wouldn't like it, I wouldn't like it, Stephen, no, I wouldn't like it.'

At that point I'd never visited a psychiatric ward nor been in danger of being placed in one, but none of the books or films I'd read or watched would have given them a high Trust Pilot rating. Stephen was under a section 3, which meant he was held on a locked ward, but if he was deemed well enough, he was allowed out with a 'responsible' adult to specific events, hence his appearance at the Yews drop-in. I invited him to come to my church. I invited him to coffee at my house. He couldn't thank me enough.

I hadn't passed by on the other side. I was the Good Samaritan. The one who took pity on the poor beaten man, brought him to an inn and paid for food and medicine so that the recovered victim could go on his way rejoicing.

I had no idea.

*I look over at Stephen to see if he will react but, no, he is leaning back on his garden chair, cigarette almost finished, listening.*

I didn't ask him why he was under section, that seemed rude, and I didn't ask Mark who ran the drop-in. I agreed to take Stephen out the following week to have coffee at my house. It would be just myself and my three-year old daughter to greet him. Risk assessment has never been one of my strong points.

A few days later, I drove up the hill to collect him. I felt good. Nothing like driving to a 'prison' to make you aware of your own freedom. The property he was resident in was on hospital grounds and called Sycamore Lodge. It was a converted old building, standing on its own in a cheery green patch of land. I remember the wild flowers and grasses. The building was Victorian with high ceilings to trap all that cigarette smoke. But once inside, it didn't feel spacious. It is many years ago now, but I still remember that heavy door. A three-headed dog should have stood at the threshold.

*Stephen nods approvingly at this description.*

A short corridor brought you to the centre of the house. To your left was the big common room with patients ranging around lopsidedly and purposelessly, occasionally cadging cigarettes off each other. To the right, more corridor and a staff room with the door firmly closed. Just approaching the door required an act of courage. It opened onto a small room crammed with staff, none of whom offered me help or welcome. In the worst places, you can normally find at least one kind soul. I did not meet one at Sycamore Lodge. Stephen said that there were good staff members, not many, but there were people who were good to him.

I never asked the staff why he was under a section, what he'd done or even what his diagnosis was. And no official or member of staff vetted me or interviewed me or even gave me a form to fill in. Presumably he was under section for a reason? Instead, they just waved me in Stephen's general direction and carried on drinking their coffees. I found Stephen in the common room and we headed for the exit, both of us completely unaware that this was to become a weekly tradition that would carry on for nearly a year.

Stepping through that door was always stepping out into sunshine. I remember the building like a cartoon, permanently crouched under a black cloud of rain while all the surrounding area laughed under clear blue sky. We'd drive back to my house. Aiming for the kettle, I'd stride into the long thin kitchen/diner with its strip neon light, orange walls and large wooden kitchen table.

Stephen, meanwhile, would be waiting awkwardly at the door. One of the first things I discovered about Stephen was a need to ask permission for everything: May I come in? May I take my jacket off? May I sit down? May I drink my coffee? It didn't matter how many times I said you don't have to ask, he would ask. Every time. Saying the usual, make yourself comfortable, didn't work. I might go into another room to get something and come back to find him still standing there like a spare part. He said he was only being polite.

*Stephen leans forward, 'I'd been institutionalised Susie. I was always frightened of other people's reactions.'*

Every time he would have two coffees and several biscuits. After the first coffee he would always ask if he could have a cigarette please. He would always smoke it outside. And then he would ask me what to do with the cigarette stub.

Stephen's view was and is that it's always better to ask because he doesn't want to get into trouble and is worried people will 'cut up rough' with him. I disagree. I think the constant asking is really irritating. He tells me he has a right to his own opinion. End of conversation.

Another characteristic that I noticed on that first visit was a sort of verbal tic. Stephen would occasionally get stuck on a word or phrase, repeating it until some section of his brain finally kicked in and stopped it. It was as pointless to interrupt with 'I've heard you' as it would be to step out in front of a lorry travelling 60 miles an hour. You simply got run over.

He still does this. He might repeat the phrase three times or fifteen times. The more stressed he is, the more he repeats himself. As readers, you will get the benefit of an edit.

Then there was the 'apologising'. Stephen apologised all the time. He was sorry for shutting the door a little too hard – Its ok Stephen – he was sorry for dropping crumbs on the floor – It doesn't matter Stephen – he was sorry for wanting another coffee – No worries Stephen – or for spilling a few grains of sugar – You don't need to apologise Stephen – The effort to remain calm would leave my jaw aching.

I often teased him back then, telling him that if I charged him 1p for every time he said sorry, I'd get rich. But where did all this asking, repetition and apologising come from? Was it institutionalisation? Was it a symptom of his mental problems? Had some angry old witch cursed him? Or was it just a strict and polite upbringing?

At the time, his diagnosis didn't interest me. I'd read 'The Man Who Mistook His Wife for a Hat' by Oliver Sacks and 'I Haven't Had to Go Mad Here' by Joseph Berke. I'd watched the films (and cried loudly and embarrassingly) 'I Never Promised You a Rose Garden' and 'One Flew Over the Cuckoo's Nest'.

I knew enough.

I thought.

I do believe people can change, but the interesting question is, what can we change and what can't we? And can one person do anything to change another? For instance, I've spent years telling Stephen not to apologise, that he doesn't need to, that it annoys people. I know for a fact that I'm not the only one to say this to him. He hasn't changed one iota.

He points out that I haven't changed either. From Stephen's point of view, my on-going difficult characteristics consist of: poor hearing, lateness, lack of attention to detail, a tendency to interrupt him (my husband Tim would agree wholeheartedly with this), and a general lack of sensitivity.

My life in 2000 was a chaotic haze which settled around a few fixed points. Coffee with Stephen became as regular as attending church and transporting my three children to and from school and playgroup. Yet at the end of each visit, Stephen would always need to establish what would happen next week and worry about what might prevent it. What if there's a storm or there are gale force winds? Or it snows? What about flooding? Every single time we met.

And every single time, jaw set, fixed smile, with my reassuring voice, I would reply 'Don't worry Stephen, it will be fine.' I was not turning out as patient and understanding as I'd hoped I'd be, and instead of relaxing and laughing, I would double down on the 'calm and patient' tone.

I could have gently teased: why don't you build a boat Stephen, call the coastguard, ask for a helicopter? I could have added extra-terrestrial options: What if the aliens take over or my house is destroyed to make way for an interstellar bypass?

*Listening to this, Stephen laughs out loud – he particularly enjoys the idea of the aliens.*

As well as the weekly coffee session, every other Sunday I would also collect Stephen to come to our C of E church. This was harder work; for one thing an hour was far too long for Stephen to last without a cigarette, so he would have to get up, go outside and have a break halfway through. Then there were the Bible readings and the sermon. Stephen, unlike many churchgoers, was particularly attentive to the words and sentiment being delivered and was sensitive to anything that suggested he was required to forgive, or that he would be judged or might be found wanting. If he disagreed with what was being said, he would tell anyone in the vicinity, whether they wanted to hear or not.

As a result, he wasn't overwhelmed by the Peace. For those of you unfamiliar with the ways of the Church of England, about halfway through the service, the priest proclaims, 'Peace be with you' to the congregation, who respond 'And also with you'. At that point, everyone turns to a neighbour or two, shakes their hand, or kisses or hugs them and says 'Peace be with you'. On one occasion, having had his hand cursorily shaken by a couple of people, Stephen stood watching the love-fest of friends and familiars hugging and kissing one another all around him and complained loudly to me about how uncaring these church people were. I gave him a peck on the cheek, but no-one else offered and he went back to the ward offended.

*14 years later, he agrees with his past self: 'It shouldn't be like that in church'. I've never hugged him as I thought he didn't like it. This is awkward.*

*'So, are you alright about being... mm... touched then?'*
*'I don't mind'.*
*I hug him when I leave.*

At this stage, my view of mental illness was from the 'outside'. For me, Stephen was interesting and exotic. He was a fully classified, stamped and accredited 'mentally ill' person under Section 3 in a mental hospital. Fifteen years previously I'd found it equally fascinating to accompany a teenager to Bromley Magistrates Court and sit with her in the cells while she waited to be called into court. She was up for 12 counts of fraud and deception (to feed a drug habit). I remember how utterly bewildered she looked when I produced biscuits, drinks and a pack of cards as if we were on a picnic outing. I'd never been in a cell before.

From the 'inside' it wasn't so fascinating, either for her or for Stephen. What might it be like to be on the inside of a psychiatric ward – as a patient? Imagine being locked in a building with a variety of mentally ill people and a mixed bag of staff, many of whom are under-trained and underpaid. At the time Stephen was there, most patients shared a dormitory. So, here you are, frightened, lonely, struggling with feelings of paranoia and now you have to share a room with people who are delusional or more paranoid than you.

A few, I discovered, were allowed a room of their own. But there was no lock on the door. From the staff point of view, of course, that was perfectly logical. Who wants a patient locking themselves in, then damaging themselves or the property? But what about the patient's viewpoint? Think about it.

There you are at night in your room, with your regulation bed and bedside table. There's a locked barred window. The whole night gapes ahead of you. The door opens. A patient walks in. He's big. His bulk dominates your view. He stands there and stares at you. He's in no hurry. He asks – you got a fag? No. You got a fag? No. He walks to your table and opens your drawers. He throws things on the floor. He walks out. You look around. You can't find anything to defend yourself with. Later (is it minutes or hours?) the door opens slowly and another patient comes in, bony and gaunt, wearing an old towelling dressing gown. He stares at the window, takes out a comb and starts to comb his hair. He never looks at you. He walks out. Almost immediately after that, the next one slinks in and sits on your bed. His face comes too close to yours. He speaks with sudden fury: 'Punk! Punk! *Choild killer!*' Then in a whiney tone, 'Do you have a cig?' He proceeds to beg you for a cigarette for the next five minutes. If you're feeling brave, you might ask him to leave. It's still only 10pm on your first night. The only relief is that the medication they gave you earlier should kick in soon.

~

Safe in his garden exhaling cigarette smoke, Stephen agrees that the above description is not unlike what happened, and adds, 'there was a patient who used to come into my room and tell me I'd go to hell if I watched 'Sex in the City.' However, he refuses to talk in detail, 'it's too painful Susie.' He pauses and then: 'The fact is, you need to talk about the abuse.' What Stephen wants others to know about is the abuse by the staff, the people responsible for keeping him safe. He is insistent that I talk about what happened. He has repeated the stories many times to me. We will come to them later.

# Chapter 2

## First Signs

*'I've been cursed since*
*I was a little boy.*
*If I haven't been cursed by God*
*who have I been cursed by?'*

Stephen, July 2016

"The important thing is that the baby is healthy." That's what they always say. In April 1955 a healthy baby was born. In May 2000 I met a 45-year-old man on an outing from the mental hospital. What happened? Why isn't Stephen a respected historian in a tweed jacket or a poet living on wild Scottish island? Or a Francophile smoking his pipe in a cottage in the Dordogne?

*Stephen objects, 'I am a poet!' It is Spring 2015 as I read this back to Stephen in an overly warm front room, Classic FM gently humming in the background. He adds, 'The point is Susie, if I had a passport, I'd have been in the South of France years ago.'*

Stephen was born in a Southern English county to a teacher mother and a banker father. He was their first child and his mother reported later that he had been the perfect baby. He ate and slept and rarely cried. She would put him in the pram at the bottom of the garden and leave him there all morning while she got on with the chores. Picture the classic 1950s mother, dusting her neat English semi-detached while her Persil-clean baby sleeps in a shiny, high-wheeled pram beside a full, perfectly pegged washing line.

Yet there are questions. Did he sleep peacefully or did she not hear him? If he could be left in a pram all morning, was that normal or a sign that something was amiss? Stephen never sucked his thumb as a baby and he said his father reckoned later in life that that had been a sign there was something wrong. That's a new one.

Stephen's mother went on to have three more children, James, Kathy and Sarah. The family took holidays in Bournemouth, Devon, France, the Channel Islands and Spain. One set of beloved Grandparents lived in Bournemouth and Stephen remembers holidays there with a fondness that I rarely glimpse from him.

From the outside, Stephen's family sound like good, solid, English middle-class stock but from his point of view it was not so, 'There were problems.' Whether there was mental illness, he didn't know, but there were certainly on-going problems with the marriage and at least one of his siblings did not share the same father. Idyllic post-war image slips, Salvador Dali style.

Co-incidentally, my father was also a banker, who travelled around Asia with my mother in supporting role. I was born in the Philippines, the only daughter and the third of four children. We took holidays in Australia and England. By the time I was two, all my grandparents were dead except my mother's mother who we visited once every few years. My parents had servants, and I had an amah (like a nursemaid or nanny). I definitely sucked my thumb.

I ask Stephen about his family history, in case there are some clues there, any hint of something passed along the genes. Stephen knows of a great uncle who suffered from schizophrenia, and he adds that his grandmother killed herself much later, at the age of 80, apparently because 'she didn't want to be a burden'.

These could be significant as there is strong evidence that genes could play a role in conditions like schizophrenia and bipolar disorder (put very briefly, schizophrenia is associated with delusions and hallucinations while bipolar relates to extreme mood swings).

And me? My maternal grandfather had a nervous breakdown

and my paternal grandmother, just like Stephen's, killed herself, but at a much younger age, in 1964, aged 57.

*On hearing this Stephen responds with great feeling: 'I'm sorry, Susie, I'm sorry.'*

One of the reasons given was, like Stephen's grandmother, that she didn't want to be a 'burden' (on her second husband's career. It was frowned upon because he'd left his wife for her). Another explanation I'd been given was that she was already dying of breast cancer. Finally, in 2005, I found out that she'd never had cancer but instead had spent several months in a mental hospital voluntarily, before she died, suffering from depression. There were also hints of bipolar disorder, family stories recounting her effusive surprise appearances followed by long silent absences.

Despite this, neither I nor any of my siblings have yet been diagnosed with any form of mental illness.

What of Stephen's siblings? From the little that he shares, I know that James and Kathy are working and contributing members of society, both married with children. And Sarah? 'She was lovely, I always thought she was very special and when she was a little girl, when she was a baby, I used to call her fantastikabulous Sarah. She was so special.'

As an adult, Sarah became seriously depressed and aged 29 she took her own life. Stephen won't talk about her.

*Stephen has been listening intently. The room feels so quiet. He says gently, 'She was special, Susie, she was special' – He starts to cry.*

So there were family issues and maybe something in the genes. But up to a point, no clear warning signs. Stephen says he was fine until he was three years old.

His earliest memories go back a little earlier, to when he was two-and-a-half. 'I used to go to the loo and have an egg cracked up my backside. To help me "go". 1957, the same year as Sputnik.' I'd never heard of this strange constipation remedy before and could find nothing about it when searching on-line. However, I could check out Sputnik, the first artificial earth satellite, launched by the Soviets on the 4th October 1957. This was two years, six months and one day after his birth. Sputnik was a small metal sphere, two feet in diameter, possibly reminiscent of an egg shape. Stephen had chosen an event that matched the dates and possibly the image in his memory.

Stephen then recounts in a flat voice that from the same age, his mother would deliver him to the care of a taxi driver to take him to nursery. It takes a moment for me to shift from egg cracking sputniks. 'What? She put you in a taxi to nursery? When you were 2½? That's outrageous!' Stephen chuckles approvingly at my response.

For my part, I was not left in a pram at the bottom of the garden but instead left in the care of an amah. My mother told me that once when we were in Hong Kong and I was about two, she came home to find that the amah had locked me in the walk-in airing cupboard. She remembers that I was distressed, and she was upset herself, yet she did not dismiss the woman. There is no way of knowing whether this had happened regularly and if it carried on. I cannot say what effect it had. My mother tells me I was a very easy child.

By the age of three, Stephen reports that he began having problems. He became ill with rhinitis and a bent septum. The technical term is a 'deviated' septum, something often present from birth and which can cause nasal congestion and infections, like rhinitis - an inflammation of the inside of the nose. At one point when Stephen was five or six, he needed a breathing tube and he has had issues with rhinitis all his life.

I don't know what, if any connection there might have been between these medical issues and the fact that when Stephen was three, his mother took him to a psychiatrist who according to Stephen, pronounced him to be the sickest child he'd ever met. Stephen cannot tell me why his mother took him to a psychiatrist, or what diagnosis or treatment was given.

From perfect baby to sickest child in three years. No wonder people believe in curses. As parents, most of us will feel distressed and guilty and search for reasons why this has happened to me, to my child, wanting some resolution. Celtic folklore used to blame 'the fairies.' Perhaps Stephen was a 'changeling,' the deformed, stupid, or strange creature that the fairies switch with the pretty human one. It would certainly explain the frightening change from beautiful baby to unresponsive or difficult child.

Moving to a modern-day equivalent – bad science – some have blamed vaccinations for the onset of autism in children. The most prominent doctor to have made this claim has been discredited, and study after study shows no link, yet the belief persists. When a child begins to show signs of autism it can be very frightening. They become withdrawn, not responding to human affection, perhaps engaging in repetitive actions or becoming suddenly upset at a sound, smell, taste or touch. This is not an illness that they can recover from but according to the National Autistic Society, 'a life-long developmental disability.' Parents desperate to avoid such an outcome may decide that refusing an immunisation seems a simple solution.

We've looked at folklore and bad science but what about bad religion and superstition? 'Recent UK government statistics suggest that almost 1,500 child-abuse cases a year are linked to notions of witchcraft and demonic possession.'

The Church of England, the Roman Catholic Church, many Free churches and sects still perform exorcisms although I hope, only on consenting adults.

We would (most of us) discount the possibility that Stephen was cursed or demon-possessed and it looks likely that nature may have given Stephen a poor hand genetically but what about the role of Nurture?

Having apparently been declared the sickest child the psychiatrist had ever seen, Stephen was not pronounced 'defective' and put in a home. Instead he carried on going to nursery in a taxi. One childhood event that he remembers well, occurred in October 1959, when he was at nursery school aged about four and a half. Miss Sticker took his marbles off him and he 'went berserk'.

*On listening to this, Stephen nods adding, 'totally berserk!' and starts chuckling.*

She tried to explain to him that she was doing it so the other children wouldn't swallow them but it had no effect.

I tell him that my first memory of nursery school was vomiting all over the floor.

*We're laughing so much, Stephen is struggling to speak: 'I went totally berserk. They had to call the social worker, it was so bad!'*

*We laugh loudly.*

They called in a social worker but Stephen's wonderful memory cannot stretch to telling me why a social worker was needed nor what the outcome of this intervention was. Were there concerns about this child and the parenting he was being given?

It was the year of the new Mental Health Act, which began the move away from institutional care, and also four years after the 1955 Underwood Report which looked at the treatment and prevention of 'maladjustment in children.' A maladjusted child was rather vaguely defined as, 'one who is developing in ways that have a bad effect on himself or his fellows and cannot without help be remedied by his parents, teachers and the other adults in ordinary contact with him.' The report mentioned nurture in the early years as an important factor: 'People dealing with a maladjusted child will often need to seek in his early childhood for the cause of his present trouble.'

At the time the theories of psychologists, psychoanalysts and psychiatrists placed varying degrees of responsibility/blame on mothers. John Bowlby's 'attachment theory' postulated that a child needed an attachment to one significant care-giver, normally but not necessarily the mother, for the first five years of its life (the first two being the most crucial) and that if the attachment was weak or disrupted, this could result in long-term difficulties.

Leo Kanner, the psychiatrist who in 1943 recognised 'infantile autism' as a specific condition, later suggested that it could be related to a 'genuine lack of maternal warmth.'

*Stephen interrupts forcefully: 'Susie! It's the shape of the brain.'*

The term 'refrigerator mothers' followed (attributed to the psychologist Bruno Bettelheim) and the 1955 Underwood Report, reflecting on 'maladjusted' children considered that, 'there is much evidence that failure in personal relationships is the most important factor in maladjustment. The relationship between mother and child in the early months of the child's life is... of vital importance.'

My mother's memory of the 1950s and 60s echoes this. She said the mother got blamed for everything and that Dr Spock's advice (best-selling author of 'Baby and Child Care') was 'the child is always right and the mother is always wrong'. Dr Spock was actually revolutionary in telling mothers to trust their own instincts, but my mother only picked up the general zeitgeist: if there's anything wrong, it's the mother's fault.

I'm curious to know if Stephen's mother was ever accused of being a refrigerator mother. He isn't aware of it. Carol, Stephen's first primary school teacher (more of her later), had a succinct view of his mother's character:

'In this world, Susie, there are givers and takers. Stephen's mother was not a giver.'

While this is not an endearing epithet, it isn't evidence that there was poor attachment or that she was a cold 'refrigerator mother'. In the case of autism, The National Autism Society makes very clear: 'It is not due to emotional deprivation or the way a person has been brought up. Evidence suggests that autism may be genetic.'

Perhaps when we look at 'Nurture' it is useful to have a broader perspective. As well as our genetic make-up, and our family backgrounds, we're all powerfully influenced by the society we are raised and live in. Stephen was born into a particular society, at a particular time in history which was for the most part neither tolerant nor compassionate towards those who were 'different'. In 1955, homosexuality was a crime, as was suicide. Racism & sexism were normal currency, divorce was a sin and single mothers were pariahs, some of them put away in homes and forced to give up their babies.

What about our society now, with all its scientific and technological advances? How compassionate and tolerant are we?

*2000*

*Getting to know Stephen*

When I first met Stephen in May 2000, he had been held under Section 3 for over four months in a local psychiatric unit. A Section 3 lasted six months, but could be extended to a year. If the patient showed improvement, they would gain privileges as they prepared to go 'informal' (become a voluntary patient), which is why he'd been allowed out with me. Finally, on October 5th, a little over 9 months after he was sectioned, he became a voluntary patient with far more freedom. Suddenly, he didn't need me to pick him up in a car. He could walk over. It was less than a mile away.

I hadn't thought this through.

It's one thing being a Good Samaritan. It's quite another when the poor beaten man doesn't get better and go away.

*I'm embarrassed reading this back to Stephen. He is immediately, 'very sorry'. We embark on a farcical round of 'I'm the bad person', 'No, you're not', 'Yes, I am', before Stephen states with finality, 'I'm a nuisance and I harass people. Now get on...'*

Planning and long-term analysis have never been strengths of mine. Things seem like a good idea at the time and then I improvise.

At this point, I knew very little about Stephen's diagnosis. He mentioned having a 'personality disorder', which didn't mean much to me. At the time I was firmly in the 'nurture' camp when it came to causal analysis. If he'd been properly loved and cared for by his family, I thought, then he wouldn't be in this mess. And once Stephen had got into the mess, NHS psychiatric care had clearly failed to get him out.

My own experience of psychiatric care was limited. In my mid-20s (1986-8), I'd worked as an assistant at a residential Christian rehabilitation centre for women with drug addiction problems. It was a detached, sand-coloured Victorian house, pleasantly refurbished to accommodate ten women in a rundown corner of an English seaside resort. Some squatters lived opposite us, with a hangman's noose swinging from the first-floor window.

The drugs the women had been taking often masked mental health problems which we weren't equipped to deal with, and occasionally we'd need a psychiatric assessment. The first time I met a consultant psychiatrist, he rolled up one morning in an E-type Jag to assess a resident. The resident had razor scars up both arms and her acceleration rate from 'delightful human being' to 'screaming bitch' would have put his E-type Jag in the shade. He had a brief private consultation with her (she was wearing long-sleeves), gave her the all-clear and left. Two days later, from across the room, I saw her slice open her scarred arms with a kitchen knife. I patched her up, reported the incident and went home surprisingly composed. The following day my body began to shake with delayed shock. A week later, she was removed from the house, bloody and screaming, by three policemen.

Contrast that with Father Benedict Ramsden, the Russian orthodox priest who'd inspired me a couple of years earlier (1985). He shared his family home with patients, many of whom had been referred by psychiatric units that couldn't deal with them. The only time he had a violent incident, he recalled, was when he and his wife went away for a few days and the authorities insisted that he couldn't leave his teenage children in charge. They sent a 'professional' over and within half an hour the place was in chaos.

These and other experiences had confirmed my view that if nurtured properly, people would find healing. Lack of love was the cause of our problems. Love conquers all. All you need is love. God is love, God's love is eternal and for everyone, and sharing that love brings healing.

You love people, they get better.

And they're grateful.

Having lived as part of a Christian community in my twenties and found healing there, I was hopeful that our church family would help Stephen. The people were warm and friendly, the services were structured but informal in feel and the building was light and modern. The difficulty was that Stephen was… well, he was mentally ill. And perhaps more importantly, he wasn't very 'nice.'

*He agrees: 'I wasn't very nice.'*

He had that awkward, wary institutional look. He wore baggy unfashionable clothes with cigarette burns in them. He wasn't imposingly tall (5'8") but he was tense and restless. In the middle of a church service he'd insist on going out to have a fag. He'd complain. He'd hang around at the end and ask people for money, especially if the Bible reading had been anything to do with caring for the needy. Eyebrows lowered, he'd mutter dark things under his breath: 'No-one asks me to lunch', 'I thought they were Christian', 'The people who hurt me should burn forever.' He didn't ask people how they were or show any interest in them.

*I'm not enjoying reading this to Stephen – he responds sadly, saying 'My fault, my fault.' I keep repeating that it isn't, and reminding him that he was ill.*

And he wasn't grateful. People avoided him.

*Stephen takes up my suggestion: 'I was really ill.' But he adds: 'Was that my fault? I'm not saying it was or it wasn't. I'm asking the question, was it my fault?'*

No-one invited him over to their house. No-one seemed keen to approach him at coffee in the church hall afterwards. I was indignant. These were Christians, they were supposed to love and welcome everyone, irrespective of behaviour or looks. Where was the so-called Christian love in action?

I didn't have the courage to challenge anyone because I couldn't think of a way of doing it that wouldn't have sounded repulsively self-righteous. 'Have you spoken to Stephen yet? What would Jesus do? Hmm?'

This 'love' thing was not turning out as easy as I thought. As Stephen began to demand more, the compassion I felt became trodden underfoot in the battle between self-preservation and my guilt about not doing enough.

Stephen was no longer content with coffee once a week. He wanted to come over after church and at other times. If I made excuses, he'd remind me about 'Christian love in action'. In October 2000, I had three children aged 7, 5 and 3. I would attempt to listen to him while the kids fought over a toy and Tim was ensconced in his study. I felt angry with everyone. No-one was grateful to me.

Stephen kept reminding me I was a Christian, that I was following someone who preached the way of love. 'Love your neighbour as yourself', 'If someone asks, give'. I'd been a fully paid-up Christian for 17 years. What was the matter with me?

*In my mind, rather floridly, the Guilt Queen, meticulously dressed, appears; one smart shoe firmly on the windpipe of Self-Preservation.*

No-one was helping to share the load and I couldn't lift the weight.

*The Guilt Queen purses her lips:*
*'no-one said it would be easy, Susie'.*

One Sunday I was standing on the drive of our house with

Stephen. He was expecting to come in. I waffled. I fumbled. I said very nicely that it wasn't a good time for him to come over today. He wasn't taking the hint. He glowered at me, grumpy and miserable. He didn't want to go back to the hospital. It was horrible there. Horrible. Horrible. Horrible. Did I know how horrible it was?

*The Guilt Queen stands behind Stephen, inspecting a booklet entitled,*
*"Hypocrites of the 20ᵗʰ Century".*
*She holds Self-Preservation in a headlock.*

Did I know how horrible it was? Yes, I knew, yes, yes, yes of course… He pulled his trump card: 'If you were Jesus, you'd invite me in'.

*Suddenly Self-Preservation emits an elemental roar.*
*Guilt Queen is thrown. White noise.*

'I'm not bloody Jesus!' I screeched into his face, before storming off, slamming the front door and bursting into tears.

Tim, my lovely husband and also vicar of the church, offered some basic theology,

'You're right. You're not bloody Jesus.'

He then added, 'If Stephen turns up whenever he wants, you'll end up being overwhelmed and shutting him off for good and then nobody wins. Lay down some ground rules.'

*Stephen surprises me by leaning forward and firmly agreeing with this: 'Obviously, I needed some ground rules. I didn't have to go back there. I was informal, I could have gone somewhere else. There was no excuse for my behaviour. All I can do is apologise. Quite frankly,*

*I was a menace.' He warms my heart; I hadn't even thought of the other options available to him.*

Without that piece of crucial advice, my connection with Stephen would never have survived.

Then, as Tim got up to return to his study, 'and stop him ringing all hours'. Thanks. I found setting boundaries excruciatingly difficult and relied on people picking up social cues and not making unreasonable demands. This was going to be awkward. Fixed-jaw, smiling, teeth-grindingly awkward.

When we next met, I eventually got round to stuttering that coffee once a week was enough, that's what I could manage. He was not happy. Couldn't he come at other times? Erh, No. What about a coffee after church? Pulse rate rising, I reminded him there was coffee at church. Stephen kept pushing. What if he was desperate?

*The Guilt Queen appears again displaying*
*a beautifully printed verse,*
*"Love one another". Self-Preservation wilts.*

I suggested that he could ring me. This wasn't good enough. He reminded me, I was a Christian, I was supposed to help him. With Tim's voice echoing in my head: 'You'll end up shutting him off for good,' I told Stephen that was the best I could do. He started ranting: 'I'm having a terrible time. I hate it there. I hate it. I hate it.'

*The Guilt Queen towers over me.*
*Self-Preservation pushes from behind.*

Digging my heels in, I insisted, 'If I'm going to stay your

friend, this is what I can offer.' Then, remembering the phone calls, I asked him not to ring me after 10 o'clock at night, 'It's not good social etiquette, people don't like it.'

'Carol never minds what time I call.'

*Guilt Queen plants a manicured hand on my heart.*
*Self-Preservation shouts in my ear.*

'Call Carol then,' I managed between clamped teeth. Stephen had one card left: 'You're not a very good Christian.'

*Guilt Queen digs her nails in. There's blood.*
*I give up the fight and laugh.*

'Ha-ha… you're right. I'm not.'

'I'm disappointed in you, Susie. Disappointed.'

*'That wasn't right of me to say that.'*

Stephen tried ringing me after 10pm. I didn't answer. He tried inviting himself round. I said no. Mostly, I felt like crap. A small part of me felt quite pleased. It helped that Tim would have stopped Stephen coming if I didn't. He wasn't Jesus either.

When I ask Stephen about his memories of those times, he's reluctant. 'It's too painful, Susie'. He doesn't want to remember anything about that time and especially that town. It was there that he suffered the worst abuse in his life.

# Chapter 3

## Primary School and a Fairy Godmother

*'I loved school.*
*School was easier than home, obviously.*
*Obviously, I preferred school to home.'*

Stephen October 2012

The story so far: perfect baby at birth, 'sickest child' psychiatrist had ever seen at three years old and social workers called in to nursery when he was four. Did he go to a special school? Did Stephen's mother take him anywhere to help him? He's adamant: 'No. She made me walk to school when I was four years old, on my own, to cross three busy roads. I was four-and-three-quarters. The County Primary School. After I left the nursery school.'

I get caught up in the detail: 'Four busy roads?'

'Three busy roads. I was four-and-three-quarters.'

She sent her disturbed four-year-old son to school on his own? I imagine little Stephen standing by the side of the road with his satchel and lunch box and my heart clenches. Stephen says decisively: 'She was a very bad mother.' Perhaps independence at that age was considered normal back then? 'My aunt thought it was terrible that my mother made me walk on my own.' I ask him about his father's parenting and he responds with less interest; 'Average, he was average.'

*'I'm hearing voices Susie.' It is a late spring afternoon and Stephen is crunched up in his chair looking miserable. He rarely admits to the voices but I know he hears them often. I suggest we don't carry on but 'you need to write this book'. I begin to read.*

It was at this point that Stephen's fairy Godmother appeared in his life. She couldn't undo the curse on Stephen but perhaps she could lessen its power. We shall call her Carol and she was Stephen's first primary school teacher. When I first met her in 2002, I loved her instantly. Like any decent fairy Godmother, she twinkled and sparkled. Short, with wavy light brown hair, round bright eyes, a prominent nose and chin and multiple smile lines, Carol was also warm, direct and irreverent. And rather deaf. Genuinely deaf, unlike me.

*A visit to Carol - 2012*

In September 2012, Stephen, Charlie the dog and I drive the 20 minutes to her house for our inaugural recording. The low beamed ceiling, the dark wood furniture, the deep fire-place all off-set by untidy piles of cheery magazines and cushions, provide a comforting and easy setting for our conversation.

In her early eighties now, Carol's mind and memory are still sharp and she provides me with details from Stephen's early life. 'I remember Stephen very well. I remember his first day in my classroom. He wouldn't speak to anyone except me. I taught him to read.' Stephen adds, 'when I was five and a half.' He continues solemnly, 'I was reading the Encyclopaedia Britannica a lot at five-and-three-quarters.' I gape at him and repeat like a parrot: 'you were a reading the Encyclopaedia Britannica?'

*Hearing the surprise in my voice, Stephen remarks stiffly, 'Lots of children did that.'*

Carol agrees that he did learn to read very quickly but that writing took longer. He found it difficult to hold a pen.

At the time, Carol was unaware of any diagnosis or label for Stephen. No-one briefed her, gave her advice or offered support. As she puts it, 'There was just something wrong with him'. She describes how, when she sat on a chair to tell the children a story, they would all gather cross-legged on the floor in front of her except Stephen, who would crawl under her chair and stroke the stockings on the back of her legs. It seemed to comfort him, so she let him.

Stephen doesn't know what was the matter with him either, 'I used to crawl under the tables, crawl under the tables. They didn't understand, none of them, no.' In that first year, 'Young children wanted to play with me but I didn't want anything to do with them. I wanted to read my book. I stayed in the classroom and they went out in the playground playing.' He becomes more and more intense: 'I hated playing, I hated socialising, I hated, hated, hated, hated it.'

I assume he's referring to school and I joke, 'So, you weren't fond of school then?'

Stephen fervently corrects me, 'I loved school!' He repeats, 'I loved <u>school</u> – I hated socialising. I didn't like children and playgrounds and sports. I loved school. School was easier than home. Obviously. Obviously, I preferred school to home.' He preferred school to home? Why? 'I'm not well.' End of conversation. I don't get another word out of him on this subject.

As Stephen's mood dips, Carol asks, 'What would you like to talk about, Stephen?' and he puts his teeth in and begins to tell us about France and then adds: 'Mummy taught me French when I was about five years old, special, special.' Carol remarks drily that his mother was a strong woman.

When Stephen's mother became pregnant with her third child, who was born in late 1960, she consulted Carol about it. She was considering putting Stephen into care for a few months. Carol recalls this with a cool anger and my throat constricts as I listen. Carol offered to have Stephen stay with her and Stephen's mother gratefully accepted. Stephen lived with Carol for a couple of months. It was as simple as that.

Carol comments, 'His mother was not a very easy lady. She tended really to push her children to one side.' Stephen responds defensively, 'She didn't mean it.' Carol doesn't hear him and carries on, 'She did her own thing and they just grew up alongside her. She was quite good friends with friends of mine.'

After that first year, Stephen moved up to another class and teacher but he kept in contact with Carol. 'She used to take me out in her car – went to see the bluebells, went to see the primroses – picked primroses – fantastic.' Was this with his mother as well? 'No. Carol on her own and Mummy on her own. Not both together.'

Carol adds that he enjoyed teaching himself and he agrees: 'When I was six-and-three-quarters, six-and-a-half, Jan '62, I taught myself spelling and arithmetic.' He did this at school, not at home. He also began reading the kids' factual magazine 'Finding Out' at the age of nine. 'I never read comics. I hated comics!' (I feel suddenly frivolous for having loved comics as a child. I keep quiet).

Stephen describes his life between five and nine as 'fairly quiet.' What happened when he was nine?

'I became more disturbed'. Why? 'I don't feel well.'

Sometimes Stephen will go on to tell me more, but on some subjects, the door remains closed. Fair enough.

'I was a very serious child, Susie. You know I never smiled, don't you?'

'Not once?'

'Not once.'

'You must have smiled once. You've got a lovely smile.'

He does. It is full and open and accompanied by a lively warmth emanating from his eyes.

'I never smiled when I was a child. Door slamming, rages, tantrums. Very serious. Watching the news and 'Panorama' and intellectual programmes, reading books, reading heavy fiction and non-fiction books. I was a very serious child, a very serious child.'

*Stephen nods, repeating 'never smiled' and adds, 'I never ate hard-boiled confectionery, you should write that down.' He cannot abide the sound of the word 'sweet' and he doesn't like me using it.*

He insists that he just wanted to be left alone as a child. I suggest that he must have felt lonely and didn't he want to play with his brother and sister? He shakes his head and won't speak.

We pause and Carol makes us some coffee. Stephen takes his teeth out for this but then asks, 'You mind if I smoke?' and Carol doesn't hear.

I enunciate his question more loudly. 'He says do you mind if he smokes?'

'Not at all. As long as I don't have to smoke.'

Stephen, however, needs further clarification. 'You don't mind if I smoke?'

Carol confirms loudly, 'Stephen, you can smoke.'

Stephen looks around the room. 'There's no ashtray, so I can't.'

Again, Carol misses this. 'What?'

'HE NEEDS AN ASHTRAY. I'LL FIND SOMETHING!'

I shout, while Stephen apologies profusely in the background, which Carol can't hear either, 'I'm sorry, sorry, sorry.'

While people and socialising were (and are) problematic, Stephen found comfort in nature and pets. 'As a child, I never had dogs but I had mice, hamsters, cats and a tortoise.' He pauses, inhales the smoke from his cigarette, exhales. 'He's probably still alive somewhere.'

I'm confused. 'Who?'

'The tortoise.'

Stephen got a bike for his eighth birthday, and then he was off, biking in the countryside, on his own of course. Stephen loves the countryside. 'One thing I hated as a child and hate now is electricity pylons.' Their appearance? 'Yes.' It ruined the look of the land.

Stephen's mood suddenly drops again, his voice becomes a whisper. 'I can't talk. I can't talk to you now.'

'Tell me about France then.'

He puts his teeth in and begins speaking with great tenderness. 'Paris is beautiful…'

Later, Carol leaves the room with the coffee things while Stephen recovers enough to tell me that when he was nine, he won a singing competition at a Butlin's Holiday Camp. The song was 'Money Can't Buy Me Love.' He adds that he also played piano: Tchaikovsky's 'Swan Lake' and 'The Nutcracker Suite'. He couldn't hold a pen but he could play the piano? He nods. He stopped playing at around nine or ten and when I ask if that was because he'd got bored (as I did) he replies, firmly, 'No, I was too busy, taking my eleven-plus.'

Despite being 'more disturbed' during this time in his life Stephen still managed to do well enough academically to be permitted to sit the eleven-plus exam. This exam would determine whether he went to grammar school or a local secondary modern. He recites that he was eighth in the class in 1965 and 21$^{st}$ in 1966. It is the 1965 grade that matters as he would have sat his 11+ during 1966 but why did his grade drop so badly in the final year? 'Leave it.'

*Stephen interrupts gruffly: 'When I was 11, May 1966, I went to Ivy Holdman's house and threatened to jump out of the upstairs window. I was ill, I was unwell. May 66 when Sarah was born. Ivy was a friend of Carol's. They never forgave me.' I get no more from him.*

Carol returns and as I bring this recording to a close, I mention that there must have been gaps when she didn't hear from Stephen. 'Oh yes, but we knew where to find one another, didn't we Stephen?' And they smile at each other, the smile of a warm shared history.

~

So, here we have a boy who is very serious, likes facts, watches 'Panorama', reads the *Encyclopaedia Britannica*, plays piano, has poor social skills and doesn't like sports. Added to this he works, as Stephen puts it, 'like a Trojan' to pass the entrance exam for grammar school. The diagnosis is obvious: Stephen was a middle class egg-head destined for Oxford.

He doesn't sound too unlike my little brother, who liked reading instruction manuals and at ten years old preferred to stay at home for the Budget Special on TV rather than see the new Star Wars movie with me and my elder brother. He ended up at Cambridge University.

Comparing Stephen's early years with my own childhood in the 1960s, when I was living in Hong Kong, I played with classmates, I loved swimming and the sea, I read Marvel comics and watched cartoons on TV. I remember very little about school.

I had two elder brothers, but I barely saw them. Ex-pat parents didn't need to consider putting their children in care, they sent them abroad to English boarding schools, usually at the age of seven. Both of my elder brothers had been sent off before I turned three, and afterwards we saw them just once a year. It was 'normal.' I cannot speak about this with any impartiality; it was an atrocity and it took away my brothers.

Despite difficulties, Stephen remained at home with his siblings. Although Stephen won't talk about it, occasional comments he makes suggest there was an on-going involvement with a psychiatrist. However the family gave no indication to the school or Carol of any diagnosis or treatment.

It is perhaps understandable that the family chose to keep quiet. For a start there was a lot of shame and blame being bandied around at the time. Added to this, the diagnosis and treatment of children with mental disorders was in its very early days. It was not until the 1959 Mental Health Act that there was any legal recognition of a type of child who was 'mentally disordered' yet treatable. It would take some time for this to be translated into actual care and provision for such children.

Huge changes were swirling round this child as he began

his bed-time reading of the Encyclopaedia Britannica, negotiated those three busy roads on his own, and sat stone-faced watching 'Panorama' on TV. His passion was learning and he had a goal. If he worked hard enough maybe he could pass his 11+, maybe he could achieve the holy grail of grammar school.

### 2001

#### *Stephen, God and Godmothers*

In the spring of 2001, 42 years after the 1959 Mental Health Act, and 25 years after first going into psychiatric care, Stephen was offered the possibility of moving into a half-way house in the community. He just had to wait for a vacancy to come up.

By the spring of 2001, my children were aged four, five-and-a-half and seven-and-a-half. None of them was watching the news or reading the *Encyclopaedia Britannica*. All of them loved comics. They were fun, boisterous, demanding and argumentative.

> *Stephen remarks, 'Nothing like me.' I smile,*
> *'you can be pretty argumentative!' He accepts this. I don't mention*
> *'demanding'.*

None of them displayed signs of being mentally ill. Not that I was looking, of course. We lived in a vicarage, a modern semi-detached house with a colourful décor that we'd chosen. We'd over-reacted to previous magnolia walls, hence: royal blue sitting room, lime green toilet, orange kitchen. It was not a place of tidy order. Toys, school bags and miscellaneous clothing were heaped on any available surface. Fortunately, an obsession with cleanliness was not one of Stephen's ailments.

*Stephen asks for clarification here. I make a long-winded explanation which he concludes with, 'you mean, I'm not fastidious.'*

I was nearly 39, with no developed career behind me. We'd been in the present house a year and a half, moved three times in the last eight years and there was no immediate possibility of me getting a job that could cover triple childcare. To be honest, I wanted to be at home with the kids. This had nothing to do with the ongoing arguments about whether mums 'should' stay at home or go to work. I stayed at home because I wanted to, and I could.

As well as parenthood, I was involved with the church and being naturally gregarious, I invited people over. Various church groups, parents and individuals met at the vicarage. Children from around the estate appeared and played with my kids.

I also met various parents while waiting at the playgroup doors and one rolled up a cig and carelessly unrolled her life. Maggie had been into heroin but when social services threatened to take her kids, she and her partner managed to kick the habit. She was articulate and funny and I invited her to coffee, not mentioning I was a vicar's wife in case this put her off. Our house didn't look like a vicarage so I could get away with it. Maggie showed up and as we sat chatting in the kitchen, she was just asking me if I 'had a man' when her face went rigid. Tim had appeared in the doorway in full priestly regalia, ready to sail. He smiled a welcome to her, but all that came out of her mouth was an asthmatic 'fuck'! She did become a friend and I am a godmother to her daughter.

Other parents and children came and went, and then there was the Church Social Action group and hey presto, here was Stephen. However, as fast as I was 'collecting' people, Stephen seemed to be shedding them. By spring of 2001, he had become thoroughly fed up and it wasn't helping his relationships with others.

He would ring and complain, 'I'm not going to the drop-in anymore. Someone there was very rude to me.'

'I've fallen out with Rachel. She told me to stop ringing. She said she'd ring the police. I'm worried sick.'

'I can't get hold of Robert. He never answers the phone.'

The one person he never fell out with was Carol. He could ring her any time of day or night, and when he could get a lift, he would visit. I will always be grateful to Stephen for introducing me to her. When Carol and I met, after hearing I was a vicar's wife, she scrutinised me with those sharp blue eyes of hers and then declared: 'Would you be a darling and secure me a burial site at my local parish church? I want to be buried in my boots facing the hill.' Carol described her religious affiliation as 'lapsed Catholic,' and I had no idea of burial etiquette, but I agreed to try and help.

After that initial meeting, she invited me to bring Stephen over to her house for a Sunday roast. Thus began our regular trips to Carol's house. Long and low and lots of dark wood. A kitchen with every surface covered and a half-frozen chicken slopped into the sink – just how I liked it.

*Stephen is listening, remembering, nodding.*

A sitting room with oak beams and comfortable saggy sofas and an oil painting of one her blonde children, whose direct gaze unnerves me even now, remembering. And Stephen standing there every time, asking 'May I smoke?' and every time Carol does not hear and I have to relay the message. And every time she responds, 'You don't need to ask, Stephen'. And every time, I'm sitting in one of the chairs, watching his long run of ash that never quite makes it to the ashtray but Carol won't mind.

Sometimes Charlie the dog is there, on the short blue lead which Stephen will not release. And occasionally her lover, or a friend or a neighbour. If Stephen is lucky, it might be someone French.

And I'm happy. Because I'm in the house that Carol built. Because she makes you feel good. She supplies coffee, then a full roast dinner, followed by an apple crumble and more coffee. And all of this with conversation, stories, snippets of her life and favourite aphorisms:

'Darling, always make decisions with your heart, not your head. The only times I've made bad decisions are when I made them with my head.'

'I was a typist and one of my employers suggested I'd make a good teacher. I laughed because I had no qualifications but he contacted a friend and away I went!'

I've been reflecting on what it was about Carol that I loved so much: For starters there was welcome, warmth and hospitality, humour, wit and intellect. There was not a thread of self-pity. The central plank was this: acceptance and directness. There was no game-playing, no judgement, no self-effacing dishonest, English politeness. She had an unorthodox private life, but lived it with a pragmatic integrity. 'I decided I needed an affair, so I went to the party. In the last room I saw him and I thought, "he'll do".' 'He'll do' became the love of her life, but that is another story.

She was a fabulous fairy godmother to have. A Psychology Today article suggests we all need one: 'Someone who would reassure us and tell us that things were all right and, far more important, that *we* were all right.'

How precious is that?

Carol had been there for Stephen all these years. She couldn't save him from the hell of mental hospital but she could keep accepting him and treating him as a human being, reminding him that hospital was not the only reality.

There was, however, another type of hell that Carol couldn't help Stephen with, although her Catholic background would have given her plenty of information on the subject.

The phone goes. It's Stephen. There is no polite preamble:

'I'm worried sick Susie, I'm worried sick! I think I've sinned against the Holy Spirit. I'm going to hell.'

'You what?'

'Sinned against the Holy Spirit. The Bible says I'll go to hell if I've sinned against the Holy Spirit…'

'I'm sure you haven't.'

'Am I going to hell?'

'Of course not'

'How do you know?'

He wasn't convinced. I did a quick theological foray and then rang him back. I explained that it meant claiming white is black, that the Holy Spirit is evil but Stephen was not encouraged. He'd cursed God on a number of occasions and that sounded very similar to him. 'I said I hated God. I said he was evil. I'm going to hell.'

*Stephen stops me here. He wants me to know that I'd told him that God would hold him to account only for what he said out loud, not for thoughts that ran through his head. This had helped him a great deal. I have no memory of this at all.*

The phone goes. It's Stephen.

'This horrible woman at the URC upset me. She told me animals don't go to heaven. I don't want to go to URC church anymore.'

The phone goes. Stephen leaves a message.

'I'm worried sick. The pastor told me that if I don't forgive, I'll go to hell. If I don't forgive, I'll go to hell.'

*Stephen adds, 'If it hadn't been Good Friday, I'd have decked him.'*

The phone goes – it's Stephen.

'I cut up rough with a patient here. He told me that if I take my life I'll go to hell. He shouldn't say that.'

Stephen needed more than a fairy godmother to help him on this one, and his black and white response to this issue was a sharp challenge to me. In 2001 I was a fairly orthodox Christian: Jesus was God and human, born of a virgin, died for our sins on the cross, rose from the dead and was the only route to heaven. I'd stepped away from the fundamentalism of my twenties, but I still accepted the authority of the Bible, as 'the Word of God'.

I spent a lot of time telling Stephen that no, he wasn't going to hell; God loved him, Jesus had died for him and that he, Stephen, had suffered plenty enough hell here on earth. It never fully satisfied him. After all, there was a lot about hell in the Bible.

Something was niggling me. 'What if there is no hell?' My evangelical background had taught me that I couldn't play pick 'n mix with the bible, and I certainly couldn't have heaven without hell.

*Stephen growls at me. I explain, 'This was me back in 2001.' He relaxes and chuckles, 'Back in the early seventies, I was a God-Fearing Damnation Evangelical!'*

Stephen did and still does, however, have one very definite use for the idea of hell.

'I think he should burn, burn indefinitely, burn, burn, burn, burn indefinitely, he should burn indefinitely, forever and ever and ever, burn, burn in agony – that's what I think, that's what I think should happen to C*. To C*. That would be justice.'

(C* was a member of staff at St B's hospital.)

On another occasion in the summer of 2013, he takes up this theme while we're sitting in the small grassy garden of the flat, next to a large hedge which I'm hoping will absorb his voice:

'I hate C*. I hate C*. C* should burn. C* shall burn!'

He takes a breath and looks down at the ground. Something

catches his eye.

'That woodlouse… that woodlouse is more important than C\*. Is far more important than C\* can ever be. Evangelicals said I was going to hell if I didn't stop smoking. I have to forgive. I'm not going to forgive! I hate them. I hope they rot in hell; I hope their families all die and they die slowly from horrible illnesses.'

At one level, his rage made me very uncomfortable. My upbringing did not permit such expressions of personal anger and hurt. But at a deeper level, I found his honesty a great source of relief. I recognised the raw unedited pain in his voice, a guttural response to cruelty and betrayal. It helped that there was biblical precedent for such visceral outpouring of rage:

Psalm 109: 8-9 'May his days be few; may another seize his position. May his children be orphans, and his wife a widow.'

*He nods: 'That's right.'*

Psalm 68: 21 'But God will shatter the heads of his enemies, the hairy crown of those who walk in their guilty ways.'

*He's happy with this.*

Psalm 137: 9 'Happy shall they be who take your little ones and dash them against the rock!'

*'Going too far, too far.'*

For a long time, no-one, including myself, was willing to see past this roaring torrent and engage fully with the gross injustice that had provoked it. Instead, some of the Christians he met would tell him earnestly that he must repent of his anger and forgive his enemies, or he would go to hell. I could not do that. It felt literally disgusting, like telling someone who has been raped, or whose child has been murdered that they should forgive; responding to inexpressible pain not with compassion but smug, crushing dogma. And what about justice? Stephen was beginning to challenge me at levels I barely knew were there.

Stephen considered himself a Christian, but had not always been religious. His parents had done the traditional thing and sent him to Sunday School. 'I went away from God, I decided to turn against it when I was six. My parents still made me go.' When I ask Stephen why he went against it, he says he didn't like them firing cap guns in Sunday School. I raise my eyebrows, but he ignores me.

As a teenager Stephen became a 'God-Fearing, Damnation evangelical' and later in life adapted his faith to a form of Christianity flavoured with Buddhist elements. He still has a relationship with God, but it has been bumpy.

> 'It's one crisis after another. God has been so cruel to me that I lost my faith and then got it back. If God carries on, I will crack up.'

> 'On Good Friday, I had the sensation in the garden, Susie, of love from God.'

And my personal favourite,

> 'God can be very annoying.'

Back in the 1960s, Stephen was not so interested in God and getting into heaven. Back then he just wanted to get into Grammar School.

# Chapter 4

## Education and the Adolescent Poet

*'Dear Susie, In honour of survival and poetry of survival and something better than survival.'*

(in my copy of "Sorry for Your Troubles" by Padraig O'Tuama)

It was 1966, the year that England won the World Cup. In his final year of primary school, Stephen prepared to sit his Eleven Plus exam. If he passed, he could go to grammar school. 'I worked like a Trojan.' I imagine that dark-haired boy sat at an old wooden desk in his bedroom, curtains closed, concentrating intensely on his books, angry with interruptions, struggling with his writing, anxious but oh so hopeful.

We're sitting in our usual positions in Stephen's front room, Stephen with fag in armchair and myself on an upright chair holding a notebook. The recorder sits on the arm of Stephen's chair. Charlie's claws are clack-clacking, Classic FM is playing something gentle behind me.

In my mind's eye I watch Stephen sitting down amongst rows of pupils for the test, and it occurs to me that this must have been highly stressful for him. I wonder whether his family had taken him to a doctor or psychiatrist. Was he prescribed any drugs to calm him? As I'm asking this, Classic FM intrudes cheerfully with the title track from 'Fiddler on the Roof', 'Yubby dibby dibby dibby dibby dibby dibby dum!' Stephen is indignant: 'No! Why would I take drugs?' I explain loudly over 'Yubby dibby dibby dibby dibby dibby dibby dum' that children are given pills like Ritalin these days, but Stephen is adamant. 'No. In those days they didn't. There's no way I'd do that!' 'Dum dum dum dum dibby dibby dum.'

I sat my Eleven Plus in Hong Kong in 1973 around a small table in the Headmistress' study with a few other pupils. We came to a Maths problem that we'd never been taught and she explained it to us. I was confused, as this looked like cheating to me, but the person doing the cheating was the Headmistress.

Both of us passed. Stephen was very proud of his achievement. For me, it was just a test I had to do, with no cheerful outcome. It resulted in me being sent to a boarding school in the faraway land of England.

Stephen was accepted into the local grammar school and he loved it. Built in 1958, it was big, grey and modern, part of a commuter town and built close to the train station. It took up to 800 pupils. Stephen smiles at the memories. 'I enjoyed the work. I liked to stay after school finished at four p.m. I got told off when I got home, you see, they didn't like it. They wanted me to come at four o'clock, didn't like me staying there. I liked to stay afterwards and do my homework. I thought four o'clock was too early, do you understand?'

I nod. I wonder why his parents would have wanted him home, but I don't ask. Stephen has moved on and wants me to know that he only just missed being in the upper set for English. Then, 'I loved Latin. She reckoned I was one of her best, the Latin mistress. One of her best! Mathematics – hopeless!' He chuckles. 'The dunce of the class at mathematics. Dunce of the class!'

I ask him if they were strict at the school. 'Very strict. Once I was late. Once. I was warned. The next stage was to go on report. In disgrace, as it were. I was warned and that was as far as it got. Mr C…' He laughs at the memory. Stephen liked the strictness and the rules. 'Nice and quiet'.

Sport was a different matter. 'I was useless at sport. Cross-country running when those two bulls chased me across the field. You know that.' I don't, but I nod.

Did he get on with other students? 'Absolutely, I kept myself to myself.' That is not my definition of getting on with others. He agrees he didn't talk much to the other boys, but adds, 'I was good at public oration, public speaking, but you know that.' This time, I bite the bullet and admit ignorance. 'Well I've told you enough times. Public oration.'

He's in his stride now and too happy to berate me for not remembering what I am quite sure he's never told me before.

'I made long speeches at the grammar school and they all listened to me. One or two heckled me.' I was part of a debating society at University, so I assume he's talking about formal school debates, but it seems I'm wrong. 'I just made speeches in public areas.' An image arises in my mind, of Stephen in smart school uniform with jacket and tie, dark hair blowing into his intense eyes as he stands stiffly on a bench and bellows out a speech to a crowd of bewildered students in the playground.

In the background, Classic FM starts to play carols. As he muses about the students and his speeches, Stephen comments, 'I *hated* socialising. I call myself a socialist, but I hate socialising. I call myself left wing and yet I hate change.' I laugh and realise I've caught Stephen making a joke. Within two sentences, he shifts subject and mood and asks me, 'Do you like carols?' Before I can answer, he says, 'My favourite is "In the Bleak Midwinter".' I'm not surprised. His usual gloom descends, and he remarks, 'It's all my fault. My whole life. I mucked it up.' At that point, we go off on a tangent. I don't realise until I listen later to the tape, that it was the background radio that had set off his train of thought.

Eventually we return to Grammar School and to a seminal moment, when he wrote his first poem. He recounts this to me in the voice of one honouring the sacred: "The Passing of Steam". You should write that down. I wrote it. I spent a long time writing it. Four o'clock one Monday afternoon. I wasn't in detention at all. My English teacher stayed there. My English master was sitting at one end of the room and I was sitting at the other end. He was looking after me while I wrote it. I began writing it at four o'clock and I left there at half past five. I got the late half-past-five train. What a rollicking I got when I got home too! And I'd written that poem. I'd written that poem!'

This was the inspiration, the catalyst for Stephen's creative direction in life. He carried on writing poetry for the next 50 years.

I'd also written what I call 'sort-of' poetry since I was a teenager. I didn't understand what drove me, until I heard Padraig O Tuama, an Irish poet, explain that he wrote poetry to survive. This from a gay Irishman who lives in Belfast.

*I ask Stephen if he agrees with Padraig. 'Absolutely right.'*

Stephen's poems are written by hand on A4 pads of lined paper with amendments and crossings-out. Whenever I can, I type them up before they disappear into the mole hills of old post office receipts, charity letters, shopping lists and care agency/DHSS correspondence.

Certain phrases and sentences strike me:

'An acrylic sensation of despondent desperation and despair.'

'As the rain so intensely and monotonously yet
luminously falls tonight.'

And occasionally surprise me:

'The sheer ecstasy of the intrepid blackbird protruding
onto the waving branches of the tree.'

*When I read this back, a deep delighted chuckle emerges from the
armchair. 'Did I write that?' I confirm that he did and we both laugh
with pleasure.*

This passion can be traced back to that fateful day in 1967,
when Stephen's English teacher sat so patiently at one end of
the room, giving Stephen time, space and encouragement to
write 'The Passing of Steam,' a poem mourning the passing
of the era of the steam engine. Through the 1960s diesel had
been taking over from steam, and the last coal-fired engine
to run on British Rail mainline tracks would be the 'Fifteen
Guinea Special' on 11th August 1968.

Whenever I ask Stephen about grammar school, his voice
lifts and lightens. He was happy there, he liked the teachers,
he felt safe. 'I used to talk with the teachers. Once, when
I was late to a lesson, the Geography master criticised the
Biology one, saying "he made you late, he made you late." He
said he'd have a word with him.'

Even when Stephen mentioned being 'doffed around the
head' by an exasperated maths teacher, his voice was cheery
and he chuckled to himself. He particularly liked his English
teacher and recounts that he'd gone on a trip organised by this
man, to see the London Philharmonic Orchestra. Stephen
felt encouraged and cared for, 'I was doing really well there.'

Then his mood changes, 'I had a bad spell at home, didn't I?' At the end of that first year at the grammar school, his parents made a decision which blew apart his world. They moved him to a boarding school, for the maladjusted. 'I went berserk.'

Was it because he was having trouble at the grammar school? He reacts strongly, 'No! I was coping well with the work, doing perfectly well. It was the problems at home.' When I ask what the problems were, his mouth clamps shut.

Internet photos of the school he was sent to in the autumn of 1967 show a red-bricked main building with large bay windows, an array of chimneys and a sweep of lawn. It looks grander than his grammar school and remarkably like the front of the girls' private boarding school which I was sent to.

What was it like, this boarding school for the maladjusted? 'It wasn't a nice place. They used to make you do things. They'd make you go on long country walks against your will. They'd force all the boys to go on long country walks.'

Compulsory country walks were standard boarding school fare. I never liked them much, but I couldn't see why this would be a problem; 'Stephen, I thought you liked walking in the countryside.'

'I'd have preferred to go walking on my own. I felt trapped.' He adds, 'I used to cry a lot. I was homesick. Teachers and pupils didn't like it.' So, no warm pastoral support then.

As for the food, 'Awful food! Egg and chips on a Sunday. I liked to have a roast on Sunday. I used to get weekend leave or go home on a Sunday - for the day. I got a roast meal that way.'

When I attended boarding school, I accepted it as something 'everyone' did. I had no choice in the matter, and no sense that there could be any choice. I did not cry once and I displayed no signs of being homesick. The food was terrible, the pastoral care was non-existent. It wasn't a 'special school', but I meekly accepted it for four years. Recalling that time now fills me with helpless rage and nausea.

*Stephen responds with feeling: 'I'm sorry Susie, I'm sorry.'*

Apart from crying a lot, Stephen was well behaved: 'I had an excellent record, bar one incident when I got caught lighting matches with two other inmates.' Stephen laughs, 'Three of us got caught throwing lighted paper out the window. I didn't get the cane. One of the boys did because he'd rung the fire brigade! The Headmaster said to him, "I'm going to use this cane hard!"'

Like Stephen, I kept out of trouble, bar one incident where I and three others were marched off to the Headmistress for making too much noise and disturbing those revising for exams. After standing silently in the corridor for what felt like hours, we were ordered into the study and stood in a row as the Headmistress addressed each of us in turn, using personal invective to reduce us to tears. I was asked how I could be considering getting confirmed that year, when I was so insufferably selfish. Another girl, whose younger sister had cerebral palsy, was reminded of the pain she was inflicting on her already-burdened parents. I'd have preferred the cane.

Stephen says the worst part was that the education was so poor. 'I did quite well in History and Geography in the first year. In the second year, I learned nothing. It was a bad school.'

*We have a brief diversion as Stephen asks, 'Why didn't they send me to Oxbridge?' I explain gently that he'd need to have done 'A' levels to go to Oxford or Cambridge. He goes quiet and a sadness descends on us both.*

'Why did they send you there?'

'Dr S, my psychiatrist decided along with my parents that I needed to go. My parents couldn't cope with me at home. Both of them.'

It's getting late and I need to head home, but this nugget is so tempting. I can't resist asking again if I can speak with his mother or one of his siblings. The answer, again, is no, I cannot.

Stephen was sent to a school for the maladjusted on the advice of a psychiatrist but on what grounds? Perhaps because the maladjusted child was one of eleven types of 'defective' minor for whom the authorities had to provide special education. 'Mentally disordered' children were now recognised under the law but by 1967, gathering the necessary information and providing appropriate care had barely begun. In 1960, Conservative MP William Carr was the first to bring the subject of autism up in Parliament where he suggested the government should be at the forefront of:

'the work on causes and treatment of so-called autistic
– sometimes called schizoid, sometimes psychotic –
children, which is almost unknown territory.'

In 1962, a group of parents looking for more research and support for their children, formed 'The Society for Psychotic children,' before opting for the less terrifying, 'The Society for Autistic Children.' By late 1963, a Special Education

Sub-Committee attempted to define autism thus: 'Autistic is the name now given to severely disturbed psychotic children suffering from a form of childhood schizophrenia. They are unresponsive, withdrawn, non-communicating children who live in a dream world and are unable to form or sustain relationships with people...' A report in 1966 on children showing autistic traits, recommended small-scale, family-type units with behavioral and speech therapies available, rather than large institutions.

That would have been nice.

We do not know what diagnosis the psychiatrist gave Stephen's parents. Perhaps the school for the maladjusted was all that was available at the time. As far as any diagnosis of autism was concerned, it was not officially listed in the UK as a disability requiring special education until 1970 when Stephen was 15 years old. Stephen himself would have to wait much longer to be diagnosed.

### 2001

*Moving Town and a New Diagnosis*

In April 2001 Stephen was finally offered a place in a half-way house in another town, and on 9th May 2001, he left the psychiatric ward (hurrah!). As a result of moving town, he also moved health authorities for the first time in 25 years and this prompted a review of his diagnosis. In February

2002, at the age of 47, Stephen was finally diagnosed as having Asperger syndrome which is on the autistic spectrum. This was in addition to other diagnoses of which he had only disclosed 'personality disorder' to me.

By 2002, there had been extraordinary strides in the understanding of autism. There had also been an exponential rise in the number of children and adults diagnosed with the condition. The Society for Autistic Children had become The National Autistic Society and was now 40 years old.

In 2000, the fourth addition of the bible of diagnosis, the American Psychiatric Association 'Diagnostic and statistical manual of mental disorders' (4th ed., rev) recognised that autism related to persistent difficulties with social communication and social interaction together with repetitive patterns of behaviour, interests and activities. Autism was also associated with delays in cognitive and speech development whereas people diagnosed with Asperger's syndrome could be highly intelligent with a very able grasp of language.

I personally like the simpler explanation that the Autism Society gives for those with Asperger Syndrome. They, 'see, hear and feel the world differently to other people.'

This diagnosis finally helped Stephen make sense of his own behaviour. At the time I was unaware of the National Autistic Society, understood very little about the condition and didn't recognise the need to find out more. By now I also reckoned I'd done a good stint supporting Stephen and after he moved, I wasn't expecting to carry on. Life was opening up for Stephen now and it was also opening up for me. I'd finally found my own creative drive.

As a lover of drama, I'd recently helped the church youth club with some drama sketches and what came next was not so much a 'desire to write' as the feeling of being picked up and hurled into writing. I signed up for an evening course and dreamt of becoming the next Tom Stoppard – meanwhile, Stephen would conveniently get better and live happily ever after.

*Stephen interrupts brusquely: 'You were wrong.'*

He had freedom now, a new life, possibilities for voluntary work, it was all going to be good.

*Stephen glares at me, his eyebrows heavy.*

Stephen was initially happy with his new residence.

*'I was not!' I compare it with being on a psychiatric ward and eventually we agree that the new set-up was 'so-so'.*

Stephen carried on ringing me and asked me to visit him, so I went, thinking this would all tail off in time. Beech House was a semi-detached Victorian building just off a ring road and I parked in the home's small car park facing the conservatory. Through the clouds of cigarette smoke, I could see the patients sitting in comfy chairs. The place felt much more open and friendly than Sycamore Lodge.

Stephen was regularly attending a couple of day centres, went to a local URC church, had signed up for various courses (one was the history of 'The Beatles') and had started talking about doing voluntary work. It was all sounding positive. He wanted to work with animals. As he said with regularity to me (with no heart-warming exceptions), 'I hate people, but I love animals.'

He may have hated 'people' in general, but some he managed to put up with; single women in particular. They certainly liked him. He complained to me about one woman who kept demanding chocolates and flowers from him. He was as ever, short of money and needed every penny for cigarettes. Consequently, he thought she was being very unreasonable.

While Stephen was taking his medication and going along to day centres to enjoy the music of The Beatles, nothing expressly therapeutic appeared to be on offer.

*Stephen remarks, 'I was offered therapy. I didn't properly get it. It was no good'. When I try to find out more, he clams up.*

There was no sense of him being helped to develop, or move on. While I was diving into evening classes and writing intense early scripts, Stephen could have been attending poetry classes, learning French, how to use a computer or the ins and outs of animal husbandry. A course on social skills would have done him no harm. In 2001 was there no money in the council budget for this, or was there no expectation that after 25 years inside psychiatric wards, Stephen might benefit from some proper input?

I'd assumed that once he got out of the mental hospital hell hole and into normal living, Stephen would feel happier and behave better. As someone who'd lived in many different places during my life, I didn't recognise how overwhelming he would find it to move somewhere new after 25 years, let alone after leaving a psychiatric institution. On top of this, Stephen was also dealing with a whole new diagnosis of Asperger syndrome.

Very soon, the cracks began to show. There were issues at

Beech House and also Stephen didn't feel cared for in the new URC church. He tried another church but didn't like that either. He started having problems at the day centres. The pressure was building up. Stephen says that people would 'cut up rough' with him. On one occasion Stephen rang me up in a state. Earlier that day, while in town, he'd gone to the local public phone booth (remember them?). He was in a hurry to make a phone call and then get to the chemist before it closed. The large bloke in the phone box was not in a hurry. Stephen had all the patience of a black rhino, combined with the self-preservation skills of a lemming.

*I feel the glare from the chair. He reminds me that he's autistic, and we agree that he can lack empathy, and struggles with communication.*

He started banging on the phone booth, telling the bloke to hurry up. The response was an abusive tirade. Stephen shouted back and walked off. A few minutes later, returning from the chemist, he met the bloke on the street and it kicked off again. The man threatened him and wouldn't leave until a woman shouted at them both to stop the racket. What did Stephen do? He rang the police. Presumably from the phone box.

*I smile at Stephen. He doesn't smile back.*

Eventually Stephen was banned from one of the day centres after falling out with a number of people. He also fell out with staff at Beech House.

Possibly his greatest fear was (and is) being sent back to mental hospital. Those in charge at Beech House thought they could use this to control his behaviour, so the sword of

Damocles was constantly held above his head.

*he nods approvingly at this phrase.*

A 'behavioural contract with staff and residents' was signed by Stephen on 29th May 2001 and states (spelling as original - this document was handwritten in capital letters):

## *Code of conduct relating to the following:*
1. Use of residents pay phone - at all times Stephen to be aware and responsive to the rights of other residents waiting for the phone. This is especially important between 6pm and 8pm. During this time Stephen should limit his calls to one or two only (depending on que) and for max 5 mins.

2. Time spent away from home – at all times Stephen will negotiate with staff the length of time he wishes to be away.

3. Inter-action with others – at all times Stephen will inter-act with staff and residents in a reasonable way (ie looking to negotiate and to compromise if possible) without resorting to any sort of aggression.

NB: Stephen has been made aware of the consequences of any violent behaviour ie: 1) return to psychiatric ward 2) Police involvement and risk of prosecution

*Signed and dated 29-5.01*

It didn't work.

He would ring me in a state. 'Susie, they've told me this is my last chance, my last chance. If I'm difficult again they say they'll send me back to Sycamore Lodge.' I was angry with both Stephen and the half-way house.

*Stephen stiffens at this: 'It's not my fault!'*
*I waffle uselessly – 'No, I'm sorry, it's just that, that's what I felt back then, um, I...'*
*Stephen interrupts: 'Go on!' I return to the text, feeling exposed.*

If I could see that his aggressive anger stemmed from fear, then why couldn't trained staff? Threatening him with another section only increased the fear and led to more anger. How could they be so stupid and patronising?

*'Quite right!' Stephen is listening intently. I feel embarrassed to read him the next bit, but I do. My turn to act the lemming.*

I was also angry with Stephen. Why couldn't he be a bit more 'reasonable'? Or at least willing to make some compromises to avoid these threats? He was so intolerant.

*I stop and wait. Stephen replies with straightforward clarity: 'I was given so little help. That's why I was being so difficult. You couldn't see that.'*

Despite powerful motivation to do so, Stephen was unable to moderate his behaviour. There was much I didn't understand at the time. For instance, anxiety is a real difficulty for many autistic people particularly in social situations or when facing change. The National Autistic Society explains: 'It is very important that autistic people learn to recognise their triggers and find coping mechanisms to help reduce their anxiety. However, many autistic people have difficulty recognising and regulating their emotions.' I didn't 'get' this back then but what about the staff at the half-way house? Why did they not understand this? Stephen had certainly escaped the hell hole of the psychiatric ward but was Community Care going to give him the support he needed? On first indications, it seemed not.

# Chapter 5

## Keeping a Stiff upper lip

*'A person who is said to have a stiff upper lip displays*
*fortitude and stoicism in the face of adversity, or exercises*
*great self-restraint in the expression of emotion.'*

Wikipedia

In the summer of 1977, I was 15 and enjoying school holidays in Hong Kong with my father and younger brother (aged nine). In the early hours of one Sunday morning, three men broke into our house. A stranger appeared in my bedroom and pulled me from my bed, and as I was led across the landing, in the shadowy light I glimpsed someone else with my brother. They brought us into my father's bedroom, where a third man was demanding money from him. The men had what looked like screwdrivers or wrenches as weapons and my father, terrified, had opened his wall-safe to show them he had nothing else to give. Once they had whatever money my father could find, they hog-tied him, tied my brother and I up by our hands and feet, laid us on the king-sized bed, put pillows over our heads and, after ransacking the house, left.

The three of us did what we were told without question. My one act of rebellion was to tense my wrists as they tied me up. After the burglars had gone, I finally managed to untie myself just as one of the servants came in and found us (yes, we had servants) when they arrived in the morning. Later, after the police visit, 'You were lucky, these were professional burglars,' my father and brother stayed at home while I insisted on going on a planned boat trip with family friends. By the end of the trip, I was blind drunk, swearing at everyone and incapable of standing up, something I'd never done before and felt very ashamed of afterwards.

The following day, my brother and I were taken to a police station to stare at rows of photos of Chinese men to identify the intruders. I was hungover, my brother was just about to go down with mumps and identifying people is hard enough without crossing ethnic boundaries. No-one was ever brought to trial. My memory of my father's response to the burglary was him declaring: 'Thank God I had some cash to give them.' He then installed a solid metal door halfway up the stairs.

Nobody hurt, solid metal door in place, trauma sorted. For 40 years, we never spoke about this incident. We kept the great British Stiff Upper Lip.

My father is dead now, but recently when I raised the matter with my younger brother and mother, my brother remarked that we'd all been fine, so what was there to talk about? My mother remembered that I'd handled it all very calmly, and had assumed there was no problem.

No Problem.

My 15-year old self had agreed. I had not been raped, assaulted or maimed, so what was there to complain about? My body said otherwise. On the quiet, I spent the following few years regularly waking up in the night, frozen with fear that someone was in the bedroom. Eventually I would force myself to edge my hand almost imperceptibly towards the bedside light before switching it on. I was so ashamed of having these 'girly hysterical' feelings that I didn't tell anyone.

No harm done. No problem. As a postscript, a short while after our burglary, a similar burglary took place at a house up the road. This time they murdered the inhabitants.

While I was taught from early on to hide emotions, Stephen never learned how to do this. Perhaps it wasn't possible for him. Having been sent to the school for the maladjusted in 1967, he was utterly miserable and he let his parents know. He openly cried, was homesick and went home as often as he could.

During that time, he had one brief moment of relief. In the Easter Holidays of 1969, he says, 'My mother took me to Paris on my 14th Birthday. For the day. All around Paris. It was a lovely day, it was a lovely day, Susie, it was a beautiful day.' Was it just the two of them? 'Yes, a lovely day.'

This was one of the happiest days of Stephen's life.

After two years of misery, in the summer of 1969, Stephen's parents took him out of the school for the maladjusted and moved him back to mainstream education. So, was he 'better'? Had the school for the maladjusted 'worked'?

Stephen replies abruptly, 'No, it didn't. The school thought my parents were mad to take me out of it. I wanted to get away from it. I hated it. My parents took me out because I hated it.'

He hated it, he let his parents know and they responded. Wow. My brothers and I all hated our schools but were unaware either that we could complain or that it might make a difference. I did move to a different school in the sixth form, but only because most of my year group were already doing so. I still have the carefully crafted letter to my father, explaining how it would be much better for my academic advancement to go to an all-boys school where they admitted girls to the sixth form.

Stephen's parents even gave him the choice of where to move to. He'd lost his place at the grammar school, so there was either the Catholic school or the local comprehensive. He chose the latter, built in 1955, with large characterless classrooms and huge windows.

Even for a socially adept child, changing school at this stage is a challenge. Stephen was a vulnerable, sensitive lad with very poor social skills, who had been moved three times in four years between the ages of 11 and 14. Not only that, but he'd studied so hard for a place at the prized grammar school and then had it taken from him. Now he'd spent 2 crucial years unhappy and making little academic progress. How was he supposed to settle somewhere else, let alone succeed in his 'O' levels?

'My parents ruined my education by sending me to the special school, ruined my chances and then ruined my chances again… ruined my chances. They were so selfish.'

Because, just when it seemed things couldn't get worse…

*Stephen is listening intently and immediately delivers the punchline: 'My parents split up'*

It was early 1970, a few months before the Tories came into power and Stephen was still 14. His parents had a massive argument – 'the big Friday night row', as Stephen called it, and after that they decided to separate. Stephen says no more so I ask: 'Did that upset you?' He looks at me, incredulous: 'It affected my whole life.'

He tells me I sound like Jeremy Paxman (an abrasive BBC interviewer).

In September 1975, when I was 13 years old and Labour was in power, my parents also separated. There were no arguments and I had no idea this was coming. My parents chose the last night of the holidays to tell me. My father explained that I'd have two homes now, while my mother sat on the bed next to me and cried. They told me not to share this news with my younger brother who was 7 years old at the time. The school was informed but no-one there spoke to me about it. At the end of the term, I received the following report from my housemistress, who had been told about the situation at home:

> 'This has not been a very satisfactory term. Susan has been very self-absorbed and not very co-operative about doing her share of tasks.'

Clearly at 13 years of age, the stiff upper lip needed some work.

For Stephen the separation and the months that followed were a time of misery and uncertainty. Later in 1970, aged 15, Stephen went to live with his father. Both parents stayed living in the same town, so geographically at least, it made almost no difference. Was he given a choice? 'I had a choice,' he says. 'I made the wrong choice.'

I question him. 'What makes you think it was a wrong choice?' He doesn't like this; his voice hardens, 'You're not going to know. I don't want to tell you.'

Silence falls between us. I offer to make some instant coffee and go to the kitchen. There are five large jars of coffee lined up on the kitchen counter. He likes his coffee black, with half a teaspoon of demerara sugar. It must only be three-quarters filled and half of that must be cold water. I bring it back, he drinks it in three mouthfuls and then speaks: 'My father assaulted me when I was 16. I'd had a bad day with exams and when he came home, I spoke out of turn. I was too noisy. He started punching me.'

Stephen's words are clear and his tone is steady, the effect like a clean punch to my chest, knocking the air out. I splutter, 'Your father punched you? Did you hit him back?' Stephen is horrified, 'I couldn't do that!' Then adds, 'My step-mother tried to restrain him. Not physically but verbally: "You better stop that or else a neighbour will call the police."' This wasn't a single punch, then, his father was laying into him big time.

Stephen then feels compelled to confess that there had been an incident with his mother, also, when he was 14. He physically threatened her, and I think he may have hit her but he is so deeply ashamed of this incident that he later asks me not to detail this. I argue that it's part of painting a truthful picture of his life. He allows this but wants no more questions, 'It's too delicate a subject.' I leave it alone.

Stephen's father hit him in 1971, the same year that the first British soldier was shot dead in the Northern Ireland 'Troubles' and the UK changed to decimalised currency. Aged 16, Stephen sat his 'O' levels in the midst of mental vulnerability, the aftermath of a family break-up and being assaulted by his father. At that time, grades 1-6 were recorded as a pass. His results were mixed: 'I took History. It should have been a grade 1, but it was a grade 3. Grade 4 in Geography. I just failed my French. English Language grade 5, English Literature grade 6, Grade 7 French.' I ask about Maths. 'I was poorly, I couldn't cope.'

In the summer, Stephen had some welcome relief from his father. A friend of the family drove him down to France to meet up with his mother and siblings for two weeks' holiday. 'A lovely time. Wonderful times in France, the sh... sh... sh...'

'You went on the shuttle?'

'Chateaux.' He spells it out. 'C.h.a.t.e.a.u.x. You must do something about your hearing.'

In the autumn, Stephen was allowed to start studying for 'A' Levels at a local Sixth Form College. He chose History, Geography and English; three hefty, essay-based subjects for a struggling student.

He was also still doing a paper round. Stephen stayed away from home and his father as much as possible. 'I was always there on a Sunday afternoon when my brother and sisters were there but, on the Saturday, I'd be out all day and not come back till 11.20pm at night. Be in bed about midnight and up at 5.30am.

*Stephen adds: 'I was out EVERY night until 11.20pm. I was at school in the day time.'*

Stephen was a 17-year old boy who worked hard, didn't 'mix with the wrong sort', didn't smoke, didn't take drugs and rarely drank, 'Only time I got drunk was at the school leavers' party in 1972. Wasn't properly drunk even then.'

By the age of 17, I'd been at the boys' school for nearly 2 years and I was drinking, smoking and partying. Working? Not so much.

In May 1972, Stephen had a 'shattering experience of Christ' at an evening church event. For years he wouldn't talk about it, it was too personal. Then in 2016 he gave a few more details.

'It was Sunday May 21st, 1972. After the youth group, they stayed behind with me. The Christian minister asked me, "Do you want to go on making your own messes? We can stay here all night and it won't make any difference. Say, "Jesus is Lord." In the end I did. In the end after staying there, sitting, saying nothing, I did.' He'd been going to the youth group for some time by that point and he adds, 'I was disillusioned with the past, felt suicidal and was ringing Samaritans on a regular basis.' He pauses and then, 'I might need to go to the loo, Susie.'

'That's fine, Stephen, just tell me when you need to go.' He says no more so I gently probe, 'Did you find a sense of peace when you became a Christian?'

'I felt it when I first became a Christian, yes, for a while. Not for long.'

In that final year of school, one of Stephen's teachers who was a member of the church, invited Stephen to his home, so Stephen would visit most weekends and attend church with this man and his family. 'He was a very kind man.'

Even so, the pressure was rising, Stephen was only sleeping about five-and-a-half hours a night and his academic work was suffering.

'I read the books thoroughly, but didn't do the writing. I want to smoke now but I've got my false teeth in. Is that fair enough?' I agree, before remembering that without his teeth in, understanding him will be difficult. Before we continue, I have to confirm several times that it will NOT be his fault if I don't understand him. 'I was unable to take the 'A' Levels because I was too ill. After that, I had a nervous breakdown, an emotional nervous breakdown…'

It was April 1973. Stephen had just turned 18.

He hadn't managed to keep the stiff upper lip.

On many counts, 1973 was not a good year for the UK. Stephen reminds me that Edward Heath's government introduced the State of Emergency, the three-day week and power cuts. However, the British government had been confident that by this time, the nation's mental health problems would be sorted. There were new approaches, new drugs. Our problems would be over.

Back in 1961 the Health Minister, Enoch Powell, had embraced the prediction that by 1976 the need for hospital beds for the mentally ill would be halved: 'Expressed in numerical terms, this would represent a redundancy of no fewer than 75,000 hospital beds.' He was inspired to make his "Water Towers" speech referring to the forbidding lay out of the old asylums:

'There they stand, isolated, majestic, imperious, brooded over by the gigantic water-tower and chimney combined, rising unmistakable and daunting out of the countryside.'

Enoch Powell became known as 'the father of Community Care.' He laid out a ten-year plan, in which the old prison-style asylums were to be knocked down and those who still needed care would be provided for 'by a whole new development of the local authority services for the mentally ill and mentally subnormal.'

They certainly reduced the number of beds. Between 1960 and 1969 psychiatric hospitals lost 24,000 beds. During the same period, the prison population doubled from around 20,000 to 40,000. Just saying.

Enoch Powell did not under-estimate the cost of the changes. Those who came after him, did. It appears (you will be shocked and appalled) that the Government had declared a new revolution in mental health care without supplying the finance to achieve it.

*2001*

*Solving the Problem*

By 2001, 28 years later, it seemed the British Government had been over optimistic about solving the 'problem' of mental illness. The shift from the Asylum model to Community Care was seismic. Not only did the huge asylums need to be closed, a whole network of skilled local care provision needed to be put in place. By 2001 the number of beds available for mental illness and learning disability in the NHS had dropped from 150,000 in 1955 to less than 39,000. While much good was done, for many people 'care in the community' meant no sort of care at all and they fell through gaping holes in the net, ending up on the streets and in prisons.

In 2001, Stephen was not one of those statistics but he was not thriving in his half-way house and the staff didn't seem to know what to do other than threaten him with section. He was being very difficult. He still hadn't discovered his Stiff Upper Lip. He was in a 'half-way' house provided for by the state. He had a roof over his head, enough to eat and he could go out to the day centre. Was he grateful? No.

There are those, with the stiff upper lip in place, that internal solid metal door, who would have put up with this situation, repeating phrases like, 'I'm lucky to have somewhere,' 'Mustn't grumble', 'Others are so much worse off than me.' People who would accept poor treatment without complaint and even apologise for putting others out. But is that right? Should we applaud such behaviour?

Stephen was not finding the support he needed, and he was not slow to say so. In his old stomping grounds, he'd been part of the local URC church for over 20 years; they knew him and accepted him. Now he tried various different churches but couldn't settle anywhere. From my perspective at the time, he was being too picky. From his viewpoint, the people he met were not kind or tolerant. On the subject of 'putting up with things' Stephen and I were chalk and cheese. I had a lot to learn.

With regard to churches, I knew about putting up with what I didn't like, I'd been doing it for years. My present church was warm, modern and friendly but I'd endured four years of Tim's curacy in a cold, Victorian church with people who thought 'welcoming children' meant allowing them to sit silently in a box pew for an hour. The older ones got to go to the portacabin round the back, but I had three children under the age of four and I brought them to the church every Sunday and took them to the cold, damp vestry during the sermon and prayers. There we would act out bible stories or play. I never publicly complained even when given the opportunity. As I write this, the coldness of the time penetrates. I'm sitting here crying. Why did I comply?

My upbringing was clear. Unless I'd been raped, stabbed or beaten senseless, there was nothing to complain about.

The additional commandment was: 'Whatever you do, don't embarrass other people.' This is as firmly entrenched in my psyche as the fear of Hell is entrenched in a cradle Catholic. It goes down to the bone.

Even though the rational side of me understood from early on that Stephen could not 'put up with it', 'cheer up' or lock his feelings behind a metal door, still it annoyed me. Why? Perhaps because it challenged my own approach to life.

It was certainly one of the reasons why it turned out to be a long and bumpy journey for both Stephen and myself. Over the years it was, and at times still is, almost physically painful for me to stand up for what I want or challenge someone else's poor behaviour towards me. At the same time, I repeatedly made the mistake of expecting Stephen to be more understanding of other people. I had no tenderness towards myself, and so had precious little to offer him.

After Stephen moved into his flat, he complained frequently about the carers who came twice daily to support his practical needs. They held the phone too close to his ear, they were too cheery in the morning, they told him he looked young.

*Stephen interjects forcefully, 'I don't like it!'*

In 2014, Stephen complained to me during a phone call that one of the carers had behaved 'outrageously'. She had accidently trodden on his foot, laughed and not apologised. Then when he got angry with her, she said that he'd ruined her day. He told me he wasn't happy with her, and that on another occasion she'd split his toe-nail. When I asked how, it turned out to have been an accident as she was helping him put some clothes on.

I reminded him that people make mistakes, but he wouldn't have any of it. Carers were supposed to look after people and she didn't. And she didn't even say sorry. He'd made a formal complaint to her care agency and was refusing to have her back.

I felt concern for her and asked, slightly bitchily, 'So how is your foot now? Is it injured?' He didn't answer and I pushed the point home. 'Stephen, you're too critical.' He was furious with me. If they sent that woman back, he'd barricade the house, he'd barricade the house! I wanted to stamp on his foot myself.

The incident was not over. The following day I got an answer machine message from him. The care agency was planning to launch 'an investigation'. Now he was terrified the police would be involved and the carer would sue him. I wanted to ring and shout at him, so I didn't ring him. I just hoped they were bluffing [they were]. I'd known him 12 years by that point, but still his behaviour infuriated me. Why couldn't he put up with minor inconveniences? Why didn't he see the damage he was doing to someone else? When I told Tim, he looked at me with surprise and said: 'What did you expect? Stephen can't do this.'

As the National Autistic Society reminds me: Stephen sees, hears and feels the world differently to other people. Looked at through the prism of autism, Stephen's point of view becomes clearer. He is very sensitive to pain, cannot easily recognise the difference between a mistake and deliberate cruelty, finds it hard to notice any nuance in social interaction (for example, the carer's laugh might have been embarrassment) and struggles with empathy.

There was another matter that I hadn't picked up on immediately, the things that 'trigger' us. Stephen had told me that when that carer laughed, it reminded him of a time at St. B's hospital, when they'd beaten him up and then laughed at him. The incident had triggered a traumatic memory in him, but instead of sympathising, I remonstrated, 'This is nothing like that, Stephen! They deliberately hurt you and laughed at you. She made a mistake and didn't understand it was a big deal.'

It was not until later when I got home, that I wrote in my diary, 'If that laugh brought back his time at St. B's, no wonder he doesn't want to see her.' However, Stephen wasn't the only one being triggered; his rage with the carer had triggered something in me. I realised I was reacting to old, locked-up memories of being shouted at for making unintentional mistakes. It was these memories that made me empathise with the carer rather than with Stephen. Finally, I was beginning to catch on to what was happening, not just to Stephen and to me, but between us.

The incident blew over, but Stephen never forgets. In 2016 he rang me, very tired: 'My right toe is in a lot of pain. One of the carers stamped on the toe and ruined it two years ago.' This time I listened and simply offered sympathy for the pain he was experiencing.

That was all he needed.

Later it turned out, 'I've got a fungal infection that doesn't need treatment.'

In 2001 Stephen needed so much love and care. I couldn't offer it then, but maybe there was someone else who could.

# Chapter 6

## Humpty Dumpty:

## Breakdown and Beyond

*'The average standard of psychiatric practice in Britain is*
*abysmally low…*
*The evidence is overwhelming.'*

1974 report by The Royal College of Psychiatrists

In April 1973, aged 18, Stephen had a nervous breakdown.

We've been sitting for some time in Stephen's front room. It's a warm spring afternoon, with a breeze coming in through the open window. Without much thought, I ask, 'Do you know what caused it?'

'I couldn't come to terms with my situation.'

'In what way?'

'Leave it there.'

Did he know what caused it? Apart from a troubled mind, severe lack of sleep, fear of his father, suicidal thoughts, and pressure to complete 3 A levels?  All stewing within the unstable pot of adolescence.

Stephen stayed at home for eight months, cared for by his step-mother and receiving outpatient treatment which consisted of doses of the drug Largactyl (the trade name for chlorpromazine).

Largactyl was the first anti-psychotic drug released onto the market in the 1950s and it signalled a revolution in the use of drugs to treat mental illness. It was considered a 'wonder drug' but Stephen said it didn't help much, it just gave him sunburn. For God's sake! Stephen's insistence on making causal connections between unrelated facts drove me nuts, and still does. I looked up Largactyl and found that common side-effects were: body movements that you cannot control, trembling, muscle spasms, producing more saliva than usual, slow movement, feeling restless. However, before that was a warning: 'Chlorpromazine can make your skin more sensitive to sunlight. Keep out of direct sunlight while having this medicine.'

*That's what I got!'*
*'I apologise.'*

Reading all those side effects makes me wonder whether it's the drugs or the condition that makes a person look like a stereotypical image of 'madness.'

Detractors call Largactyl a chemical cosh. I saw it in action at the drug rehabilitation home where I worked in my mid-twenties (1986-88). As I welcomed a new dazed woman into the TV room, I released the door, assuming she was going to take hold of it. She didn't. It was a fire door and it shut firmly, fixing her to the door frame. I could see her blank face and one arm flapping a little.

*'I knew lots of people like that.'*

If nothing else, Largactyl would have knocked Stephen out a bit. After a few months, he was considered well enough to move to phase two, voluntary work. No counselling, no talking treatment of any kind, no-one exploring with him the causes of his breakdown. Instead he was told to do voluntary work, caring for vulnerable people.

'I worked in an old people's home for two months and then at a blind people's home for one month.'

Knowing how he feels about people now, I blurt out, 'But you said you hate people!'

'This was a long time ago. I enjoyed working at the old people's home, helping the blind people. I was happy doing it. I enjoyed it.'

'If you were happy, why did you stop?'

'The psychiatrist in Jan 1974 decided to send me as a day patient to St Bs.'

At this point I ask him to repeat something which I didn't catch. He's not happy, 'I shall have to put my false teeth in. I've got no choice, have I?' I admit to poor hearing.

We return to 1974 and the psychiatrist sending him as a day patient to St B's. What was on offer? 'Occupational therapy – making things, painting pictures mainly – there wasn't a great deal to do.' They told him to give up voluntary work, which he'd enjoyed, to paint pictures all day. He stayed as a day patient there for nearly a year and left in October 1974. 'I discharged myself.' He was 19.

'You were the same age as Peter,' I find myself saying. The same age as my beautiful eldest son, Peter. I am no longer on the outside looking in. My protective metal door has cracked.

*As I read this to him, Stephen asks what I mean. I explain that comparing Stephen with my Peter and thinking of Peter having a breakdown fills me with pain. The pain does not diminish in this awkward exchange. On the contrary.*

As for me, by the age of 19, I had garnered three decent 'A' levels and a place at university. On my 19th birthday, I was living at home in the UK, on a year off, doing voluntary work, bar work and learning to drive. I headed off to France with a boyfriend in May 1981.

Aged 19, Stephen would have liked three 'A' levels, a girlfriend and a trip to France. Instead he was living at home being looked after by his step-mother. 'She was kind, very kind.' His step-mother was NOT a wicked step-mother. Stephen was having paranoid delusions about getting poisoned, but not with an apple from her.

*'My father and step-mother thought that I thought that they were trying to poison me.'*

Without realising it, we then enter into profound and murky waters.

'I kept worrying her about things that didn't matter.'

'You were unwell.'

'It made her mentally unwell.'

'I don't think it MADE her. I don't think you can blame yourself.'

'Course I made her ill.'

'No.'

'You're entitled to your opinion.'

'I am. Thank you.'

'It defeats the evidence. It confutes the medical evidence.'

'You haven't made me mentally ill.'

'I probably would do, if I was with you for long enough. Not now, but in the old days.'

'You couldn't help being what you were like.'

'I could've had a different attitude. Could have got a grip on things.'

'Maybe you needed some help to get a grip on things.'

What can we do and what can't we? When is it because we 'can't' and when because we 'won't'? To what extent are we responsible for our actions and for the way people react to us? Leaving this complex area for now, we move on to equally tricky terrain: love and girlfriends.

'I was doing very well for a while. But silly school girls made me ill. Then I fell in love with school girls, I was worrying irrationally. Illness caused me to worry irrationally. Worried I'd be poisoned by touching bad water and germs so I'd be poisoned, worrying irrationally.'

His interest in girls became obsessive. He was still taking his pills but it didn't seem to help.

'I became very, very ill. I became iller and iller. I followed a school girl. Got in trouble following a school girl home. I nearly got into trouble with the law. Her mother complained and I was threatened that I'd get into trouble if I went around to their house again and harassed her.'

> 'Sitting in his armchair, Stephen is back in 1974, and now he adds more characters: 'The social worker threatened to have me put away but a kind policeman told me that no social worker could grab me and I'd make myself into a hospital case if I keep worrying – that reassured me.'

He tried another approach: 'I became involved with Dateline because I wanted a girlfriend.' Dateline was established in 1966. In the 1970s, before the internet, they publicised themselves by putting ads in the local newspapers. People would then fill in a profile and send it back to Dateline who would match them up. Nothing came of this. 'I got iller and iller, Susie, iller and iller and iller.'

We move on to the subject of politics:

'I was making long telephone calls, involved with the local Labour Party, campaigning for Nationalisation of Heavy Industries, which Tories in the early 70s mucked up. Tony Benn nationalised ship building, which I thought was a wonderful thing – referendum 1975 – I got a vote – you didn't, you were too young. I voted to stay in Europe.'

At University, one of the subjects I studied was Politics. I didn't make long phone calls but I would verbally blast my flatmates with my latest theory or outrage as they walked in the door after a lecture. On one occasion, I woke a friend at 3am to tell him I'd become a Christian Marxist.

Stephen meanwhile, aged 20, had not made it to university, and thus had no flatmates to regale. Instead his political obsession resulted in huge phone bills for his father and step-mother. Once upon a time, back in the 1970s, there were no mobile phones, only one line and one or two fixed phones in a house. Teenagers would regularly run up large phone bills and annoy their parents. This was so common that it became the butt of jokes in TV soaps and sitcoms. The stereotypical scenario involved teenage girls talking to each other about make-up and boys. Instead, Stephen rang a friend for hours at a time, three times a week in order to talk politics.

'One of my great regrets. Edith Piaf had no regrets, *je ne regrette rien* but I had. I made all those phone calls and high phone bills and made my step mother ill with worries. I'm disgusted with myself. I could have controlled that. My parents didn't like it.'

I somehow doubt if Stephen's father shared his left-wing politics. My father, also a banker, thought Margaret Thatcher, "The Iron Lady" was a bit soft.

*I ask Stephen if his father was left wing in case I might be stereotyping bankers. From the depths of the armchair, his head shakes. Stereotype wins.*

Putting up with his son's opposing political views would

have been one thing but <u>paying</u> for Stephen to spout left-wing tirades on the phone?

*'He didn't like it, no.'*

What Stephen's father wanted was for his son to get a job. That would solve the problem. Finally, in June 1975, aged 20, Stephen got one. As a road-sweeper.

'As soon as I got the job my step mother and father were all very relieved and my mother, very, very relieved.'

June 1975 was a good month for Stephen. On Thursday 5th June the EEC Referendum was held. We voted to stay in Europe and now he had a job. Hurrah!

By this time, Stephen had moved onto another anti-psychotic medication called Mellaril. Stephen reckons that it did help with the stress. However, one of its common side-effects was drowsiness.

'I got this job road-sweeping and these silly girls kept chatting me up and then I fell asleep and lost my job, only proper job I ever had.'

Stephen lasted road-sweeping for 6 weeks.

'The Tory councillor found me [asleep]. The Labour councillor spoke up for me. The Liberal was undecided. Tory majority on the parish council decided to sack me so I was on the dole.'

I enjoy his political take on this.

So, what happens next? It depends on who's telling the story. Looking from the outside in, Stephen's father might have put it like this: he and his wife finally asked Stephen to leave because he was an adult and they could do no more for him. For five years they'd had him at home, looking after him through a nervous break-down, erratic and obsessive behaviour and occasional police involvement. Stephen had left the supportive day care of the psychiatric hospital and was refusing to go back. He, Stephen's father just wanted his son to get a job, get some independence; that would sort him out. What Stephen needed was to get out into the real world and find his way. He was 20 years old, it was reasonable to insist he left home at this point.

However, Stephen, 'from the inside' might have seen it differently.

*Stephen is watching me attentively as I read my take on his 20-year old former self. I read it slowly.*

Stephen was only 20 years old. He was seriously ill. He did not know how to handle himself. He wanted to be like other people. He didn't want to be a mental case in a hospital. He wanted a girlfriend, he wanted to work. He had just lost the first proper job of his life. And now his father and step-mother wanted to throw him out onto the street.

*Stephen reflects on this. 'They had no choice. It was my medical condition. I'm not at all cross with them. If I'd stayed as a day-patient I'd have been fine.'*
*I'm cross with them. I have friends who've had similar difficulties with their son, but they'd still make sure their son had somewhere to go.*

They gave him two weeks' notice and Stephen planned to find lodgings in a nearby city but either he didn't get organised in time or they grew fed up, because on Sunday 6th July 1975, 'They packed my bags and I had to go, I had to go.'

The police were called to 'escort' him from his father's home. Stephen did not tell me, so I do not know what he felt like being manhandled down the drive. I do not know whether he was angry or terrified, shouting or begging or crying. I do not know what Stephen's last sight of his father was as he was taken away.

I know only one thing.

After Stephen left home on that day, he never returned.

Was it Stephen's fault? Could he have 'pulled his socks up', 'made an effort' or 'stopped being so negative?' The anti-psychotics had helped to some degree but Stephen had still not managed to cope with normal life. In his book 'Psychiatry in Dissent' in 1976, Dr Anthony Clare (famous for his BBC Radio programme 'In the Psychiatrist's Chair') remarked that patients and relatives complained most about a lack of time with doctors, and the over prescribing of drugs. They wanted the doctors to spend more time listening.

As well as the drugs, day care had been available for Stephen at the hospital, but did anyone there sit and listen to Stephen? He loved history and politics and wrote poetry, but they just told him to paint pictures. Nobody asked about the things that mattered to him. My chest hurts as I write this. Don't get me wrong, I know that art can be a vital means of communication. The Largactyl door-trapped woman at the drug rehab I worked at, early on produced an extraordinary painting, a picture of her head with half of it blacked out, because, as she put it: 'I'm only half there'. Art can certainly be part of the healing process, but how about offering something specific and tailor made? Asking patients about their hopes and aspirations and seeing what can be done to support them? Is that really so impossible?

In 1975, it seemed that that all options had been exhausted.

Except they weren't. If money had been available, Stephen could have undergone psychoanalysis or psychotherapy. There was also an array of alternatives, due to the 'anti-psychiatry movement' of the 60s and 70s spearheaded by figures like Thomas Szasz, R. D. Laing and David Cooper.

Thomas Szasz was a psychiatrist and psychoanalyst who didn't believe in mental illness. He would have interviewed Stephen, asked him what he considered to be his particular 'problems in living' and then helped Stephen find tools to resolve them. He would not have used drugs and it would have cost Stephen's family a lot of money. I didn't have a Thomas Szasz but I have been to see counsellors and psychotherapists to sort out my issues on two or three occasions. It was extremely helpful but also costly.

As far as David Cooper would have been concerned, Stephen was the sane one and society had driven him mad. What Stephen needed was a safe place where he could re-discover his own autonomy. Cooper, a psychiatrist and communist, set up a therapeutic community outside 'the system' called Kingsley Hall together with the Scottish psychiatrist R. D. Laing, and had it still been open, perhaps they would have invited Stephen to stay.

One of Laing's major concerns was the way in which the psychiatric profession approached patients as 'objects,' or 'organic systems' that had gone wrong and needed 'fixing'. He wanted to re-affirm that such people were not 'other', they were still people like us. Amen to that.

At that time, there appeared to be two main 'answers' to mental illness. The medical model was about fixing: eliminating or suppressing symptoms so that the patient could function well enough to fit into society. The psychotherapeutic and anti-psychiatry approach was more about working with the patient as a human being, in order to discover what they needed to fulfil their own potential and to be happy. The attempt to fix Stephen certainly didn't work and as far as I can tell, it was the only approach used.

There were also more old-fashioned answers. One was 'go out young man and get a job', the option favoured by Stephen's father. In fairy stories and folk tales what was needed was the love of a good woman or man. In 'Beauty and the Beast', the prince, turned into a hideous beast by an unkind act, is saved by the love of Belle's pure heart. In 'The Snow Queen,' Kai's heart, warped by shards of an evil mirror, is saved when Gerda's loving tears penetrate his heart.

*Stephen hasn't heard this story before and is visibly moved.*

My great uncle Hugh was the least favourite child of his parents, the only one of three brothers to survive the First World War and probably suffering from PTSD (Post Traumatic Stress Disorder) when he was saved from an alcoholic ditch by a remarkable woman, aptly named Grace. I remember Hugh as withdrawn and grumpy but also kind with a good sense of humour. He liked to recount the story of standing sipping drinks at a cocktail party, where a woman he'd never met made conversation by pointing at Grace and remarking 'She's such a wonderful woman but I hear she married a hopeless alcoholic.' Raising his glass, he replied drily, 'Yes, I know. I'm the alcoholic.' Grace was indeed a wonderful woman, a fabulous, vibrant and warm human being and she loved my great uncle deeply.

Some things you can't prescribe.

*2001-2002*

*Finding Home*

In August 2001, Stephen had been at Beech House for three months. It was a half-way house so the idea had always been for him to move on and move out, but instead Stephen was in danger of being removed, sectioned and placed back in a psychiatric ward. It seemed that nothing had worked.

And then he met Mandy. The date was the 20th. A Monday.

I have the recorder on and ask Stephen to tell me about her:

'I went to Moorhaven (mental hospital) day centre – I hated that place. I went to Moorhaven with this other silly girl and er... came across Mandy. Mandy then went to the half-way house I was in. I fell in love with her there and went to live in her house.'

When I ask him to say what he liked about her, he bristles,

'I don't think it's any of your business. Is it any of your business? I don't think so, no.'

So, I'm going to tell you a love story, a fairy story.

'There was once a sensitive prince, a poet, who was cast out of the kingdom by his evil step-father and cursed to appear as a great ugly beast to those around him.

*I look apologetically at Stephen. He doesn't seem bothered.*

'He wandered the lands, shunned and feared, at times beaten up and chained or chased out of town. Wounded, scarred and angry, he held longings in his heart that no-one knew.

'After many years of journeying, he came to a new land and approached a village there. He was tired, thirsty and in need of food. The people of the village showed him some pity, fed him and sent him to the nearby forest for shelter. As he limped through the trees, he heard ahead of him someone sobbing as if their heart was broken. He found himself, standing there shaking, crying unfamiliar tears. Then the sound faded and there was only a skittering of leaves in the breeze. He carried on walking and shortly afterwards came upon a clearing. From that clearing a deep earthy voice began to sing, singing to the sky, to the trees, to life. The voice belonged to a small, rounded woman in a simple blue shift dress with faded red hair flowing to her waist, her arms and face reaching to the sky, her body undulating, her hair rippling. He could see her feet were crippled but still, she danced. When she stopped singing and looked at him, her eyes were bright and curious as a blackbird's and she was not afraid. She came right up to him, her head as high as his shoulders and she sniffed. "I smell a curse," she said and laughed aloud. "But I see a handsome prince with jet black hair and clear eyes, just the one tooth and a wounded heart." She smiled at him, a smile that reached from one side of her wide-open face to the other. He did not know he was smiling back, or how long he stood, fixed as a maypole to the ground, while she danced in waves around him, swaying, singing, murmuring and sighing. 'When she came to stillness, she declared solemnly, "You are the one I will marry. The gods have put me on this earth to love you. I shall <u>always</u> love you." With that she took him by the hand and he followed her into her cottage and into her life. And his life was never the same again.'

Stephen and Mandy married in March 2002 at the local registry office. I have a photo of them; Mandy looking solemn in a pretty blue dress while Stephen, stands beside her smiling broadly, wearing a dark suit with a carnation buttonhole, white shirt and blue silk tie. It was a lovely spring day. Mandy's mother and adult children were there, plus some members of Stephen's old URC church, Mark his advocate, Carol and myself. No-one from Stephen's family was present,

*I look at him to check, he nods in agreement.*

It was here that I first met Mandy.

My own experience of Mandy was of a lovely and complicated human being. She was short with a wide, warm smile and a wide, worn face. She had a wild encasement of greying-red hair and she was a similar age to Stephen, whom she visibly adored. She was caring and generous and she had a heart two sizes too large.

*I look up. Stephen is nodding, the memories alive and present.*

She suffered from bi-polar disorder and swung from wild energy to debilitating anxious depression. She had tried to take her life on more than one occasion. She was a devout Christian who attended a 'happy clappy' type of evangelical church and who loved listening to worship songs on her tape-recorder.

She saved Stephen's life.

She and her dog Charlie.

*Stephen smiles a deep warm smile.*

Charlie was a delightful little rollmop of a dog. He continually chased balls and if you threw one for him, then he required you to repeat the action for the full length of your stay. If he wasn't chasing a ball, he was humping one of his soft toys. To Mandy's irritation, Charlie became Stephen's dog almost immediately. Charlie loved Stephen. It was mutual. Stephen anointed Charlie, 'King of all Dogs'.

*'He is King of all Dogs!'*

After the wedding, they headed off to the chippie to celebrate. By the time they married, Mandy had moved back to her own home, a two-bedroom house with a garden, but Stephen was initially only permitted there for weekends.

Finally, four months later, in July, Stephen left the half-way house and moved in with his wife, Mandy. Now at the grand age of 46, he had found himself a beautiful (if equally middle-aged) princess.

And a house.

And a dog.

And step-children.

And a mother-in-law.

*I look over at him and we smile at one another.*

For the first time since leaving his father's house in 1975, aged 20, Stephen had a place called 'home'.

*We sit in silence after this sentence and then I ask him, 'Is that true?'*
*He nods and then adds, 'Then things went wrong. And then they went right.'*
*After all, this isn't a fairy story.*

# Chapter 7

## Down the Rabbit Hole

*'The rabbit hole went straight on like a tunnel for some way and then dipped suddenly down, so suddenly that Alice had not a moment to think about stopping herself before she found herself falling down a very deep well.'*

From Alice in Wonderland by Lewis Carroll

Our recording takes place on a damp October afternoon. The backing track as usual is composed of Classic FM and Charlie clacking up and down the hall. Today Stephen sports his black beret.

Back in early August 1975, the 20-year-old Stephen had just been removed from his home by two policemen. Where was he supposed to go? In 1975 unemployment was rising and homelessness was a major problem. If they weren't roaming the streets, many mentally ill people ended up in prison as a result of the reduction in psychiatric beds available and the problems around the introduction of community care.

*'I was in a very perilous situation,'*

Over the next five months the story of this young 20-year old resembles a dystopian version of the already surreal, *Alice in Wonderland*. In the book, Alice chases a white rabbit down a hole, falls into Wonderland and spends a large chunk of the book trying to get through a very small door into a beautiful garden with 'beds of bright flowers and cool fountains.' A golden key to unlock the door sits on a nearby table but she is too big to get through the door. She finds a bottle that says 'Drink me', drinks it and becomes small enough to go through the door, but the key is on the table and she is now too little to reach it.

*'Alice looked along the passage into the loveliest garden you ever saw'*

On 6th July 1975, Stephen had just fallen down the rabbit hole. At this critical moment, some Christians took him in. 'I went to a Christian evangelical house; I was an evangelical at the time. They were very kind. They didn't have to.' The family who took him in were part of the Baptist church he'd belonged to since the age of 17. Here was hope, a vision of a beautiful garden. That August the family took Stephen on holiday with them to a residential Christian Conference & Holiday Centre in the South West. I shall call the Centre 'Holy Spirit' House as it housed an independent, evangelical, charismatic church. Charismatics believe that the Holy Spirit of God has power to work miracles, heal physical ailments, and change people. Stephen wanted some of that.

*'What a curious feeling! Said Alice;*

*'I must be shutting up like a telescope'*

Alice found a bottle that said 'Drink me.' Stephen was also offered something that would alter him. The elders at Holy Spirit House diagnosed Stephen with 'demon possession' and Stephen agreed to undergo exorcism. When I ask him what happened, he comments, 'They came out gently'. This intrigues me enough to ask 'so did you have a sense of demons leaving you?' He shrugs.

*'She was now only 10 inches high... now the right size for going through the little door into the garden.'*

It was a good week, where Stephen made friends and lots of well-meaning Christians gave him their contact details and phone numbers. Was the exorcism enough? Now could he get into the lovely garden these people inhabited?

At the same age, 20, in August 1982, I came into contact with devout charismatic believers. I was in Hong Kong for the holidays with my father and at weekends I was mixing with Chinese ex-drug addicts and a woman called Jackie

Pullinger, who'd spent 20 years standing outside opium dens telling people that Jesus loved them (in Cantonese). Now she had a small flat where ex-addicts lived together with Christian volunteers. They prayed and worshipped in Chinese and English, and it was here that I had my own 'shattering experience of Christ' amongst people who had suffered deeply but who experienced a God of genuine love and power. They didn't talk about Hell except the real hell of their own broken lives and I didn't see anyone exorcised. I sat next to Jackie late at night in an underpass as she talked tenderly to a pile of rags that still housed a precious human being. The love being shared was shared with everyone, even me, a wealthy, lonely, white daughter of the British Empire and it broke me open. I too had seen a magical garden, a place of transformation and hope.

At the end of that holiday week, Stephen travelled the two hundred miles back with the family to their home and lived with them until October 10th.

*The Golden Key is on the glass table out of reach*

Through the autumn, living with the family became increasingly difficult. 'She wanted me to leave, several times. She thought I was making her children unwell, her unwell, even her husband unwell. Then the lady said something I took exception to. She said that only her sort of evangelical Christians were Christians. So I walked out of there. I had terrible times.' These were kind, generous people who'd put Stephen up in their own home for three months. I couldn't have done that. Yet here they were, stating that there was only one key into heaven and Stephen didn't have it.

*'She tried her best to climb up one of the legs of the table,
but it was too slippery'*

Stephen was now homeless for the second time in three months. He went to the house of another Christian, who promptly took him to his mother's house. She wouldn't take him in and wanted him to go to St B's hospital but he wasn't having that. He had lots of Christian contacts now and decided to head off to a nearby town where there was a big church centre. 'My stepfather cut up rough with me. Gave me a lift to the Evangelicals' big centre but said I'd be poaching off their food. Called me "a bloody villain!" I was a bloody villain.' So that was it; Stephen was just a lazy good-for-nothing scrounger.

*I explain to Stephen that I don't think this, it's supposed to be irony. Ha-ha. He is not amused.*

*'Come, there's no use in crying like that!' said Alice to herself rather sharply;*

Stephen did attempt to hold it together with the help of various Christians, but the next two months sound like a pinball game with Stephen as the ball and his Christian friends not knowing which way to flip him. The people at the big evangelical centre put Stephen on a train down to Exeter, where he stayed at a Christian hostel for two weeks and then 'I was transferred to Holy Spirit House.'

Here they performed a second exorcism: 'I went berserk.' After another two weeks, on 7th November, a young man was appointed to drive Stephen the 200 miles back to the evangelical centre near his home. This time Stephen wasn't going to be 'transferred', instead he persuaded the young man to drop him off earlier and went to 'Londinium' (Stephen always talks about Londinium, NEVER London). He stayed a couple of nights with a Christian there and then hopped on a train back down to the south west. Stephen was putting the contacts he'd been given in August to good use.

Back in Exeter, Stephen found another Christian Hostel, 'They weren't like the evangelical ones. They put up drug addicts and down and outs – the very lowest of society on account of Christ.' This time he lasted three weeks, 'I kept getting kicked out of their Christian meetings for verbal abuse. I wasn't violent. They showed me the door several times. I ended up outside a church and fainted on the pavement.' The police found him and took him to a doctor.

*'The Queen shouted, "Off with his head!"'*

By now it was early December and this next episode has a Wonderland twist to it. Stephen told the doctor he had a weak heart. The doctor examined him and then, Stephen laughs,

'The doctor poked me in the right eye.'

'He did what?'

'He poked me in the eye and said, "Did that hurt?" I said, yes and he told me "that was for wasting my time". He gave me a black eye. If you look, you can still see the mark.'

Forty years ago. No, I didn't look.

Having been entirely failed by the doctor, Stephen went back to the hostel but ended up in a nightmarish loop:

'I wanted to go back to my home town but they didn't buy me a ticket. I had money but I couldn't find the booking office. I spent the day charging about on buses. One bus conductor was genuinely concerned and told me to go to Social Services but I was trying to avoid that.'

*'At this the whole pack rose up into the air and came flying down upon her.'*

Alice's adventure ended with a pack of playing cards attacking her. As she beat them off, she woke up from her dream. Stephen did not have a dream to wake up from. Instead, the Samaritans picked him up and as he was refusing to get in the ambulance to the mental hospital, the police transported him. He was sectioned.

> Except he wasn't. One more surreal twist comes as Stephen sits forward and stubs his cigarette out. 'I wasn't sectioned Susie!'
> 'Then why did you stay?'
> 'They said that if I tried to leave, then they would section me.'
> Joseph Heller eat your heart out (author of the satirical novel 'Catch 22').

Stephen hadn't been able to find his way into the lovely garden. Instead he was delivered into the care of Exe Vale mental hospital just in time for Christmas. It was a proper asylum, sprawling redbrick buildings with towers, chapel, and farm, segregated by gender.

'It was a hell hole, Susie.'

He stayed there for nearly ten months as a 'voluntary' patient. Four months in, on April 3rd 1976, he celebrated his 21st birthday.

'Horrible place. They beat me up.'

'You got beaten up a lot in your life then?'

'Oh yes, a heck of lot. Beaten up a heck of a lot. Exe Vale

is closed now but you know Farleigh in Somerset? They [hospital staff] were sent to prison. Exe Vale was nearly as bad as Farleigh.'

Stephen is referring to the 1971 scandal at Farleigh, when three male nurses were convicted for the ill treatment of patients.

Remembering this, Stephen's mood drops and he returns to a theme that becomes familiar to me over the years, his desire for this difficult life to be over. 'It scarred me and now I shall move on from this life, far away from this mundane life and seek peace with God in the next life.'

Was Stephen really beaten up, or was this part of a paranoid delusion? There was a lot of patient abuse going on at the time. As well as the Farley scandal there were complaints and enquiries at Ely, Whittingham, Napsbury and Ockendon. And they are the ones that came to light.

As well as being beaten up in the hospital, Stephen insists that everyone there hated him. Not just there, in fact. Back in October, his step-father had called him a 'bloody villain.' This phrase had clearly hit home because now it was on national TV. He tells me: 'The newscasters were saying, "he's a bloody villain". Tony Blackburn said I was a bloody villain. Apparently, I'd prophesied the long, hot summer of 76.'

I take on a careful neutral tone, 'When did you prophecy it?' Stephen replies without a hint of irony. '1976. Stephen, Martyr of the last days.' His voice rises, distressed, 'They were going to poison me. You don't believe me, do you?'

I try to give a non-committal answer. 'It does sound quite difficult to believe.'

It doesn't work. 'You don't believe me, do you?'

No, I didn't believe that Tony Blackburn (who I remembered presenting 'Top of the Pops' on TV when I was a teenager), was talking about him, I didn't believe Stephen was a martyr and I didn't believe the staff were trying to poison him. Stephen believes it. He saw it and heard it with his own eyes and ears. He doesn't trust people, but he trusts what he sees and hears. This was his experience. He certainly isn't lying. Stephen doesn't lie. I don't think he could lie to save his life.

Stephen carries on, 'They called me Stephen, Martyr of the last days. They were talking about it all over the world. And yet Gareth [support worker] reckoned that was a paranoid delusion. But it wasn't. They knew me. Everyone knows me.'

I try to gently challenge this, 'Lots of people where I live don't know you.'

He is adamant, 'They all know Stephen Martyr is mental, he is mental.'

'No, they don't.'

'They won't remember me now, Susie, but in those days, yes, in those days, yes.'

I try another tack. 'When you start believing that everybody in the world thinks something is true about you, then it's a delusion, Stephen.'

'They were talking about it on TV, radio, Stephen Martyr of the last days.' His tone becomes intense, his voice rising again. 'There was nothing I could do about it. They [staff at the psychiatric ward] were laughing, saying I was paranoid. They were just laughing. There's no justice for me. They said they were going to poison me.'

'Who said they were going to poison you?'

'Staff. Staff at Exe Vale. If you tell them that, I'll be going down for a hundred years.' He's forgotten the asylum is closed, he's back there now.

'That's not true, Stephen,' Amateur psychology, here we go. 'You put your fears on everyone else.' Stephen is listening intently. 'You feel so bad inside that you think that's what people are saying all the time about you. But they aren't.' Stephen connects this with what happened to him after Exeter. 'On Monday August 16th 1976, they transferred me back to St B's hospital, I told them that the staff at Exe Vale wanted to poison me. They said, "That's anxiety – that's an end of the matter".' Such sensitivity.

It's here, at St Bs, that he says they gave him ECT, against his will and with no anaesthesia. 'Then they transferred me from the main hospital. W ward wasn't too bad. They didn't abuse me there.'

I respond brightly, 'Oh, that's good!'

'They didn't abuse me too much until 1979, 1980.'


What is true? How do we differentiate between reality and delusion? How could Stephen tell? Whom could he trust? The apparently sane church people who showed him love had also told him he was possessed by demons and insisted that it was only their particular group who would get into heaven.

Then there were the various mental health staff. One set apparently beat him up and threatened to poison him and another set told him it was just 'anxiety' and then forced

ECT on him. Whom could he trust?

Pioneer of the anti-psychiatrists R. D. Laing argued in his book *The Divided Self* that no delusions are without content; they all have a logic and a rationale. They relate to real deep feelings that a person has, and often to an external truth. We cannot know for certain what happened, but we can know where Stephen felt safe and where he didn't.

A huge problem arises if Stephen says he wants justice. If he cannot differentiate between reality and delusion then in a court his testimony would be undermined. If it is true that he was beaten up and abused in hospital then these were criminal actions and no-one thus far has been brought to account.

Talking about trustworthy testimony, what about the rest of us, who variously believe in UFOs, conspiracy theories, ghosts, God(s), stars, 'signs', Holy Books, fairies, string theory or a 'unified theory of everything'? How sane are we and how reliable is our testimony?

You might say that that's the job of a psychiatrist. They're the ones trained to diagnose mental illness. But there are problems here. In 1976 Dr Anthony Clare admitted that consistency in diagnosis was problematic in the UK and long-term studies have suggested that the profession has been slow to improve its record.

In the early 1970s a famous study by Stanford University psychologist Dr David Rosenhan showed just how poor diagnosis was in the United States. He and seven 'pseudo patients' presented to various doctors saying they heard voices. They were all transferred to mental hospitals, where they behaved normally and then asked to be released. Despite this they were held in hospital for between 7 and 52 days, given drugs and not permitted to leave until they agreed with the diagnosis. In an article Dr Rosenhan wrote afterwards, he described witnessing patients being beaten and verbally abused by staff for no justifiable reason. He also noted that one of the most distressing things that the pseudo patients discovered on the wards was the overwhelming experience of powerlessness and depersonalisation. They felt 'invisible'.

This is what it felt like from the inside.

Stephen may or may not have received an accurate diagnosis, but the psychiatric wards stripped him of agency and left him feeling powerless. What could he do? Primo Levi, a survivor of Auschwitz, wrote in his 1959 memoir 'If This Is A Man' that in the face of the total deprivation of our rights we still have one power left: "and we must defend it with all our strength for it is the last – the power to refuse our consent."

Having given up this power myself, so many times, with so little understanding, I am in awe of Stephen's capacity to hold onto it no matter what it costs him. He knows its true value.

*2002*

*Early Days with Mandy and Charlie*

In July 2002, 27 years later, Stephen was back in normal

society. He had a wife, a dog and a home.

As we sit in his front room in October 2013 recording this time, I ask for the date that he moved in with Mandy; 'I went there on Monday July 8th 2002. I wasn't discharged from Beech House until Thursday August 22nd 2002.' He growls, 'They kept tabs on me, I didn't like it.'

On 18th July, only ten days after his move, Stephen had a spectacular fall out with Rose, Mandy's daughter. 'I lost my temper. We had a row. Extreme. In the middle of Ramsay Road. We held the traffic up. Police were called.'

Stephen is still incensed as he describes what happened next. 'The police arrived... sprayed gas in my eyes. They said don't move. It was in the street. And my fag was still alight. The fag moved. And they sprayed gas at me. What do you make of that? That's why I don't like the police too much Susie. I don't want anything more to do with them. I don't like the police or criminals, Susie.' He pauses, inhales his cigarette smoke and then, 'I still haven't got over it. That's why I got cataracts probably.'

*'Too painful talking about it.'*
*'Is it alright for me to read it to you?'*
*'If you must.'*

Stephen was put in a cell and two police doctors assessed him. He wasn't sectioned, but sent to Beech house just before midnight. 'I stayed up all night. I thought they were going to put me in St B's, under a section. I went back to stay with Mandy, thank goodness, thank goodness.'

Consider your own response to that story. Take a moment. Who do you have sympathy with?

In 2002 at the beginning of my journey of knowing Stephen, my sympathy was with Rose. Why did Stephen always have to start an argument?

*'My fault.'*

By 2013 when we recorded this, I was more sympathetic but still felt a tug of irritation that he blamed the police gas (probably pepper spray) for his cataracts.

Then I read it to Tim and he remarked: 'That's a bit over the top, isn't it? Do they normally gas people in the street for an argument?' That thought hadn't occurred to me. I went back to Stephen, 'If the police had simply asked you to stop, would you have?'

'Yes, I would have.' He did make a complaint via a solicitor, he told me, but: 'The police never replied. Too busy, I think.' Was this institutional prejudice against someone with a diagnosis of mental illness?

In 2002 I had a long way to go. At the time I felt that Stephen brought it on himself. It felt the same with my middle son, it was always him behaving badly.

*Listening to this, Stephen fervently defends my son:*
*Of course, he was alright! He didn't misbehave. He did not misbehave!'*
*'But you don't know.'*
*'I say he didn't! He's not like me, He's not like me!'*
*These last two phrases are uttered in a desperate, pleading tone which move me deeply. I want to cry.*

I was continually telling him off for punching his (older) brother.

*'I say he didn't!'*

These days, he tells me how unfair it felt because his brother verbally wound him up but it was only him who got punished.

There was one person who didn't blame Stephen or diagnose him as an unsolvable 'mental case.' That was Mandy. To Mandy, Stephen was always her precious, wonderful, special husband, 'the gentlest, the kindest, the most handsome'. While she did struggle with bi-polar disorder, she had not spent her life in psychiatric units. She'd been married before and she had warm relationships with both her adult children and her mother. She knew about mental illness and she knew how to love people. She also owned her own house.

The house where Stephen took up residence with Mandy and Charlie was in a pleasant residential area and had its own, overgrown back garden. There was a small patio area looking towards the central apple tree and then the brambles took over. I attempted 20 minutes of weeding on one occasion, but it really needed a weekend and an enthusiastic working party.

*Stephen smiles: 'I remember.' He gets out a cigarette and snaps the lighter.*

Coming in from the patio, you stepped through sliding glass doors into the utility room. Beyond that was a small crammed kitchen and on the other side, facing the road, a decent size front room. Although there were two bedrooms upstairs, the double bed was in the front room. As a result, there was very little room to move. The bed faced the bay windows and the rest of the room was taken up with a sofa, a couple of tables and some pine upright chairs. On the right of the bed was a cabinet with a tape recorder for playing

Mandy's Christian worship songs. The room had a south-facing aspect, but it never felt light. Perhaps the constant clouds of smoke dulled it.

*'My fault, my fault. I was the one who smoked.'*
*'Mandy smoked as well didn't she?'*
*'Mandy smoked, but not much.'*

The cleanliness of the house varied, depending on how Mandy was. When she was 'high' she might hoover the house at three in the morning but when she was depressed, she could barely get out of bed. Stephen's institutionalisation meant that he didn't have any idea about cleaning and Mandy didn't push him. On top of this, Stephen's right arm became increasingly useless. Together with his dyspraxia, that meant he found it hard to eat without spilling food and Mandy was forever washing his clothes.

Through the mental health support team, a cleaner was brought in to support them but Stephen fell out with her and every subsequent cleaner and they eventually stopped coming. My impression at the time was that it was 'just Stephen'.

*Stephen apologises sadly. I wonder aloud whether there are cleaners trained in autism and he responds, 'The one who came recently couldn't even speak English.'*

Mandy found support in a local evangelical church which Stephen didn't like but he went with her sometimes as he didn't want to upset her. She was generous and hospitable, often gave me boxes of chocolates for the children and kept reminding Stephen not to be mean. She taught Stephen to ask after other people. As a result, at the end of every single phone call, he invariably asks me, 'Are you all well? And Zozzi?' (our dog).

*'I got that from Mandy, I got that from Mandy.'*

It wasn't perfect but they were together, it was home. In 2003 he and Mandy went on holiday to Hampshire for a week which went well. Stephen still rang me on a weekly basis and every two or three months, I'd drive down to visit and take Stephen and Charlie out. We either went to see Carol (for the fabulous roast lunch) or to a local beauty spot on an open hillside, with a fabulous view of the English countryside spreading out before us. Sometimes I would bring the kids, and Mandy occasionally accompanied us.

*Stephen speaks huskily: 'Please don't go on much longer - it's getting too painful.'*
*'Do you want me to stop now?'*
*'A little bit longer.'*

There would be kites flying, families rambling, ice cream vans and plenty of dog walkers. While the kids chased each other and ran after Charlie, Stephen worried: about the dog, what other people thought, whether he'd get in trouble and what to do with his fag ends (he always put them in his pocket). However, in the midst of all this, he did enjoy it, especially the ice-cream. He always was a big fan of Mr Whippy.

While Stephen sometimes worried irrationally (in my view), I wasn't aware of him being delusional and hallucinating. Perhaps the drugs kept this under control.

*I look at him - he nods.*

He did occasionally let on that he was going through a bad patch and hearing voices. I was always sworn to secrecy, in case this information might provoke a return to the psychiatric ward.

Stephen may have got out of the system but his extraordinary memory tortured him. Justice had not been done, he couldn't forget and he did not forgive. His right arm was becoming increasingly useless and he blamed this on restraint techniques introduced to psychiatric wards in the 1980s.

There were also the nightmares – the ones where he's back on a ward under section, the staff are approaching him and he is totally and utterly powerless.

# Chapter 8

## Institutions and Patients' Rights

*'There is a fundamental contradiction at the heart of mental health, between care and control.'*

MIND report on physical restraint 2013

*'There is a fundamental contradiction at the heart of the church between love and judgement.'*

Me, 2015

'I can't help you this time.' Snap. Stephen is flicking a lighter, repeatedly failing to light his cigarette. We're sitting in Stephen's garden on a grey April afternoon in 2013 and my recorder sits on the green metal table between us. Snap, snap, snap. Irritably, I take his lighter and snap! I light it first time and finally find some inspiration.

'Stephen, if you could stand at Speaker's Corner, in Hyde Park, what would you want to tell people?'

'It's all in the past, all gone. I must move on to another dimension, another sphere, another life. Far, far away from this world.'

Charlie ambles out untainted by existential despair. Stephen sees him and comments, 'He's come out.' Charlie wanders into the house again. 'He's gone in again.'

At that point, my recorder packs up.

In November, we're back inside and I try again: 'Stephen, if you could stand at Speaker's Corner, what would you say?' This time he responds crisply: '"Patients' Rights". The right to be a danger to yourself without being sectioned.' This is not a definition of 'Patients' Rights' I'm familiar with. He expounds on his theme, carefully enunciating each word for my benefit:

'The right to take your own life, without people breathing down your neck, without people raising concerns, interfering in your private business.'

'But surely people should be protected from harming themselves?'

Stephen scowls, I clearly know nothing; 'Susie, as long as you're threatened with section, you can wave goodbye to any of your rights. Abolition of section. That's what I would do. I still believe in that.'

'What if you're a danger to others?'

There is silence and heavy breathing before he reluctantly agrees, 'Danger to others, but not to yourself. People should be allowed to be a danger to themselves. I hate section. I was sectioned myself for many years.' His voice picks up an energy, a horror. 'I hated being sectioned, I hated sections. Look at the abuse! The appalling abuse I've suffered. Nothing was done about it. It just went on. I wish I could die now. I see no point in this earthly life, Susie. That's what you should understand before you go home this evening, Susie. I see no point in this earthly life.' As he takes a breath, he's distracted by Charlie poking his nose into the new slow-feed dog bowl. 'I still don't see how that thing works to stop Charlie eating so much. You show me?' I show him and then he returns to his theme: 'Susie, I see no point in this earthly life.'

~

Institutions, institutions, institutions. Many of us spend our lives involved in one, with varying degrees of choice. We may love them, hate them or endure them. How do we keep them alive and healthy; how do we create an environment which fosters mutual respect and prevents abuse?

For Stephen, the first time the institution formally sectioned him was in July 1977 aged 22. Three months earlier, he'd been released from St B's, after 16 months as a 'voluntary' patient. No support, no provision, no follow-up but Stephen was young, it was the 1970s, he was stepping into freedom. At this point, he stopped his medication. This wasn't because he deliberately chose to but because he couldn't get hold of any. I ask, 'Did you ever choose to stop taking your medication?'

'Once, in 1975.'

He then joined a squat run by the Divine Light Mission, set up by Guru Maharaj Ji. The aim of the Divine Light Mission was inner peace leading to Universal Peace. When I ask him how it went, he replies, 'I got involved in several punch-ups.' After two months, Stephen gave up on the Divine Light Mission. There were always 'bags of drugs' there, but not the ones he needed and he became ill.

Stephen stayed in London and met up with friends. He is still in contact with one of them, a chap called Will.

*'Really, really nice bloke.'*

In my mind, I'd imagined Stephen as a loner at that point. 'Susie, I had loads and loads of friends!' Stephen's friends helped him find a Christian hostel in South London where he stayed for a month. When I ask about money, he says he had a savings account. He then fell out with the proprietors of the hostel and 'I got the train from Londinium, got off at G and walked 22 miles… 22 miles!'

'Why?'

'I hadn't got the money for the bus.'

Stephen went home to his mother's and she delivered him back to St B's psychiatric hospital. He stayed there as a voluntary patient for a month and then in July came the section. When I ask why, he is brusque, 'I don't like questions like that.'

He was locked up and could not refuse treatment. Stephen's

section remained in place for an entire year until July 1978 when he was 23 years old, and he then stayed on at St B's as a voluntary patient.

Despite this, Stephen reckons that St B's hospital 'wasn't too bad' through 1978 and 1979. It was doing its job. He had a girlfriend there, but then she dumped him. He was so distressed by this break-up that he jumped off a local bridge and suffered a hair-line fracture to his back. He took a long time getting over her.

Stephen reports that abuse began at St Bs in 1980. At first it was intermittent. When Stephen talks about 'abuse', he doesn't delineate between legal 'restraint' and illegal 'abuse'. They're all same to him.

Lovely soothing music is playing on classic FM, as Stephen recounts that in January 1980, staff member SL*, 'twisted my arm around my back for the first time, introduced me to C & R.'

'Introduced you to what?'

'Control and Restraint techniques. He told me to do something, I swore at him, I told him where to go and he got my arm around behind my back and I was in absolute agony. First time it happened. Jan 1980. SL*. He's a key figure in my past.'

This technique was repeatedly used on Stephen over the next 20 years.

Five months later, in June 1980, Stephen was having a row with his girlfriend. Many of us have been there, but normally it's a private event. Stephen's row took place on a psychiatric ward. His girlfriend was an alcoholic and she had a terrible temper. Into this tense emotional situation, he says 'a posse of eight' staff appeared and restrained him. The duty nurse put him on an emergency three-day section (section 30). Stephen is still furious about this,

'He should have let it go. I was just shouting.'

'Was she shouting as well?'

'She was shouting. Loads of people were shouting.'

Ten days later, now off his section, Stephen threatened the offending nurse with a table knife. He wanted to get his own back. His consultant psychiatrist, Dr F, then put him on a section 26 which again allowed them to keep him involuntarily locked up, for up to a year.

Did shouting at his girlfriend constitute a threat to safety? Was Stephen's subsequent knife-wielding a sign that the staff nurse was correct or that he had misused his powers and escalated the situation? Stephen has no doubts about it: 'They should have let it go.' He thought Dr F. was too strict, 'He kept sectioning patients.'

Stephen's argument with his girlfriend sounded like a lovers' row to me and as such needed those around to calm the atmosphere not wade in and raise the temperature especially with an onslaught of staff. I was outside our local psychiatric hospital once when I heard shouting from the grounds. There was a woman screaming 'get off me!' while at least 5 staff surrounded her, gripping her, telling her to calm down. They were probably following procedure but the effect was frightening and oppressive. I wanted to run away but I made myself stand and watch them, so they'd know they were being witnessed.

As for Stephen, as a result of the knife wielding, he was sectioned for a full year. Fortunately, this was eased a little by Carol visiting him. 'Then, when I got day-passes, we used to go out for afternoon tea and cream cakes.' Thank goodness for fairy godmothers.

It was after this experience, in 1981 that Stephen started a 'Patients' Rights' campaign with a fellow patient. He doesn't explain how they went about it, only, 'I became more militant and more rebellious.' At the same time, a new consultant psychiatrist took over from the strict Dr. F. In Stephen's words, Dr R. was: '… a happy-go-lucky, forward-looking, young, dynamic, progressive psychiatrist, who let the male patients eat with the female patients - which Dr. F. would never do. He took me off the section, put me on an open ward, gave me all my privileges back: responsibilities, day passes, t-shirts and all sorts of things.'

Let the good times roll!

Stephen's friend Will told him to leave St. B's and get a flat, but despite being happy-go-lucky, his consultant would not give permission because 'if I was left to my own devices outside it would cause too much adversity.' When I ask Stephen if he agrees with this he nods, which I'm not expecting. Then he surprises me further by adding, 'I was quite happy at St B's. People whose houses I went to would take me back about 9.30 or 10 pm.'

He pauses: 'Can we get something to eat? I'm very hungry.' We get something to eat and later on return to the 1980s.

The people Stephen visited were church people and local friends and he also attended church services. On the wards, he wanted more 'Patients' Rights', but basically the institution was providing a safe space for Stephen and he was 'happy'.

However, the institution couldn't protect Stephen from a broken heart. Later in 1982, Stephen walked out and went AWOL, 200 miles back to Exeter, because he was having problems with his girlfriend. 'Every time I had problems with a girlfriend or broke up with her, I ended up in Exeter and I would meet up with Will there. In 1982 he taught me to smoke.'

Stephen has never quite forgiven Will for teaching him to smoke. Three decades on, he is smoking at least 30 a day.

Unfortunately, learning to smoke wasn't the worst thing that happened on that visit to Exeter.

'I shouldn't really talk about a man who indecently assaulted me and abused me. He gave me a lift in his car and indecently assaulted me and abused me. He got scot free away with it.'

I've been interviewing Stephen for four years now, and known him for 16. He has never mentioned this before.

'He abused me and then he said "Get out now, get out of the car". It was my fault, it was a stupid thing for me to do, to accept a lift from a stranger.'

I find my voice, 'It was not your fault!'

*As I read this back, he speaks with rare compassion for his younger self: 'I was only a young man, vulnerable, very vulnerable.'*

The people who ran his lodgings thought the man should be locked up, but no police were called. Stephen goes on in an almost casual tone:

'I was indecently assaulted by gay people when I was at St B's hospital. That's why for years and years, Susie, I was wary of gay people, but now I just accept them. They're just as good as anyone else. If anyone's inferior, I've told you before many a time, it's me because of my behaviour.'

Why has he never mentioned any of these events before? I ask if he's he willing to tell me more but he's not willing:

'It's like some of the nightmares and the voices. I get these idiots asking me, "What do the voices say?" I can't tell them what the voices say, because the voices are so horrible and would make me feel far too embarrassed and far too small if I told them – I'd probably be in a lot of trouble if I did tell them what they said. Do you understand? In an indirect sort of way - do you see what I mean?'

I understand.

Stephen never told me more and to be honest, I was relieved. Stephen is usually precise about the terms he uses, so I looked up 'indecent assault'. Indecent assault happens when no consent is given; it is sexual in nature, but does not involve penetration. This may include being touched intimately or being forced to watch sexual activity.

Stephen had stepped out of the institution and so far, it was not turning out well. Soon after this assault, he made up with his girlfriend, travelled the two hundred miles back to a town near where St B's was situated (he was still AWOL) and stayed with her family and then in local lodgings. 'I was living in guest houses nearby, being abused, beaten up.' To top that, his girlfriend finished with him. 'She wasn't at all well herself. They [support staff] talked her out of having anything to with me. They thought my illness was bad for her. I became suicidal.'

By now he'd had enough and he shared his distress with everyone in a local post office: 'A Christian there took pity on me, took me to the guest house to pick up my things and then to the police station. They were very kind to me. Gave me loads of cups of tea, loads of roll-ups and took me informally to St B's mental hospital and V ward. And there I stayed for quite a long time.'

He stayed in that hospital for 18 years.

After the break-up with his girlfriend, 'I wasn't interested in girls for three whole years. Just interested in going out with my mates in town having fags.' At first the hospital was mostly supportive, but from 1985 it changed. 'I was informal for years, then sectioned for years.' He raises his voice, 'There was no way out. No way out!' This is not a film or a novel, this is real life. I want to get up and leave. I want to go home. I don't want the world to look like this.

I never did. I wanted to believe in a God powerful enough to change people's lives, to make everything ok. Having found that God in Hong Kong, I had also become deeply embedded in an institution, the institution of the church. However, in contrast to Stephen, that was my choice. After graduating from University, I went to live for two years in a Christian community & Conference centre in Devon. It sounds similar to the one Stephen visited but it was a bigger, broader Anglican-based community, welcoming people from a wide range of Christian traditions. It was a precious time for me and it was where I met Tim.

After that I worked in the Christian residential drug rehab

and attended an evangelical C of E church, where the vicar wore a suit and preached long sermons, and some of us young ones produced drama and played guitars. In my late twenties, I married Tim, who was working at American Express in Brighton. I moved there, got a job at another Christian-based rehab and joined the church that Tim attended, which had an idiosyncratic Anglo-Catholic, 'smells & bells' approach and provided a night shelter for the homeless at the back of the building. The vicar wore robes, we had a daily eucharist (blessed bread and wine), we sang chants unaccompanied and the drama was provided by the cast: energetic vicar, contemplative monks, diverse homeless characters and a few harassed parishioners. The Vicar, Father Alan, would harangue us all to be more active, while the monks would extoll stillness and contemplation. On one occasion, Brother Martin intoned sonorously, 'I have two words for you, Father Alan: patience and fortitude.' To which Father Alan growled back, 'And I have two words for you, Brother Martin.'

In this church, homeless people were not 'clients' but sisters and brothers, and twice weekly we cooked and shared meals with any who came. I found the shift of tradition shocking and I felt the raw pain of people's lives throb in me, but surely this was what church was for, sanctuary. Jesus ate and drank with the outcasts, brought them back into community and insisted they too were children of God.

There was so much that was good here, yet the underlying structure of the Church of England was patriarchal and women priests were not acceptable. While I had feminist ideals, had even looked up feminine images of God in the Bible, I did not challenge the institution because I saw my own needs as subservient to the greater needs of others.

Stephen certainly needed sanctuary in the church and on the psychiatric wards yet both these institutions kept threatening him with different versions of 'Hell', whether it was sectioning or eternal damnation. Sectioning is enshrined in British law and for some Christians 'Hell' is just as non-negotiable; it's 'in the Bible.'

Stephen's experience on the wards was 'as long as you're threatened with section, you can wave goodbye to any of your rights.' It certainly didn't support a sense of safety, mutual respect or sanctuary.

In 1985 and 1987, staff member C: 'violently restrained me and beat me up in W ward upstairs dormitories.' In 1987 Stephen was told by staff member D that he needed 'a f****** good hiding.' 1987 was a bad year. Stephen's mother wanted to take Stephen on a trip to America. The doctors didn't agree:

'They said the USA was too far away. My mother didn't like that. I didn't like it much, but I did nothing. She was escorted off the premises. Later, after they'd all gone to bed, I stayed up. This horrible man comes towards me, grabs me by the scruff of the hair, drags me along the floor and beats the hell out of me, drags me upstairs. I went to bed. I was in a terrible state. Half six in the morning, he dragged me out of bed, got hold of me, punched me, kicked me down the stairs… beat me up again. He went off duty. The day staff weren't at all happy with it. He nearly lost his job, but he kept it. He should have gone to prison. The excuse he made was that I hadn't gone to bed like everyone else.'

I take a moment to recover from the vividness of this description and then ask if Stephen tried to do anything. 'I wasn't in a position to do anything. I reckon I'd have been sectioned if I'd tried to do something. I didn't have a solicitor until 1992.'

What else happened in the 1980s? Stephen is sitting up, eyes sparking. 'Hidings were commonplace. Mentally ill people got them frequently in the 1980s. Mentally ill people were just dirt. Scum. But the people who abused them were scum. Can't you see that?'

The 1983 Mental Health Act was supposed to improve the protection of patients' rights but Stephen doesn't feel it worked. 'My worst abuse was in the Eighties and the Nineties – sheer, absolutely hell, Susie.'

The Act required that patients should be informed of their rights [Part 2 32c] including 'rights of applying to a Mental Health Review Tribunal' and on leaving hospital, should be provided with after care. After 1983, in theory, Stephen could have demanded a Mental Health Review Tribunal and then requested a community support package. However, 'In practice, patients legally confined in mental hospitals were rarely successful in their challenges to the system.'

Why did things get worse for Stephen on the wards in the 1980s and 90s? It would probably take a whole thesis. My view is that much of it goes back to the fall-out from the tectonic rift taking place as the UK shifted from the big institutional asylums to 'Community Care'; In practice, few community services were developed and large-scale closures [of asylums] did not start until the 1980s, with the first closure in 1986.

Huge changes were taking place but the funding was not there. This created at least two major problems. Firstly, a large number of vulnerable people ended up 'in the community' but not properly cared for, which was a recipe for disaster. Secondly, this led to an increased concentration of patients with complex needs on the psychiatric wards. Resources were stretched, so wards tended towards containment and control, not care. Staff needed to feel safe as well as patients.

Stephen's campaigning for his own version of patients' rights carried on through the Eighties and his highlight was Election Day 9th April 1992. 'Placards up in '92. I shook hands with Tim Renton, the Tory Minister of Arts at the 1992 elections. I shook hands with the Liberal Democrat and Labour candidates. They all supported patients' rights.'

They may have supported it in theory but, in Stephen's case, help didn't come in time.

### 2002-2006

*An Operation and its aftermath*

Since 1977, Stephen had never been formally released from a psychiatric ward. Finally, after 25 years, on 8th July 2002, Stephen left residential psychiatric care to go and live with Mandy. It is only now, writing this book that the full significance of Stephen's move hits me. We should have hired a band, set up a street party, invited the Queen. But it was a fragile moment back then, so easily broken. Perhaps instead we should have gathered in a church at night, sat in the dark and wept.

What led to this momentous change? Yes, Mandy saved him, but this was AFTER he'd made the move to the half-way house in a different town. What was it, Stephen? He doesn't know. The National Health Service and Community Care Act, 1990 had shifted policy further towards community care but it was not until New Labour came to power in 1997 that some real money and effort was put into the reform. Perhaps this provided the push. Perhaps also, Stephen was helped when in 2000 the Human Rights Act of 1998 came into force, bringing the terms set out in the European Convention on Human Rights into domestic law. Patients began to challenge the courts. And win.

In 2001 I was still within the institution of the church. There had been reform, and the Church of England now ordained women priests. Tim, as the vicar of our present church, had a liberal inclusive approach and I'd found a voice through writing drama. In 2005, I began a part-time MA in Dramatic Writing, and I'd found a loving community where creativity was encouraged: our church. Some churches are awesome.

Stephen had found his life outside the hospital but his past kept encroaching. From 2003, his right arm became problematic and he was advised to have an operation. 'The consultant said it was bad. He thinks I might be right, it's from them restraining me.' Stephen was very anxious and Mandy was terrified, 'She thought I could be paralysed by the operation.' Eventually, in 2005, Stephen was persuaded to have the operation. In the build-up to this I was of course saintly.

*My Diary Entry, 2 December 2005*

'I lost my temper with Stephen – phone rang 3 times – found out it was Carol – apologised unreservedly.'

*Stephen chuckles.*

Our family looked after Charlie while Stephen went in for the operation. The kids were delighted.

*My Diary Entry, 12 December 2005*

'Had Stephen's dog for a week. Drove me nuts. First 3 days we left him in the kitchen overnight and he howled. Tried to feed him dog food but he didn't touch it. Stephen had told me to feed him steak or chicken!'

*Stephen laughs again: 'give him the best, the very best. King of all dogs!'*

After Stephen had the operation, Carol and I visited him. It was disturbing. The operation had been 'successful' but Stephen was almost catatonic. He sat up in bed, staring and unresponsive. He was then sent home to a fragile Mandy. Alarm bells clanged inside my head.

It was then that Stephen's delusions began: 'I saw Louis Walsh from 'X' Factor outside my house, one Saturday night, December 2005. He said he'd come to kill me. You don't believe me, do you?'

'I believe you think you saw him.'

'Mandy said it was a paranoid delusion, but I can remember it happening. I saw him outside the house, Louis Walsh from the 'X' Factor. I saw him, I saw him.'

It was Christmas, I was busy, I was the vicar's wife, I was producing a Carol Service drama and a Nativity play. I felt both guilty and angry. Why was no-one doing anything? What did these so-called 'Care Workers' do?

*As I read the following to Stephen, my voice drops to a whisper. He listens intently.*

I'm no medic but even I knew that without physiotherapy that operation was going to fail. It was his right arm and he was right-handed. I rang the mental health unit. I emailed. The physio never happened. They claimed he was not compliant and in January 2006 he was sectioned again.

The operation was a complete and total waste of time.

*'It was.'*

He stayed under section in mental hospital until April. I search for something positive that I did back then, 'I came to visit you, do you remember?'

He acknowledges this. 'Towards the end. I was better then.' I wilt.

I went to see him just after his birthday, Tuesday 4th April. It was a 'proper' mental hospital and when I visited, he was on a spacious, open plan ward on the second floor, with big windows. There was a sparse, featureless 'smoking room' with a TV in it, a couple of old sofas, linoleum floor with a smattering of fag ends, white walls, strip lights and glass doors (presumably reinforced). 'It wasn't very nice at Moorhaven, horrible place. Last gunboat of being abused, Susie. The last gunboat of abuse, like Suez after the war, last gunboat business of being abused. You understand?'

Yes. The last 'gunboat' of abuse. The war had already happened.

# Chapter 9

## Annus Horribilis,

## Decadum Horribilis

*'1992 is not a year on which I shall look back with undiluted pleasure... it has turned out to be an Annus Horribilis. I suspect that I am not alone in thinking it so.'*

Her Majesty The Queen, November 24th 1992

*I want to forget the 90s, my Decadum Horribilis and Annus Horribilis.'*

Stephen, 2016

In November 2013, we sit down in our usual places in Stephen's smoke-fugged front room for a recording which I subsequently label 'V IMP'. It is a long recording.

~

The Decadum Horribilis began in 1990 when Stephen's grandmother died; the one who killed herself so as 'not to be a burden'. In 1991 aged 36, Stephen was sectioned again for six months. Why?

'I was never there at medication time. I kept walking away from the place, disappearing, being in town at awkward times when I shouldn't have been there. I was never there for medication that's why.' What time was medication? 'Different times. Morning, midday and evening. You're upsetting me.'

> Stephen interrupts, agitated: "They'll twig!" He's afraid this information will give away who he is to 'the authorities.' As I write his phrase down, he asks me what I'm writing and so I tell him - "They'll twig". He's instantly alarmed:
> "They'll twig?"
> "No. That's just what I'm writing down."
> "They'll twig!" He's now in full panic mode. We get lost in a verbal whirlpool.

We sit in silence. Then he says, 'You must go on.'

Later in 1991, according to Stephen a member of staff threatened to break his neck. Then in July 1992, Stephen assaulted him. By now I'm catching on. 'When you say you assaulted him, what did you actually do?'

'I broke his shirt.'

'Not his nose or his ribs?'

'No, I tore his shirt. He said he had a good mind to make me pay for it. It wasn't my fault. I was getting my own back, I can't remember why.'

The hospital response to this was <u>crucial</u> to Stephen's future. The doctors gave Stephen a choice: 'The doctor said, "If you stay on open ward, we'll section you. If you go to the lock-up [special care] unit you will be remain informal." I chose to go to the lock up.'

I'm now totally confused so Stephen explains. It appears that a person can agree to be locked up and Stephen calls this 'informal'. Stephen hated sectioning so much, he preferred this to being on an open ward under section. This meant, perversely, that he had less freedom. On an open ward under section, but with earned privileges, you can go out with a named person, as Stephen did with me in May 2000. On a locked ward this isn't possible.

I eventually begin to understand: 'So you can be sectioned on an open ward or informal on a locked ward?'

'Absolutely.'

'That's weird. So you agreed to be locked up informally. How was that different from being sectioned?'

Stephen answers simply, 'I chose.'

Choice – more precious than diamonds.

A door opens on his memories and now he whispers: 'They took me down there. The nurse welcomed me on to the ward and…' The hairs rise on the back of my neck, but he stops. 'You wouldn't like to be me.'

The promise, it seemed, was that this was all temporary. 'They would eventually transfer me to an open ward when

I was well enough, but they scuttled me. They abused me.'

I ask what would have happened if he'd said he wanted to leave the hospital altogether and Stephen's response startles me: 'I never said I wanted to leave.'

'You didn't want to leave?'

'No.'

'So, you wanted to be there but you just wanted to have some freedom?'

'I didn't want to be abused.'

I need a drink.

Stephen agreed to be locked up on a voluntary basis in July 1992, with the promise of transfer to an open ward later. It all turns on this. If he'd not been locked up, the following events would not have happened.

'This is it,' I tell Stephen. 'This is where we talk about the abuse'.

He has repeated this story to me over and over. He can tell you the exact time and date. It never varies. However, nowadays he's worried about getting sued, so I won't give that information.

*He agrees.*

It is enough to say that the event took place in September, two months after he was transferred to the locked ward.

~

Stephen begins conversationally. 'I expect you were in Vietnam, weren't you?'

'I was in England. Pregnant with Peter. What were you doing?'

'I was trying to get a cigarette out of the office and they'd just closed the office.'

If you were on the locked ward, the office was the only the place to get your cigarettes.

Stephen carries on, 'I was desperate, "Please may I have a cigarette, please may I have a cigarette?"'

He was begging two male staff who knew him well and they ignored him but Stephen would not leave it. He went on and on until:

'They cut my mouth, they cut my mouth, pushed me to the ground. They pushed me to the ground. C* held me down by my face and mouth. and S* jumped on top of me. I was in agony.'

I take a breath, then ask, 'You weren't fighting them?'

'Nope. Not at all. Not at all. Not at all.'

I recap, 'So C* held you down and...'

'C* yanked me, knocked me to the ground, held me down and S* jumped on top of me and broke my leg.'

'Broke your leg?'

'Yes.'

'Were you lying on your side when he jumped on you?'

'Lying flat, face up.'

'You were lying face up?'

'On my back.'

'And he just jumped on your legs?'

'He jumped right on top of me.'

'He must have been a very heavy guy?'

'Very heavy, yes, enormous, absolutely enormous, Susie.'

'You were lying on your back, you could see him about to land on you?'

'Well it all happened so quickly.'

'And then what happened?'

'I was in agony – I got up, walked away, staggering.'

'You got up?'

'Staggered around, staggered round. They walked away, covered themselves. Then other nurses found me, a ward doctor found me. He said, 'Oh you've broken your leg Stephen, you've broken your leg – you'll have to go to hospital.'

'Did you tell anyone what happened?'

'I don't know, I was too frightened.'

'Was it all a bit of a blur?'

'The Unit Officer… I was in hospital, my leg was up, and he asked me if I wished to take any action. I said no, because I was frightened they'd take it out on me.'

'You were too frightened to tell the Unit Officer what had happened?'

'Terrified. Asked me if I wished to take any action. They [the authorities] were willing to take some action because I was an informal patient, Susie, but I was terrified they'd take it out on me… And they made my life a misery anyway, Susie. Think how much more misery they'd made my life, more hell they made my life, if I'd taken action.'

Later, a fellow patient told him that she'd witnessed what happened. She had been visiting from another ward at the time of the attack but was too frightened to speak out. 'She's dead now.'

The doctor informed Stephen that his broken leg was the worst tibia fracture he'd ever seen.

*"One of the worst," Stephen corrects me.*

Once the operation was done and his leg was in plaster, Stephen was returned to the same ward. There was an internal enquiry. The staff were cleared. His present-day Care coordinator refers to this incident as an 'accident' that happened while Stephen was being 'restrained'.

*Hearing this back, Stephen states: 'You didn't believe me.'*
*'I did Stephen. I was asking these questions to get a picture of what exactly happened.'*
*'You did believe me?'*
*'Yes, Stephen.'*
*'People don't believe me, Susie – the hairdresser said it was a bit over the top.'*
*I imagine the hairdresser pulling the comb through his hair and wishing she'd got the elderly man sitting opposite instead.*

At this point, I ask Stephen, 'You were an informal patient. Why didn't you leave? Why did you go back to the ward?' He is adamant there was no choice. I keep forgetting that if he'd decided to leave, they would have sectioned him. Anyway, after ten years on the wards where was he supposed to hobble off to with his leg in plaster? Stephen had been in the care of the local authorities and the staff who were supposed to protect him had abused him. Now he wasn't safe. Anywhere.

*Stephen repeats this to himself, nodding. I ask if that's a fair outline of what happened. He agrees: 'A fair outline.'*

What was he supposed to do with all this internal pain?

'I bear grudges.'

While Stephen bears grudges against a number of staff, it is C* he has talked about most. C* was the one who held him down. We pause as Stephen lights another cigarette. I check that he's ok to carry on. He is.

C* treated him badly on other occasions: '1994, 92, 93.' Was he ever nice? 'Very rarely. He gave me a cigarette once. That's all.' I ask if C* just picked on Stephen. 'He was horrible to a whole load of different people. I wasn't the only one. There was one person who got it far worse than I did. He was a nice man. C* physically abused him several times! He manhandled… the physical abuse. I can't talk about the physical abuse. I'm sorry.'

I say softly that it's alright, but Stephen is there now, back on the ward: 'They beat him. Strung him up. They held him up in the air and they punched him several times.' We sit and listen to a violin piece on Classic FM. I'm speechless. But Stephen hasn't finished. 'They didn't string me up. C* used to seek me out and beat me up on a regular basis. C* used to kick me and punch me and beat me, punch me and punch me and beat me up – several times, several times, he did that in '94.'

'Did nobody stop him?'

'No. In medication on a Saturday evening, he just weighed in through the medication patients and beat me up. I don't know why, he just did.' When I press further, Stephen insists there was no provocation at all, and nobody tried to stop the man from attacking him.

C* was a regular churchgoer.

Stephen had very clear ideas about what should happen to C*. Back in May 2013, he'd declared, 'May C* burn for what he did to me. Very often about 9 o'clock in the evening, I'll be having a coffee and a sandwich in the kitchen and I'll say "C* should burn! C* should burn!" out loud. You don't believe he will burn, and I believe he will burn. They're all scum. They abused me to a severe level.'

And on another occasion:

'I want someone to break C*'s leg and put him in the misery he put me through. Break his leg and say to him "It doesn't look likely that you'll be able to walk again", "the worst tibia fracture we ever had." I want them to say that to him, I want him to be in agony.'

'An eye for an eye?'

'Absolutely. An eye for an eye and a tooth for a tooth. That's what I believe.'

*As I read this back, two years later, his tone is calm, 'but of course, that's what I would want to happen to him.'*

Autumn 1992 and the decadum horribilis had only just begun. I'm expecting a long litany of horrors to follow, but instead Stephen tells me, 'In the summer of 1994, I went on a day trip to France. Now please let me smoke a cigarette'. I make him a coffee and wait, intrigued.

Finally, he stubs the cigarette out and says reflectively, 'I'm nothing. I'm going to dissipate quite soon into another world, going to pass away.' I quietly enjoy his use of the word 'dissipate' and then he begins to tell me about his day trip. 'I went in 1994 with K Ward, we went on the ferry boat.'

The scene from 'One Flew over the Cuckoo's Nest' comes to mind, where Randle P. McMurphy (aka Jack Nicholson) organises an illicit fishing trip for his fellow ward patients.

*Stephen hums in recognition*

I ask rather blandly, 'Was that nice?'

Stephen takes on the tone of a weather forecaster, 'It was a dry overcast day. The sun came out a few times…'

'Not the weather! What happened?'

'We had a lovely time, but I wanted to stay for the evening. The horrible Mr G tried to drag me back on the boat from Dieppe. I don't think the people of Dieppe thought that was very nice. It was the very same man who said my intelligence was average.' Stephen spits the last word out and asks me, 'Do you agree with that?'

'No, of course not.'

'It's way above average, way above average! He really upset me.'

I return the subject to Dieppe and suggest on Mr G's behalf that he did have a whole group to manage and they needed to get on the ferry. 'I wanted to stay till the evening ferry. He used C&R (control and restraint) to drag me back on the boat. They objected, the people of Dieppe. There was a lady and a man who spoke up for me. They said: "let him stay" in English and he pushed them out of the way.'

Stephen peers over at me busily writing and says, 'I wouldn't write his name down.' I suggest we call him Mr Goblin and Stephen laughs.

On his return to the ward, events took a turn for the worse.

'I told SL* [who was Filipino] that he was wanted in the Philippines on charges and he attacked me. I absconded from the ward, went away without taking medication from the open ward. A police car came and brought me back to the hospital and they sectioned me on a six-hour section. I was going to come back that evening.' He had only absconded for the day and the hospital staff used the six-hour section to admit him, and then put him on section 3 for six months, taking him into 1995. The section was then renewed for a year, and then another, and another.

In 1995 Stephen's sister killed herself following a period of depression. The staff were kind to him around this time. He was devastated. 'And yet nobody in the family seemed to be that bothered. I shouldn't say that but they didn't seem to be that concerned. Yet I'm still devastated. It affects me.' It occurs to me later that perhaps they didn't feel able to share their pain with a brother under section and highly distressed.

1996 was Stephen's next 'annus horribilis'. On Friday 11th October, Stephen experienced another form of restraint: 'face down'.

'They held me on the carpet so I couldn't breathe. They threatened to keep on doing it for two or three hours. I had to bite my tongue and not cry and not make fuss or anything.' The reason? 'I just moved from one chair to another and they did it for no apparent reason. They said it was standard Home Office procedure. They were horrible, brutal, evil, sadistic, cold-blooded scum.'

This action was legal. And it led to 'legal' deaths. A Mind Report in 2013 tells of David 'Rocky' Bennett who died in 1998 in a medium secure unit as a direct result of this face down restraint. In the same report a patient describes the terror and helplessness of being restrained face down with her face pushed into a pillow.

'Anything you do to try to communicate, they put more pressure on you.'

> *This triggers Stephen, 'I had that face down with a pillow at Moorhaven in 2006, Susie'. Just because I wouldn't go to bed'. He adds, 'And they got away with it.' He repeats this phrase until his voice breaks with distress. I ask gently if he wants to stop but it's a no. 'You go on, go on.'*

The abuse carried on and it doesn't sound 'legal'.

'I've had terrible, terrible memories of abuse. '96, '97 when I was punched and kicked, beaten up, hell knocked out of me.' As I listen to Stephen it feels like I'm in a movie. 'Heavies, The heavy mob. That's what they used to call them, the heavy mob – they'd come round and give you a good hiding. Dial 999 for the police but more often, you dial 333 for the heavy mob, five big blokes and they used to beat people up. They managed to employ one of the patients as well. Nasty patient to help them.'

Then came another happy moment in 1997. Stephen's other sister visited him. He also admits that other members of his family visited once or twice through this period.

While Stephen focusses mostly on the specific events of 1992 and 1996, he is at pains to tell me the experience was more generalised than that. 'The abuse Susie, it was intense, it just went on and on for years and years, for years and years. They got away with it, they got away with it.'

The year 1998 marks the end of Stephen's claims of physical

abuse apart from the 'last gunboat' incident in 2006. He came off section in 1998 but he was back on again by Christmas. He stayed that way until I met him in May 2000 and his status did not change until October.

*Stephen has been alive to every word of this read-through: nodding, echoing what he said on the page, expressing rage, fear and sorrow.*

I've had no experience of physical abuse of any sort that I can remember. Yes, I was tied up by the burglars when I was 15 but I was never beaten up or had any limbs broken. I can't even remember being smacked. However, I had experienced my own pain and was no stranger to other people's.

*Stephen asks: 'Don't you think you had it easy?'*
*'I'm not saying I haven't.'*

For me, the 1990s were the years my children were born (1993, 1995, 1996) and a time of transitions. Some of the experiences were very painful, but all came about as a result of my relative freedom to choose. No-one locked me up.

Between 1989 and 1993 I experienced close hand the fall-out from 'community care', through the raw pain of those homeless people sleeping at the back of our church in Brighton. Some were alcoholic, some mentally ill, all vulnerable. One evening, a gentle young man, an alcoholic, walked out to the vestry in the middle of the service and re-appeared a few minutes later with blood dripping from razor cuts up his arms. Someone calmly collected him and took him to get cleaned up. I wanted to scream. He didn't live past the age of 30.

*'I do apologise.'*

After 18 months 'trying,' I finally fell pregnant in 1992 and in

April 1993, after 32 hours labour, 16 of them excruciatingly painful, my son Peter was born by emergency caesarean. It all ended well, but when I look back, I see a hollow-eyed woman, pretending she was fine.

*Stephen responds caringly, 'I'm sorry it was caesarean. Were Aidan and Lara caesarean?' I tell him that Aidan was a forceps delivery, and then need to explain what that means. That sends us off on an interesting tangent about 'choice' which he finishes with: 'sometimes in life, you're pushed into a corner and you have no choice.'*

In 1993 Tim left his job with American Express to train for the priesthood with the Church of England and we moved three times over the next six years as he went through training and curacy and I gave birth to Aidan and Lara. Having three children under the age of four was both glorious and challenging and it was friends, not the church community who provided support. The 1990s ended well for me, with the move to a warm and loving parish in the autumn of 1999.

The 1990s was quite a decade for Mental Health in the UK. The 1990 National Health Service and Community Care Act was brought in by the Conservative Government, in the belief that creating an internal 'market' in the NHS, would result in reform. This Act split the roles of health authorities and local authorities, so that local authorities became the 'purchasers' buying services from the 'providers', which were the former health authorities, now transformed into NHS Trusts.

In terms of mental health, this was supposed to result in more effectively safeguarding the interests of vulnerable adults and ensuring they were appropriately cared for in the community.

*Stephen grunts, 'They were never interested in safeguarding mine.'*

It didn't.

In December 1992, disaster struck. Jonathon Zito, a young musician was randomly stabbed to death by Christopher Clunis, a 29-year old man with a history of psychiatric illness, including previous displays of violent behaviour. An enquiry found that Clunis had unequivocally been failed by all the agencies involved. Instead of providing funds for better care, this and other high-profile murders provoked a knee-jerk fear response and a sharp increase in the number of people being sectioned. Margaret Clayton, Chair of the Mental Health Act Commission, (December 2001) stated that most of those patients would not need to be incarcerated if there was proper care provision in place for them in the community.

Stephen tells me that as a result: 'The staff gloated in '94 and '95 and said, "You can forget all about Community Care". They said, "You will be detained for the rest of your life at our pleasure."' The last part of the 20th century had truly been a *decadum horribilis* and not just for Stephen.

'Because of all that Susie, it's made me feel worthless – it's made me feel quite worthless.' Stephen gets up slowly and walks down the corridor to the toilet. Sitting here, clasping my notes, I become aware of Classic FM and a young boy singing a haunting solo from Faure's Requiem.

*2003*

*Justice for Stephen*

Since 2001 Stephen had often told me the stories of his leg being broken and I thought it was awful and sad. I did believe him, but it hadn't crossed my mind that I should 'do' anything. It was over and done. Stephen needed to move forward with his life.

*He interjects 'Put up with it'. I nod, embarrassed.*

Beginning a 'Justice for Stephen' campaign was several layers of involvement deeper than I ever intended to go. I thought I was already being pretty bloody wonderful, to be honest.

*I shut my eyes and wait. A moment of silence and then Stephen remarks, 'Fair enough'.*

As a result, I had done nothing, but nor – I'd like to point out – had anyone else. After all, Stephen had his own formal 'Advocate'. This was someone with the authority to approach professionals on Stephen's behalf, challenge unfair treatment and push for correct levels of support. We shall call him John.

*'He was very kind'.*

John was a devoted Christian and had been Stephen's advocate since the late 1980s and yet he'd never questioned the authorities regarding Stephen's alleged abuse. I thought perhaps it was awkward as John was part of the system. He played music at services in the hospital and he led clubs in classical music and literature. Stephen fondly recalls John reading out some of Stephen's poems in the classes.

It turns out that the reason he never spoke out about the abuse is that Stephen didn't tell him. 'I knew that they'd find out and do me for slander. I kept quiet so he didn't find out until I left in 2001.'

*Stephen tells me now that John did eventually try to raise the issues, but 'they repelled him.' He can't remember when this happened.*

It was not until Stephen was physically out of the system that he gained enough independence and confidence to challenge it. Finally, in June 2003 Stephen was ready to take action. He had been out of hospital for a year, he was settled with Mandy and he felt not only safe, but strong.

He wanted me to help him.

2003 was a mixed year for me. I'd won my first writing competition in April, but my father was gravely ill. He was in and out of hospital and I was travelling to visit him, in between looking after my three primary-school aged children.

While I wouldn't have offered to take Stephen's case on at this point, I found I couldn't say no when asked directly. I could see that Stephen wasn't getting better and he wasn't able to put it all behind him. If what he told me was true (and I believed it was), then it was a grave injustice.

*Violin plays from Classic FM in the background as I read.*

In his first burst of enthusiasm, Stephen wanted to take his story to the papers. I put him off, as I couldn't see it ending well for him. Then he decided he was going to sue the health authority for the abuse he had suffered under their care. To do this we needed some legal advice and I agreed to help. Shortly afterwards, during that very hot August of 2003, my father died, and having no idea how to deal with grief, it hit me hard, intermittently and unexpectedly. I would burst into tears at odd times and then feel foolish and exhausted.

In the autumn, with my help, Stephen applied for the relevant hospital reports from 1992 and these eventually appeared in a massive thick manila envelope. After that I phoned several solicitors to find one who would agree to look at the case. In June 2004 Stephen and I drove to meet him, explained the issues and left the envelope with him.

In due course we received his answer.

There was no case.

*The violins rise to a crescendo and then drop.*

I'd thought he might say it was too long ago (12 years) or it was a matter of Stephen's word against theirs. Surely his delusions would be a problem? No, none of that. The reason we could take no action was because Stephen had a record of violence.

# Chapter 10

## Violence

*"Are you going to judge me?"*

Stephen, November 2013

Stephen had a history of violence.

It's June 2013 and we've been sitting in the garden talking about visiting the Roman mosaics at Fishbourne in our school days. We then move seamlessly on to the abuse he suffered. He mentions our failed attempt with the lawyer: 'Thanks a bunch, lawyer. He said I'd broken the law, committed affray.' At this point I ask if that's all he's done and he replies under his breath, 'Actual bodily harm. I don't want to talk about this. Just leave me alone.'

~

Until June 2013, Stephen had confessed only 2 occasions to me when he'd been violent as an adult. The first was back in 1977, while he was staying at the Divine Light Mission. As he was walking along a street, he encountered a fellow seeker of Inner Peace. 'I kicked her in the street. She contacted the police and they told me that if I ever did that again, I'd be arrested. It was unprovoked, I wanted to get my own back on her. She'd been so horrible to me in the meetings.'

So now he was on police record.

> *Stephen's acute sense of honesty demands that he correct me: 'I was on police record since 1970 and the incident with my mother. I don't wish to discuss it.'*

Three years later in 1980, he'd threatened a nurse with a hospital table knife and been sectioned for year. No police action was taken. Again, this was to 'get my own back on him.'

That was the sum of my knowledge until the 'V IMP' recording day in November 2013. We were in his front room, warm and smoky, Classic FM blessedly quiet at this point. Stephen had just taken me step by step through the abuse he had suffered in 1992. It had been a long afternoon, involving a flow of cheap instant coffee. Charlie pottered as usual up and down the corridor. We moved on to Stephen's need for justice and came up against the brick wall of his criminal record. I remarked that I couldn't believe he'd been particularly violent. There was a pause and then:

'Of course I've been violent Susie. I've been very violent.'

'Have you hurt anybody?'

'Of course I have! Loads of people, loads of people. Are you going to judge me? Cast aspersions?'

'No.'

'Are you going to?'

'No.'

'You're not?'

'No.'

'You're not?'

'No. I'm not interested in that.'

'You're not?'

'No.'

Reassured, Stephen repeats somewhat dramatically, 'Because I have been violent, I've been, dangerous, extremely dangerous.'

*I've been reading this to Stephen in a brisk, loud voice. Looking agitated, he interrupts me: 'I need to put the light on'. He gets up laboriously, switches on the light, then shuts the window and draws the curtains. It takes me a minute to catch on. I lower my voice.*

Finding this hard to believe, I ask him for more detail and he bursts out: 'I've broken someone's thumb, I've been charged with attempted rape, I've threatened people with knives, I nearly blinded a woman, I've done lots of terrible things, Susie.'

Do I judge him?

*Stephen asks 'Do you?' I insist I don't.*

This is quite a list. It raises a lot of questions. To what degree was Stephen responsible for what he did? If not him, who or what was? Is violence ever justified and what about 'incitement to violence,' or 'institutional violence'?

We begin to unpick his list. I choose the 'blinding' one first which took place in 1987. I ask flatly, 'Did you blind her?' 'I blinded her. She got her sight back in two days. It was an accident.' When I ask what happened, he becomes more agitated. 'I was playing around with fire. It was an accident.' It turns out that he was waving a fire lantern too close to her eyes.

*Stephen interrupts, 'I need a cigarette now, Susie. Careful what you say in case the neighbours hear.'*

The theme of fire reminds him of something else. 'Playing with fire, like I used to when I was a child. I committed arson in 1980, Susie. I set P ward on fire.' As I conjure up a building choked in flames and smoke and people running from it, screaming, Stephen explains, 'I set the curtains on fire and then the nurse put them out.' The fire brigade was never called. Stephen started the fire because 'I was desperate. I wanted to get out. I hated being locked in.' He was under section at the time, so why was he, or anyone able to access matches?

*Stephen answers simply, 'There were matches there.'*

We move on to 1996 and the occasion when Stephen broke someone's thumb. He was on a psychiatric ward, 'The female nurse kept shouting abuse at me, so I punched her hand. She had her hand back and I punched it without thinking. It was an accident, but I got cautioned for actual bodily harm. They blamed me.' This was a caution which Stephen must have accepted and he was therefore not taken to court.

Then there was a second time he threatened someone with a knife: 'Two nurses with a knife. 1998. I was trying to get my own back on them. It was horrible. They thought I was going to stab them.' These were male nurses who, he alleged, had abused him and one of them was SL*. From 1980 to 1998, SL* had been working at St B's and by the end of this long stretch, Stephen wanted his own back. But again, he was under section. How did he get hold of a knife under section? 'It was a table knife, Susie. They set the table for supper. They thought I was going to stab them with it, but I wasn't.'

Then Stephen stops speaking for a moment and sits up. He whispers urgently to me, 'I'm always frightened she gets to listen to me. She's not listening, is she?' I assume this is one of his voices and put on my 'calm' voice to reassure him that 'she' is not listening but then it occurs to me that he's talking about the woman in the flat above him. 'No, if you can't hear her, she can't hear you.' Stephen relaxes back into his chair, 'I went to court in 1998. Prosecuted. The police came and were horrible to me. One of my advocates spoke up for me.'

Stephen was charged with 'affray' and received a conditional discharge of 18 months. I ask if he hurt either of the nurses and he replies curtly, 'No, I certainly did not.' If Stephen had been considered dangerous, he'd have been sent to a higher security mental hospital. 'They were going to send me to Springfield [a medium secure hospital] but it fell through. They decided to keep me on D ward at St B's. It was hell.'

I realise that this (possibly together with the previous record of ABH in 1996) is the violent offence the lawyer was talking about. I look up 'Affray': 'A person is guilty of *affray* if he uses or threatens unlawful violence towards another and his conduct is such as would cause a person of reasonable firmness present at the scene to fear for his personal safety.' As a result, Stephen lost the right to bring his case against the Health Authority over the breaking of his leg.

We've dealt with ABH and Affray. I gear myself up to ask about the attempted rape. Stephen is tense and edgy.

'OCD [Obsessive Compulsive Disorder] got the better of me which is why I committed that dreadful act… I jumped on top of her. She used to thump me all the time. I wanted to get my own back on her. She kept thumping me, she kept thumping everyone. It was my OCD gone wrong and I'm disgusted with myself. It amazes me to think that I could get the better of her anyway. I held her down but there was nothing sexual in it.'

I ask if staff pulled him off her but it turns out neither staff nor other patients was around at the time.

'I pulled myself off. I left. She didn't tell anyone until the following week. There was an investigation but she elaborated the story, she exaggerated.'

'Did she say you had raped her?'

'Yes, but I hadn't.'

At the time, Stephen was under section on a psychiatric ward and the incident involved another patient. After going around the houses a bit, I gather that the inquiry found there was insufficient evidence and the woman was considered an unreliable witness. The incident was recorded as "attempted rape". Neither the woman, her husband nor any family members pursued the matter further. Although it had been formally dealt with, this incident continued to haunt Stephen. 'Three years later a nurse there said to me, "Don't worry about it". He was one of the best nurses there. He never touched me once.'

Nearly 20 years later he still worries that the police will turn up at his door. I reassure him as best I can: the incident was dealt with, he was under section, it was the staff's responsibility to keep him and the woman safe. Sometimes my words help for a while.

At the end of that long afternoon of confessions I check we're finished. 'Have you been done for GBH?'

'No, I haven't been done for it.'

Relief washes through me, but then he carries on, 'Not been done for it. I committed it. That woman was losing her eyesight. That was GBH. Waving a fire lantern at her.'

Stephen becomes agitated and repeats over and over, 'It was an accident, Susie.' I ask if this ended up in court and he replies, 'They just shepherded me away, took her to hospital and she got her sight back after two days.'

He looks so sunk and defeated in his chair. 'I'm not judging you, Stephen.'

To which he mutters under his breath, 'You've not done the

things I've done and neither has anyone else.'

*Stephen comments: 'You're judging me even now.' We do a 'no I'm not', 'yes you are' routine for a few minutes. 'The way you fire the questions like Jeremy Paxman. He sides against a person.'*

*I argue that I'm not doing that and if I can read on, he'll see. Eventually he lets me.*

Stephen's voice becomes raspy and difficult to hear as he mutters 'You wouldn't have liked me.'

'You used to leave horrible messages on my phone,' I remind him, 'but I worked on the basis you didn't really mean it.' Stephen remembers this. 'Back in 2001, I left some pretty nasty messages. Now I just want to pass away. I feel so useless and worthless.'

Still in interview mode, I ask, 'Why do you feel so useless?' He glares at me, 'You should be able to work that one out yourself.'

In the interest of fairness, I feel I should put down my own history of violence.

*Listening to this, Stephen frowns, 'I'd rather you didn't, I don't want to know, I'm sorry.'*

My preference is towards passive aggression, but events do accumulate when you've lived over 50 years on this planet. I also discover that it is unpleasant writing it all down. And worse when I know I'll have to read it out to Stephen.

*I remark lightly, 'So, we'll see if you judge me Stephen.' He rasps back, very serious,*
*'I am judging you.'*

When I was about eight, our family stayed in a friend's house in the UK for a couple of weeks. I broke a French window by mistake, early in the morning. I blamed it on my little brother who was only two and he got smacked. I never owned up.

On another occasion, when I was 16, I truly saw 'red' and kicked in a door at school. A boy had been winding me up and run into the room thinking he was safe on the other side of the door.

*Stephen is genuinely surprised as I read this: 'So you've done things wrong too? I thought I was the only one who'd done these sorts of things.'*

Then, aged 17 I kicked a bloke in the balls. I thought it would be funny. Apparently, it isn't.

*'You never! I don't believe you did.'*
*'I did. Only once.'*

Later on in life, the main times that violence came close was when trying to raise three small children. I tend to get very bad when I'm tired. On one occasion when I was holding a crying baby at three in the morning, Tim came into the room, saw my face, gently removed him from me and sent me back to bed.

I sometimes smacked my children, too. Sorry.

*'The point is, a lot of children are smacked.'*

I don't approve of smacking and I was never one of those Bible literalists who follow the 'spare the rod and spoil the child' approach. I smacked them because I'd run out of options and I'd lost it. It was shameful and I'm ashamed. I find it frightening, the violent feelings that can be generated when I feel frustrated and powerless.

*Stephen becomes reflective: 'I don't think I judge any of that. How can I possibly? Look I don't judge people. I judge unfairness and terrorism, abuse, mental hospitals and dishonesty. I judge people who are dishonest.'*

With regard to Stephen and myself, while we've occasionally lost our tempers with each other, there has never been any physical violence between us. I have never been afraid of Stephen. Tim also says he has never felt in any way unsafe with Stephen. Stephen may have been verbally aggressive at times, when he was particularly agitated, but Tim never felt physically threatened.

When I look over what Stephen told me about his violent history, two things stand out for me. Firstly, every time he attacked or threatened to attack someone, he said it was to get his own back, either for being verbally or physically abused.

The other thing that struck me in listening to Stephen was that almost all the violent incidents had happened when Stephen was inside, on a psychiatric ward and under section. No-one linked Stephen's violence with the violence of locking a person up against their will.

Through the 1970s most English psychiatric wards had been open and most of the admissions were voluntary (at least in name). In the last two decades of the 20th century this changed with more involuntary admissions and a move towards 'closed door' as the default policy. This meant that a member of staff had to let people in or out of the ward. Keeping the doors locked was supposed to help reduce absconding, violence, alcohol and substance misuse and self-harm.

*Stephen barks: 'It didn't. Locked wards made people worse!'*

A report published in 2008 by City University London suggests that it did not achieve those aims. Not only did it result in patients feeling 'frustrated, stigmatised and depressed,'

*'That's how I felt!'*

it also significantly increased the risk of physical violence to others. However, Professor Len Bowers, who conducted the research, admitted there was a problem with causality. Did increased violence cause increased containment, or did increased containment increase the violence? Similarly, we could ask if Stephen's attacks showed the extent of his poor mental health at the time, or if the more stringent controls provoked a violent reaction in him.

After the killing of Jonathan Zito by Christopher Clunis in 1992 there was an increased emphasis on control and confinement. Stephen was a victim of this trend, placed on a section in 1994 which was continuously renewed for 6 years until 2000.

*Stephen corrects me: four years till 1998 and then put back on, five-and-a-half months later.*

It was during this period that he was at his most aggressive. It seems very likely that the combination of the locked door policy together with sectioning him repeatedly, at such length, aggravated his situation further rather than relieving it.

*As I read this back to Stephen, I ask him: 'Would you agree with that?'*
*'Absolutely.'*

A review in 2015 entitled 'Service users' experiences and views of aggressive situations in mental health care' found that 'incidents are triggered when users experience staff behaviour as custodial rather than caring and when they feel ignored.'

When you have no power, no rights, is violence an act of aggression or self-defence?

*2004–2006*
*Marriage and Mental Illness*

In 2004 after the solicitor told us there was no case because Stephen had committed 'affray', I didn't push Stephen for more details or consider challenging the solicitor. The 'Justice for Stephen' campaign was over.

On a personal level, Stephen and Mandy were struggling. It was never going to be straightforward; Stephen had been institutionalised for 25 years and this was his first experience of living privately with another person, let alone the intimate relationship of marriage. Mandy had been married before and knew about intimacy, but here was a man on the spectrum, whose autism meant that he could not pick up emotional 'signals' and he struggled with empathy. To top this, while she was naturally warm and loving, Mandy's bi-polar disorder meant her moods were volatile: sometimes high and overactive, sometimes depressed and suicidal. This was not an easy combination.

Marriage is not simple at the best of times. When Tim and I were first married, neither of us had lived with a partner before, and while we were not 'mentally ill', we both brought our own baggage to the relationship. Stephen and Mandy had some serious mental health issues and they needed support, yet Stephen was very wary of care professionals. The only professionals Stephen called upon regularly were the police.

Stephen and Mandy loved each other dearly, but from 2004 I became aware of physical violence happening between them, in both directions. On at least one occasion, Mandy attacked Stephen with scissors and poured cold water on him at night.

*'Cold water at 4 am.'*

She hid his pills on a regular basis, which would send him hysterical. He rang the police once because she wouldn't stop hitting him.

### *My Diary Entry, 2004*

'Police come over very angry. Want Mandy to come to police station to be cautioned. Mandy won't go. Police threaten to have her in court if she won't comply. Mandy's mum says if they go to court, she'll tell the court all the awful things Stephen has done and he'll be put away. Stephen is in a terrible state – begs Mandy – Mandy agrees to be cautioned.'

There were also times when Stephen hit Mandy, although he didn't tell me that until later. She too would ring the police, but she never pressed charges. Either Mandy or Stephen called the police at least twice a week on a regular basis. These seemed to be the only people they could ring out of hours.

*My Diary Entry, October 2004*

'Mandy takes an overdose and goes to hospital. Stephen rings the hospital and they say they're keeping her in overnight so Stephen locks and bolts the door, takes a sleeping pill and goes to sleep. Mandy runs away from hospital and tries to return home, but she can't get in. She rings the police who come over and break a window. Stephen is woken by breaking glass and is terrified that it's burglars. He offers to pay for the glass repair.'

All this upset him but he understood: 'Mandy can't help it – she's ill.' On another night, after another row, 'I may have tapped her', Stephen took a sleeping pill and went to bed. When he woke up at 6am, Mandy wasn't there. 'I rang the police to say she'd disappeared. They searched the house and they couldn't find her. They assumed I'd beaten her up.' Stephen had dreamt he'd beaten up Mandy, so he was confused. The police found out that Mandy had gone to hospital, and without checking why, they arrested Stephen on suspicion of causing actual bodily harm, and put him in a cell for the day. In the late afternoon, they discovered that Mandy had gone to hospital because she'd taken an overdose, not because Stephen had hit her. Stephen was then released, worried that he was still in trouble but: 'They said there was nothing to worry about, no evidence whatsoever. Mandy said it had never happened.'

In between these extreme exchanges, there were good times. They had each other, the house and the dog. Mandy had her mother and her adult children nearby and Stephen would go out to the drop-in centres and visit friends or occasionally come out with me to a beauty spot or to visit Carol.

Meanwhile I got on with my life. I began seeing someone for counselling (which helped me a great deal), I started a children's drama club, attended an evening course in screenwriting, continued to collect people and spent inordinate amounts of time de-nitting my daughter's long hair.

Then in March 2005, Stephen's Advocate, John, died in a horrific car crash. It was the same day, Stephen tells me, 'that hooligans beat Charlie with sticks in the back garden of our house.' Rose's partner chased them off. John's death was shocking and Stephen was deeply upset.

Spring and summer passed, I was accepted to begin an MA in Dramatic Writing in the autumn and my family went on a long-desired holiday to South Africa, visiting friends from our Christian Community days.

Stephen and Mandy had been away in early summer, back to the holiday place in Hampshire but it had not gone so well this time, 'It was horrible and they barred us.' That's all I ever learned about it.

Then in August, 'We had a nasty row. I stormed out to a fete at the local park – when I came back everything was locked and bolted up. She wouldn't let me in, so I smashed a window and she rang the police. When the police came, instead of attending to my wrists, they insisted on taking me to the police station. Blood was spurting out all over my hand. I refused to go and they called up several cars, several men – it was horrible, horrible. They dragged me downstairs, handcuffed me, dragged me out to the car – just for smashing a window. Finally, after they put me in a cell a police sergeant dressed the injury – it took ages to persuade them. I was in a cell for the evening and had a horrible time eating their soup. They didn't know how to make soup properly.'

'I love the way you tell a story,' I comment. 'Then what happened?'

'They said "Your step-daughter is the owner of the house and if she presses charges against you, then you'll be prosecuted for criminal damage." She didn't press charges. She said it was all Mandy's fault for locking me out and made Mandy pay for the window.'

Autumn and Christmas 2005 were dominated by the issue of Stephen's arm, the operation and the subsequent fall-out and sectioning from January 2006 through to April.

'I went through hell then, hell on earth. Mandy nearly left me at one point over an affair. She came back to me and had me back at home in the end on my birthday and that all made up for it.'

Stephen starts to talk about something else, but I'm not letting him off the hook: 'Was it you who had the affair?' He reacts strongly, 'Leave me alone, leave me alone!'

We listen to Classic FM for a few minutes, before Stephen says quietly, 'I had the affair'. It must have happened on the ward but I don't push any further.

In April 2006 Stephen's stint at the mental hospital finished. Initially he went back to the halfway house he'd first gone to in 2001, 'I felt much better for going there. I had a good time there and everything was fine.' Wow! I'd never heard him say that before. But the sunshine didn't last. 'They transferred me to that horrible place at E.' This was about an hour's drive from his home, 'I hated it.'

Finally, in August 2006, Stephen was allowed home to Mandy. It wasn't until autumn that I discovered Stephen had been hitting Mandy, despite only having the use of one arm.

### My Diary Entry, November 2006

'Had an awkward conversation with Stephen. He wanted me to tell the psychiatrist to protect him from the police. I said it didn't work like that. If Stephen hits Mandy, the police are obliged to do something. He said he'd asked the social worker to tell Mandy's mother not to ring the police. I said that would make no difference. If Stephen hits Mandy and Mandy tells her mother, her mother will ring the police. The police will come to investigate.

*'She did. I got arrested.'*

'Mistake 1 – Suggesting he should consider moving out.
'Mistake 2 – Suggesting hitting your wife is wrong.
'We got into an argument over the rights and wrongs of hitting people. He disagreed that it was wrong: he can't help it, he's disabled, he's oversensitive, he's suffered hell in his life, he's different from everyone else. I wanted to shout at him but I managed to say goodnight and put the phone down. He rang me later to tell me I was no longer his friend and he loved the dog.'

I didn't know what to do. In my book, you don't hit your wife. Full stop.

*Listening now, Stephen agrees with me: 'No you don't.'*

Mandy did not want to be alone and she loved Stephen. Stephen agreed to changes in his medication and as a result he became calmer but also duller and sleepier. He was now a fire hazard because he would routinely fall asleep with a lit cigarette in his hand.

*Stephen remembers this well: 'Oh yes. The fire brigade came on numerous occasions. It was like a tinder box.'*

He would also smoke in his bed upstairs. While the main bed was downstairs, Stephen would sometimes sleep upstairs but then Mandy would pour water on him. To protect himself he'd lock the door but now there was a danger he would burn down the house. He didn't take kindly to my suggestion that he only smoke downstairs.

*I ask if he smokes in his reclining chair in the night, 'I have done. I've had nasty accidents. A towel caught fire at 6 am once, and the b... caught fire.'*
*'The bean?'*
*'The BIN – the bin caught fire – when are you getting hearing aids?'*

By January 2007, I knew that we were going to be moving to a new parish, a hundred miles away. We had lived in the same place for 8 years, the longest I had settled anywhere. For the first time in my adult life, I had felt 'at home'. I'd also discovered the creative source of my life there and was coming to the end of my MA in Dramatic Writing.

This time I had no doubt that the move would put an end to my contact with Stephen. I'd moved frequently over the years and had kept in contact with very few people. With regard to Stephen, I wanted to ensure that someone else would take over my role and I was sure I had it sorted.

# Part 2

Confluence

The Rivers Meet

# Chapter 11

## All Change

*'Nothing is so painful to the human mind*
*As a great and sudden change.'*

Mary Shelley

*How many bishops does it take to change a lightbulb?*

(see bottom of page for answer)

Answer: change?

I like change. Stephen doesn't. He's entitled to his opinion.

Stephen was not impressed that we were moving 100 miles away. Couldn't we have found somewhere nearer? It was very inconvenient. How was he going to get out with Charlie and who was going to take him to see Carol?

I told him my plan. I knew someone who could help, who was a lovely member of our church and a dog lover. Over the summer of 2006, Clare had looked after Charlie now and then and Charlie was smitten. When it came to dog care, this woman was gold standard. She was also a kind and caring human being. I had it all planned. She was the one who would take Stephen and Charlie out on a regular basis.

Stephen approved, so in May 2007 I took Clare to visit. I thought it had gone well, but when we got back to her house she was distressed. It all came splurging out: she didn't feel the house and conditions were suitable for a dog, she knew she wouldn't be able to cope with Stephen and she would end up wanting to take the dog away or perhaps even ring the RSPCA. She was sorry, but it was too upsetting. I went home and wrote in my diary: 'I'm terrified at how important it is to impress on Clare that Charlie mustn't be taken from Stephen. I'm terrified of betraying Stephen. I'm also angry because I want her to care about Stephen. All she cares about is the bloody dog.'

Clare suggested that she could have Charlie, permanently, and occasionally take him to visit Stephen. Stephen did not take kindly to this.

*My Diary Entry, May 2007*

'Sunday – Saw Clare and spoke to her, stopped feeling angry and remembered she was a very kind person. She apologised for putting more work on me. I said no way would Stephen let her have the dog, even hints sent him hysterical. I tried to re-assure her that it wasn't as bad for Charlie as she thought – her eyes filled up. I tried to make her smile by saying that of course, Charlie would be better off with her but so would half the dogs in the county! Felt that we had worked it out between us ok.'

And that was it.

I had hoped that by the time I left, Stephen might be part of a supportive church but he'd never found anywhere to settle. Mandy's church was too evangelical and while he'd occasionally visited a friendly Anglican church nearby, no-one there had invited him over, given him lifts or offered any help. What is the point of 'belief' or all this 'Jesus saved me' lark if Christians don't bloody DO anything? I didn't even have the pleasure of feeling self-righteous, because I could have rung the priest myself, gone to the church, asked for support for Stephen. I didn't.

I consoled myself with the fact that he had a home, he had the dog, he had Mandy, even if there were on-going issues. He had a care coordinator and a support worker, who had apparently offered to take him to see Carol on occasion. It would do.

July came along. We were going to move in under a month.

*My Diary Entry, July 2007*

'There's so much to do that sometimes I do nothing. I don't
mean that I stare at the wall – I throw the odd piece of
paper away – I sit and find reasons to google useful sites – I
play solitaire on the computer – I just don't **do** anything!
The biggest feeling is a sense of pressure building up –
jogging helps temporarily and offsets the huge amounts of
food I suddenly want to eat. Take one day at a time. One
day and the schools have been chosen, one day and the
carpets are decided, one day and, heh presto, we have paint.'

*My Diary Entry, 3 July*

'I know I am moving in 3 weeks and 2 days because Lara
tells me precise timings and she tells me every day. She is
10. My two elder sons act as if nothing is happening.'

*My Diary Entry, 2 August – Moving Day*

'The removals men have arrived and started packing. I
realise what a paltry level of clearing I've done when I find
men packing boxes full of small bits of wrapping paper and
half-used glue pots.

'The children are incensed. Tim is about to take them off to
family for a few days and I've had the nerve to insist they
do half an hour's cleaning before they leave. All hell breaks
loose. I stand there repeating that it seems a reasonable
request while Tim tells me I don't need to justify myself.
Finally, Lara heads off with a hoover and Peter slumps off
with a feather duster, abusing me under his breath, but
Aidan simply screams and throws himself on the floor
(he is 12), until it is made clear to him that he will not be

seeing his cousins until he has cleared one room of rubbish. And throughout this display of family good will, men keep appearing and disappearing with boxes, chairs, cupboards and bits of beds.'

## *My Diary Entry, 3 August – New Home*

'I feel like we're in a holiday let. Spent the day unpacking and cleaning. Everything was fine – sun shining, rooms looking beautiful, boxes emptying – and then – this weight built up inside me – finally, I came upstairs, sat down on our bed – and cried – I've left behind my home and friends and 8 years of my children's childhood. My youngest is 10. I can't go back.'

For most of August I sat and wrote my dissertation, 'Is Theatre An Effective Arena For Political Expression?', while Tim looked after the kids. In a nod towards my friend Clare, before I left, I'd impressed upon Stephen the need to take Charlie out for a walk every day and he followed this advice with his customary seriousness.

When I ask him about that time, he's curt: 'I didn't see you when you left. There were more problems at home. I don't really want to talk about that.'

I know that Stephen carried on ringing over August but Tim fielded most of the calls. Normally people get the hint when you never ring them. The word 'hint' is not in Stephen's vocabulary. As long as Tim or I carried on answering the phone, he would carry on ringing. He would occasionally comment, 'Perhaps you could ring me sometime? That would be nice.' I agreed that it would be nice, but I didn't. I had

10,000 words to write.

*Stephen mutters repeatedly: 'My fault, all my fault' while I feel excruciatingly embarrassed at reading this.*

In September all three kids had to negotiate new schools, Lara to primary and the boys to the local secondary school. The latter was chaotic, as the school had failed to register the boys with the LEA and the deputy head didn't even know they were coming.

## My Diary Entry, September 2007

'The room marked 'reason' has got lost. I am in a corridor with doors marked 'failed parent', 'we should never have come to this godforsaken town', 'I want to go home' etc. Tim is as angry, but calmer. We leave phone messages, send e-mails to the school and the LEA, arguing with one another over phrases like 'this is unacceptable'. Will that give the impression of strong parents? Or just stroppy ones?'

A hundred miles away, the clouds were gathering around Stephen and Mandy. Threats had been made to move him by the mental health team but these had been happening on such a regular basis that they were simply part of the texture of life.

Over the autumn, Mandy went into a tailspin and her mental health fell apart. This time she didn't take an overdose but looked for help and requested to go and stay on the psychiatric ward as a voluntary patient. So far so good. Now she was in a place of safety.

A few days later, she threw a chair across the room. According to Stephen, instead of being sectioned for her own protection and the protection of others, this behaviour was deemed unacceptable and she was ejected from the psychiatric hospital and sent home to Stephen and the dog. Apparently, trained staff shouldn't have to deal with this but a vulnerable, mentally ill husband would have to instead. He tells me,

'I couldn't take it. She was really ill and I couldn't take her behaviour. She threw hot water at me, she hit me, she pulled my hair too. I couldn't take that.' When I suggest they should have sectioned her, he actually agrees with me.

Stephen tells me that Mandy arrived back from the ward the evening before he was transferred to temporary accommodation, Stanley Place. The timing of it hits me like a slap in the face.

*Stephen growls, 'That was an awful business Susie, an awful business.'*

We listen to the music on Classic FM. I remember both these events but had not linked them in my mind before this. I ask what led to him to being moved. 'I don't want to tell you.'

I'm fairly sure I know, but I have to ask.

'Is it because you hit Mandy?'

'Yes. She hit me, she abused me that night. She called the police and said I'd done it to her and I hadn't. I hardly touched her.' He pauses, breathing heavily, 'I only hit her as a last resort. She left and rang the police from Arthur's house. All I know is at ten to three in the morning the police were coming round. Instead of handcuffing me they said, "We'll let you make a cup of coffee first to wake you up."' This shows how well they knew Stephen by then. 'They said, "Come on Stephen, you're coming with us". Three of them, two men and a woman.' He did what he was told and went with them to the police station where he was charged, but at that point he refused to go into a cell, so they handcuffed him.

The following day he was moved to Stanley Place. Mandy withdrew the charges and he was not detained under the Mental Health Act. 'I didn't want anything more to do with her when I left. Patrick [care coordinator] put me in a place of safety for my own good in Stanley Place. I know there was noise at Stanley Place in the street, but it was better.'

To my knowledge Stephen had never lived on his own before in his life.

> 'Once I stayed on my own overnight – for one night in 1998. That's all.'

I visited once, but don't recall much other than it being small, and in a central position in the town. It was, according to Stephen, a council flat, not supported housing.

Did he still visit Mandy and Charlie?

'Yes, I did. G..th too..ne…too ee.'

'I can't hear you, you've got your cigarette in your mouth.'

We wait while he slowly takes the cigarette out and rests it carefully on the ashtray.

'Never mind,' he says. 'Gareth [support worker] took me. I went for one or two nights every so often. Every week sometimes.'

'Did you get on better with Mandy?'

'It was wonderful, wonderful.'

Back then, I was relieved that he and Mandy were not living together. It seemed a better option to live separately and meet up. The mental health team were sorting it, Stephen was no longer in my sights.

*This phrase catches Stephen's attention. 'What are you saying?'*
*This is awkward, 'I was expecting not to carry on knowing you.'*
*'Why?'*
*'Because I moved away. I don't keep friends very often who live a distance away.'*
*'You made your point.'*
*We sit quietly and I feel like crap. Then a thought occurs to him:*
*'But you kept on with me.'*
*'Yeah, I did.'*

We'd moved to a town where to my eyes, everyone who wasn't homeless had a career, at least two children, a doctorate, an allotment and made jam in their spare time, when they weren't keeping fit, supporting a charity or raising awareness of global warming.

### My Diary Entry, 27 November

'Have been quite depressed. Started crying on Sunday morning – Felt loneliness. I also feel a total and complete failure. Other women pursue careers – I could have done and I didn't. I've done bits here and there – a little bit with the refugees, a little bit with Stephen – but these are tiny things. Here I am – I'm a nobody.

*Stephen adds, 'I'm a nobody.'*

Stephen gives me a sense of value. One or two people give me a sense of worth.'

*'I'm a nobody Susie, I'm a speck of dust.' He inhales his cigarette and affirms, 'Compared to the mighty statesmen, I'm just a speck of dust.' I remind him what I'd written – that he made me feel valuable. He doesn't know how to take this.*

I knew theoretically that all my value, all my self-worth came from God but I did not feel it. This particular internal wrangle was only the beginning of at least 5 years of angst. 2 days later it ebbed a little:

### My Diary Entry, 29 November

'Am feeling more upbeat – may be something to do with actually making time to write.'

*Stephen reflects: 'I'm so glad you come here Susie.'*
*'Thank you, Stephen.'*
*'You like coming here, don't you?'*
*I want to answer honestly. 'Yeah, I do now. Sometimes it's hard work when you're really miserable, but I like to see you.'*
*'I'm not that bad, am I?'*
*I smile at him, 'No, you're not that bad.'*

Stephen was at Stanley Place for nearly eight months and while it was 'wonderful' when he saw Mandy, the rest of the time was not so satisfactory. 'One night at Stanley Place I was ringing 111. I threatened to kill myself and police turned up at one am and I made several suicide threats.'

Throughout the spring, Stephen struggled with his dismal exile, made bearable by his visits to Mandy. In February: 'I was at Mandy's when I found a pink suitcase out on the pavement. Mandy came up and said, "That's a nice suitcase, I'll have that!" and I said, "You don't know who it belongs to, you can't do that!"' Stephen laughs at the memory of this.

'The neighbour came out said, "That's my suitcase!" But then she said, "You can have it."'

Through the spring of 2008 I ran an after-school drama club at my sons' local secondary school on a voluntary basis but the need for a job was pressing in on me. I no longer wanted to be in the role of 'Vicar's wife' and general dogsbody, as I saw it. It didn't help that our new church was Victorian in style, with pews, organ, robed choir and mostly traditional hymns. The thinking was liberal and there were interesting people there, but I was missing our old church.

*Stephen shows sympathy, 'You must have been having a miserable time, too.'*

On 23rd March, Stephen and Mandy celebrated their sixth wedding anniversary. Then as April approached, Stephen began looking forward to celebrating his birthday with her. He was still visiting Mandy a couple of days a week and it was going well between them. While Mandy always had her ups and downs, there was nothing to warn him, nothing to prepare him for what happened next.

*'Do you want me to read this to you?'*
*'If I find it too depressing, I'll tell you to stop.'*

On 2nd April 2008, the day before Stephen's 53rd birthday, Mandy jumped out of an upstairs window in her house. 'The neighbour found her with a broken spine.' My throat and gut clench at the image of Mandy lying there on the concrete.

I understood it to be one of her suicide attempts, but Stephen is angry and adamant. 'It wasn't!' I had not considered how traumatic this thought would be for Stephen. He explains, 'It was because the door was jammed and she couldn't get out.

Somebody closed it and I suspect that was Arthur.' Arthur was an old friend of Mandy's and this explanation made no sense to me. Stephen's view was, 'He might have done it accidently. Without thinking. Somebody did it.' Stephen accused Arthur at the time, and had upset him a great deal. I suggest Mandy might have got into a state of panic and confusion, and thought the door was locked when it wasn't. Stephen considers this, eventually agreeing that it was a very difficult door to open and that perhaps Arthur had no part in it.

I'm on the outside, looking in from a 'rational' point of view and I don't understand why, if Mandy wasn't suicidal, she didn't ring someone and tell them she was trapped? Stephen says she didn't own a mobile phone. So why didn't she shout for help? It is Tim who suggests that maybe in her mental distress she thought her only option was to jump out of the window. Perhaps it was perfectly logical to her.

At the time, the staff at the Mental Hospital, along with myself, considered it a suicide attempt. Mandy was first taken to the general hospital and then when she was considered well enough, moved to Moorhaven Mental Hospital. It was there Stephen says, 'She got a chest infection which developed into pneumonia.'

It was Rose, Mandy's daughter, who told Stephen on the Sunday that Mandy had died the previous day, Saturday 17th May 2008.

Stephen will rarely talk about that time, and doesn't like me asking about it, 'You're upsetting me.' On one occasion he rasps, 'She died in a horrific way. You know that, don't you?' I agree 'I know that' and he repeats this several times to himself before we move on.

He is at his most vociferous when talking about how she was treated, 'I don't forgive them for putting her in a cold room. They put Mandy in that cold room in 2008. That was a crime.'

> *Stephen's tone is intense. 'The grudge that I bear, Susie, is primarily [about] when they put Mandy in the cold room and she died of pneumonia. That is the main grudge – not what they did to me so much.'*

Writing this now is painful. At the time I blocked it out, I didn't want to feel the pain. Mandy had made many suicide attempts over the years; it was much easier to think that she didn't really want to live than sit with the horror and the loss. My background had taught me to avoid pain, either by rationalising in this way or by 'Christianising' it into comforting phrases. 'They're with the Lord.' Job done, move on. The capacity to accept and feel the pain has taken me a long time to develop. It is not faith but mindfulness that has helped me and it is an on-going journey. Nowadays I know other people with bi-polar, vibrant, delightful people, none of whom want to die except when a depressive episode takes them over.

I bring to mind that small vital woman. She was never dull, never boring, always smiling, teasing, anxious or weeping, rarely anything in the middle. She adored Stephen and she worked so hard to keep him clean and fed. With dyspraxia and then a failing arm, he was a messy eater. Intense and tactile, she had adult children and a mother who she loved deeply. Her mother lived to be over 100 years old.

*Rose – Mandy's daughter's story*

After Stephen died, we were sitting together in the funeral director's office and Rose told me about her mother's death. She was certain that Mandy wasn't trying to commit suicide and that her previous attempts had been cries for help. Mandy got herself locked in her bedroom and couldn't get out. Charlie was downstairs and she was worried about him. She panicked, climbed out onto the flat roof and jumped off. She was taken to hospital and then moved to the mental hospital where she got pneumonia and the staff couldn't seem to get on top of it. Rose visited her every day and finally the staff told her they couldn't do much more and they weren't going to resuscitate her mum if she stopped breathing. Rose was completely overwhelmed by this. She didn't know what to do with herself. She doesn't drink at all, but her friends persuaded her to come out for a drink. Then she went back to her mum's bedside and lay next to her mum all that night. The following day she rang her grandmother, who had felt too distressed to come up to that point, and persuaded her that she needed to because there wasn't much time left. Her grandmother, Mandy's mum came over and made her goodbyes to her beloved daughter. She then left the room and sat on a chair outside while Rose went back in to sit beside her mother. Then, Rose told me, 'She passed almost immediately with me holding her hand.' Rose is sure that Mandy waited for her mother to come.

~

On June 11th 2008, I drove down for the funeral. It was a short service in a chapel and then a burial. I sat with the care coordinator and Stephen. I'd been worried that Stephen might become hysterical and so I was tense throughout. He cried, occasionally loudly, but that was all. He wanted to attend the burial so we drove over. We all stood on a hillside and took our turn to walk past the grave. Then we stood and watched them filling in the earth.

Stephen was withdrawn and unhappy, but he did not collapse.

One year and so many changes.

Two weeks after this, I applied to work as a part-time Teaching Assistant at a local primary school. An email I sent to one of my referees explains: 'At the interview I banged on about drama. They rang later and offered me a job, 2 days a week, taking small groups of children out of lessons to do drama and creative writing – all to help the kids with literacy. I can't quite believe my good fortune!'

This was the first paid employment I'd had in 15 years.

For Stephen the big change came three weeks after Mandy's funeral.

*Stephen interjects, 'It was June 30th at 5.45pm'*

He was moved out of temporary accommodation to a ground floor flat with a garden. Mandy's daughter had been looking after Charlie but now Charlie moved in.

For the first time in his life, aged 53, Stephen was embarking on an independent life, living alone with his dog. I wonder what odds the bookies would have given him of lasting six months.

*'I lasted, didn't I?'*

# Chapter 12

## Ordinary Life

*'Oh how I desire –*
*so desperately, so intensely –*
*The yearning, the longing, the passion–*
*oh Mandy;*
*on Earth I shall never again*
*see or experience the wonder of You.'*

Extract from poem by Stephen July 2011

It was 30th June 2008, six weeks after Mandy died. Stephen was now living in an ordinary flat on an ordinary residential street; a ground floor flat with a small garden. Nearby was a park where he could take Charlie and his local health centre was in walking distance. A film would end at this moment: panning out from the man and dog to the house on the street, the cemetery and Mandy's grave, the city spreading out below us. The music would be tender, melancholic with sparse notes of hope.

But this wasn't a film, and it wasn't over. What was truly remarkable and what I'd somehow failed to notice was that, despite forcible removal from his home, six months in temporary accommodation and the traumatic death of his wife, Stephen had neither fallen apart nor gone into a psychotic state warranting a section or even the threat of it.

*I look to Stephen for acknowledgement. He responds gruffly, 'We got through that. That's all over and done with.'*

One of the reasons I didn't see this is that I didn't open up to the pain of Stephen's loss. Even if I'd recognised the enormity of his achievement, I'd still have put better odds on Sisyphus getting his boulder to the top of the mountain than Stephen lasting a year on his own.

*I ask if Stephen knows about Sisyphus? 'No and I don't want to know.' In Greek mythology, Sisyphus was a king punished by the God Zeus to push a boulder up a hill for eternity. Just as he was about to reach the summit, it would roll back down and he would begin again.*

By now I knew I couldn't abandon Stephen but I'd mostly given up on him finding ease or peace in his life. I reckoned my role was to support him by listening to him when he made his weekly phone calls, and to visit and take him to Carol's once or twice a year.

Over the next four years this is how we maintained contact as we each got on with our own lives. I now had a part-time job but this did not assuage a burgeoning mid-life crisis, which declared my life a waste of time. I had an MA and had written and produced over 50 pieces of drama, but didn't consider myself a writer. Fortunately, Hugh Turner thought I was. Hugh ran a drama project with primary school children and got me involved. Between 2008 and 2012, I worked part-time, created dramas with Hugh as well as in the church, wrote and produced a set of three short films (one based on Stephen's situation) and became a school governor at one school and chair of the PTA at another. All this while getting a dog, having three teenagers in the house and as the vicar's wife, getting involved in the new church. None of this ever felt 'enough' to appease the mid-life crisis, but there were many moments of happiness. In one diary entry in 2009 I wrote:

'I want to dance, like the branches and leaves I'm watching now, dancing in the morning breeze. I want Stephen to join in the dance.'

Stephen wasn't ready for a dance, but he did last that first year on his own – with Charlie of course – despite his grief and the many obstacles to living an ordinary life. As I'm writing this Chapter in 2017, he is still there. And as he says, 'It's been a heck of a struggle.'

From 2009 his depression set in and over all these years Stephen has been on constant alert in case 'they' should remove him and take him back to hospital. Even the word 'hospital' sets him off. At one point in 2014, I asked him to sign a letter giving his care team permission to contact me, if anything happened to him. He immediately reacted,

'What do you mean, if anything happens to me?'

'If you went to hospital, nobody would ring me.'

His eyebrows lowered, 'I don't want to go to hospital. I hate hospital!'

'I just meant an ordinary hospital.'

'I wouldn't go to Moorhaven, that's for sure.'

'All I'm saying is…'

'I hate Moorhaven.'

'I'm not saying…'

'I hate all hospitals! I loathe and despise all hospitals. If they try to take me to hospital, I'll barricade the house up. I'll…'

*Stephen echoes this as I read it.*

He did eventually sign the letter. This fear of being taken back to hospital has never left him. His life with Charlie in the flat was, and remains, provisional.

The good news was that he was in his own home, in a nice area of town supported by a mental health team and daily carers. The difficulty was how to manage the responsibility of independent life. From 2008, I grew used to the way every phone call would begin:

'Everything's gone wrong.'

## NEGOTIATING EVERYDAY LIFE

For Stephen, negotiating everyday life was like Alice playing croquet with a live flamingo for a mallet, hedgehogs as croquet balls and card soldiers as hoops.

*Stephen interrupts, grumpy. 'You made your point.'*

'Everything's been tumbling down around me.'

'The TV's packed up.'

'I had nuisance calls.'

'The washing machine won't work.'

'The major crisis of today is that my iron tablets have got lost. I could become very ill.'

Sometimes I was sympathetic and sometimes I wasn't.

*Stephen responds gently, 'I don't mind.' My heart lightens.*

## BILLS, BENEFITS AND THE COUNCIL

'I've received a letter from income support demanding forms and a bank statement.' Stephen receives the bills and demands for money we all receive. In Stephen's case, he mulls over every one, imagining the full ghastly outcome of failure-to-comply and it always involves being thrown out of his home.

Every now and then a nice letter comes through the post.

In November 2009 he had a letter from the Department for Work and Pensions, telling him about his Christmas bonus, a whopping £10. This came as a two-page printed letter with the provisos, 'You can only get one Christmas bonus each year' and 'You must let us know if you have already had the Christmas bonus this year.' Whoopee.

## WORK

Stephen would like to volunteer or work, but as he said to me on one occasion, sounding like a wartime recording: 'I'd like to contribute to the national effort at this time. I can't do it.'

A letter arrived just before Christmas 2015 informing Stephen that he needed to go to a work-focussed interview to discuss employment prospects. I laughed. Stephen did not. The letter said that failure to attend without good cause would result in financial sanctions and that the interview was mandatory 'unless you are ***terminally ill***' (their bold and underlining). Stephen declared, 'If they insist on me going to the interview and say I have to work or lose my benefits I'll have to live off my savings. When my savings run out, I'll probably have to go into care.'

'Stephen, you've gone about three steps too far. Surely it's up to your care coordinator to sort it out.'

'I hope so.' There's not a flicker of hope in his voice.

'It's absurd. I mean, what do they think you're going to do?' Stephen considers this seriously, 'Maybe they think I could write a few notes, clerical notes?'

*Stephen comments, 'It's all been dealt with and I've been ruled out of those now.' Then he says he wants me to get his pension sorted.*

I take my casserole into the kitchen to put in the microwave for lunch. When I come back in, he has decided to tell the solicitor to cancel his will, as there'll be no money to leave. I wonder if the writers of these letters know how much added anxiety they create in already vulnerable people.

## SHOPPING, COOKING AND THE HOUSE

Until 2016, Stephen, together with a support worker, went food shopping once a week and to the Post Office once a fortnight.

'I had to go on my own for a while. For about two years until Care Outlook. My mobility worsened in 2015.'

His shopping list has varied very little over nine years:

---

4 chicken roast dinners (frozen and microwaveable)

3 lamb or beef roast dinners (as above)

2 cheesy beans and sausage

Microwaveable chips

2 pints milk

3 lots of 4 Activia yoghurts

1 large brown loaf of bread

1 large Flora margarine

1 jar of Chivers marmalade

1 box of small tomatoes

Sugar

Angel cake, ginger cake

3 jars of full roast coffee

Cadbury's Smash Potato

Scottish porridge or Good Morning porridge oats

---

Seedless grapes, nectarines

1 bottle of Coca-Cola

Dettol Multi-action cleaner

Floor cleaner, air freshener, preferably OUST

2 of 4 or 6 rolls loo paper

Dog food: Bakers or Pedigree healthy Vitality

Pedigree Chum pouches, 2 Dentastix – VERY IMPORTANT

Due to the fact that Stephen does almost nothing except smoke cigarettes, buy food for his dog and eat £1 frozen meal deals every day, he manages to save money from his benefits. I only know one other person who has done this and he has a similar diagnosis to Stephen. Both, while refusing to spend money on themselves, give money to charities. Despite his claims of hating everyone, Stephen set up a direct debit in 2011 to give £2 a month to Water Aid.

Stephen has no cooker, so unless someone brings him a cooked meal or takes him out, he only eats microwaveable meals. Normally, carers leave some bread and butter out and he might eat a yoghurt and a banana mid-day. In the evening, a carer microwaves a meal for him.

And what about the cleaning? Having spent 25 years in psychiatric units, Stephen has never had to clean or cook and has no idea how to deal with either.

*Stephen interjects: 'I'm disabled!'*

He also has the added handicap of only having one arm available. To my knowledge, no cleaners have entered Stephen's flat in nine years.

*Stephen reminds me: 'one came once but they didn't speak English. They had to go.'*

The regular carers aren't paid to do it and don't have the time. Stephen is reluctant to pay for cleaning and is also deeply suspicious that cleaners will steal from him. For a long time, I felt he was being unnecessarily paranoid. The place NEEDED cleaning and Stephen was being obdurate about it.

*Stephen interrupts: 'I'm entitled to disagree.'*

It didn't help that in 2014 about £100 went missing from his secret hiding place, and it seems certain now that a carer stole the money.

*'Why are you writing that down in the book for? People are going to know.'*

*'I'm not saying where your hiding place is.'*

I'm not 'fastidious' but nine years with no cleaning? When I visit, I have time to clean the toilet or the kitchen floor but that's one small job, once a month. At this stage, he would need to begin with a "deep clean" which the council would charge him £400 for, and it isn't going to happen. Yes, Stephen has the money, but it's not his priority and more importantly, he'd hate the upheaval, having his belongings moved around by strangers and the worry that cleaners would steal from him.

As so often happens with me, it was personal experience that helped me to see Stephen's point of view. As a family we normally do the bare minimum of cleaning, but at one point when Tim was ill, I caved and paid for cleaners. It lasted six months and then the cleaning agency folded. The cleaners were good, but I noticed that I didn't like strangers being so intimate with my home and when I couldn't find something, the suspicion that they'd stolen it would drift briefly across my mind.

When it comes to personal hygiene, Stephen has a set protocol. He washes his hands carefully after using the toilet, he wears an apron when he sits down to eat and more recently when he drinks coffee. After he's finished eating, someone needs to bring him his flannel and towel and he will carefully wipe his face and hands.

Stephen has a washing machine and his carers wash his clothes regularly. He buys clothes and has a backlog of trousers and shirts piled up in his bedroom, but as far as I can see he only wears certain favourites until they are unusable.

Of course, I'm nothing like that...

## HEALTH AND GENERAL WELFARE

There's a lot to negotiate here: doctor, dentist, pharmacist, chiropodist, hairdresser, PDSA and haircuts for the dog.

A support worker takes Stephen to most of his appointments, but he is expected to walk on his own to the surgery every Friday for an injection. He has never liked the receptionist there and seemed surprised by her angry response when he asked when she was leaving.

As well as the above list, there is the caring structure: the psychiatrist he has to see once or twice a year, the monthly meetings with the care coordinator, the weekly support worker, the daily carers.

Stephen complains that his support workers and care

coordinator are always off sick or on holiday when he needs them. He also finds some of them very difficult. In 2010, after having the same support worker (named Gareth here) for three years, Stephen asked for him to be changed. The catalyst was Stephen's use of a Vick's Inhaler in public places, sticking it up his nose and making a lot of snorting noises. Gareth told him not to do it. Stephen garnered support from MIND and a representative wrote on his behalf. The key issue was Gareth's attitude. Stephen felt put down by Gareth. In addition to the Vick's event, Gareth told Stephen that he thought his Christian beliefs were 'all fairy tales.' Another support worker, Alyssa, eventually took over.

Then there are the daily carers sent from two different care agencies, who attend to him morning and evening, seven days a week, assisting him with dressing, meals, and clothes washing. Some are warm and delightful, others are sharp and brief, and occasionally (he claims) steal from him or tell him he's going to hell. As for the care managers, Stephen considers most of them 'difficult and unkind'.

Stephen's needs have increased over the years (from as early as 2010, aged 55, Stephen had been to a clinic about incontinence) but the time the carers are given has been cut.

## TV AND HOBBIES

I ask about his favourite poets: 'Byron – world's greatest poet. Fantastic poetry, brilliant poetry – how poems should be written. My poems can never be as good as his, never. Byron was the greatest poet. He was one of the greatest men, in my opinion, of all time.' He pauses and then says 'I expect you'll disagree with me – I don't care if you do.'

'I'm not arguing with you.'

'We live in a democratic society where opinions are tolerated?'

'Absolutely.'

Stephen is also interested in history, politics, music, nature, animals and sitting in the garden, listening to the birds. He surprises me by saying that he also likes football.

'I like watching Match of the Day. I support Chelsea, Southampton, Arsenal, Hull.'

Television is essential. 'I love the 'Planet Earth' programmes. 'Life in Cold Blood'. Been watching those. David Attenborough. Best programme there is, apart from 'Spring Watch'. Far better than, say, 'Coronation Street' or 'Emmerdale', far better than that.' That's saying something. I'm not allowed to ring him any weekday evening at 7.30pm because 'Coronation Street' is on. I did once just to show him how annoying it is to be rung at the wrong moment. It didn't go down well.

Over the years, the TV has sparked a wide range of interests in Stephen; 'That lovely programme about Fair Isle – lovely place to go to on Holiday. Or Corsica or French Riviera or Italian Riviera.' He clicks his lighter trying to light a fag, 'Ara ara ara. Such terrible catarrh, Susie, such terrible catarrh.' Then he carries on listing his favourite TV. 'I watched the Boat Race and thoroughly enjoyed that – absolutely wonderful. I do hope you saw it.'

*Listening to this, Stephen is warm and reflective: 'I've had some good times Susie, I have had some good times.'*

'There was a programme on Shostakovich in Soviet Russia... most interesting. I love his piano. I love Brahms,

Tchaikovsky…'

Music is hugely important and Classic FM is Stephen's life-blood. I love music but we have very different tastes. Stephen is surprised when I admit I don't like classical music.

'You don't listen to pop music, do you? You listen to classical music.'

'I think I prefer Folk or blues really.' He doesn't accept this. 'You like Classical music, don't you?'

'No, I don't.'

'Pity. I think that's a pity Susie – it's a pity a pity. We have classical here, classical, classical.'

*'I wouldn't get that in the care home. Susie, I have to stay here.'*

## POLITICS

Stephen loves a General Election. Whenever one happens, he stays up all night and gets out the cigars.

'I believe in the power of the proletariat against the bourgeoisie, Susie, although I may be bourgeois. I think heavy industry should be nationalised. If they were nationalised, they'd all work properly. I believe in the Green Party and the Labour Party. I don't think I'd vote for UKIP, having found out about their immigration policy.' He also believes in freedom of movement, and staying in Europe.

## GOING OUT

In all the years that I've known him, Stephen has not been to a cinema, theatre, football match or a show of any sort.

*Stephen corrects me: 'Once in 2009 with Will. I don't have anything more to do with Will now.'*
*'What did you go and see?'*
*'Slumdog Millionaire.'*
*'Did you like it?'*
*'It was alright.'*

In terms of going out for a meal, every Christmas Day he gets taken to a locally organised meal at the Methodist church. From 2012 I began to take him out to pubs for meals and later his support worker also took him to cafés.

## THE NEIGHBOURS

Over the years Stephen has had a variety of neighbours on either side but the neighbour living above him has been there since 2009. Mostly they have been kind. Some have mowed his lawn for him, others chat to him over the fence, give him Christmas cards or bring over a meal occasionally. This doesn't stop him worrying.

'I keep thinking I hear the CID walking around upstairs and the upstairs people telling them about me. I'm always worried that the neighbours are going to report me. The point is I've got this constant insecurity about being arrested and evicted.'

None of Stephen's neighbours ever complained about him except the one above him. 'The neighbour contacted the council in June 2009 complaining about harassment. I got a phone call and a letter from the council. A Police Community Support Officer and a Council Official were coming to see me and I was all tense and nervous and I didn't get a lot of sleep. They came around and the PCSO told me off for harassing. The neighbour didn't press charges. I was only being friendly, over-friendly and she took it the wrong way, and it spiralled out of all proportion. I went too far, my own fault. Part of my own condition. Part of my OCD.'

'I remember you were very upset at the time.'

'I very nearly lost this flat. I was in a terrible state. I really don't want to talk about it. If you're going to harass me about that then quite frankly, I don't want you to write the book.'

'I'm not harassing you.'

We sit and listen to Classic FM.

I add, 'And the person upstairs had autism. That's what you told me.'

'She's mentally ill'.

Classic FM plays some grand military stuff.

He carries on: 'She told the local Autism charity. They wrote me a very nasty letter in 2010 saying that what I'd done was extremely serious and made my neighbour's life a complete misery. I left them some unpleasant messages on their answer machine. No more after that. I haven't had anything more to do with her.'

More recently he and his neighbour have begun simply to nod in recognition of each other.

### FAMILY

We all have very different relationships with our families. Stephen's contact with his direct family has been largely via Christmas and Birthday cards and the occasional phone call. These cards are very important to him.

*Stephen intervenes: 'Kathy didn't want anything more to do with me at one point. She does now. She wrote me a lovely letter in 2009 explaining how they're all getting on and hoping Charlie was well and about her dog. Now she sends me emails.'*

His father died in 2009 but he didn't attend the funeral. He used to ring his mother on a regular basis, but then something happened and he couldn't find the number and that contact stopped.

'I think she was moved into a home.'

He also used to ring his brother but when his brother moved that also stopped. His brother always remembers to send presents to Stephen as well as cards. Stephen has been very faithful in sending cards to his family every birthday and Christmas.

Stephen's step-daughter, Rose, visits him for his birthday and Christmas and often brings her daughters with her. He has a photo of his step-grand-daughters placed proudly next to his DAB radio.

## *FRIENDS*

Stephen has had a variety of friends who ring, visit or send post cards from time to time, including church people and carers who have moved on.

Stephen knew Mick Brown for a number of years, having first met him on a psychiatric ward. Mick had been in the army and had a breakdown. After he left, Mick would send Stephen cigars. 'I was friends with him. He was good at playing snooker. They had a great big snooker table at "The Yews", you probably remember. When I moved to the half-way house, I had a lot to do with him. After I married

Mandy, I used to meet up with him at the mental health drop-in centre.'

After Stephen moved to the flat, Mick used to visit but then, according to Stephen, he 'became more and more unpleasant. He stole from me, threatened me, he hid my hot water bottle in the back of the rubbish bin.' Things came to a head in Christmas 2011, when Mick asked Stephen to lend him some money to buy cigarettes for a friend and Stephen refused. Stephen claims Mick then stole some money off him. The police got involved and Mick stopped coming over, but he 'kept ringing me up and harassing me.'

*As I read this, Stephen responds with a kind tone: 'He only stole from me when I wouldn't lend him some money for someone who was far worse off than me. It was all my fault. I was mean, Susie. I wouldn't help. Mick, as you call him, wasn't bad. I still see him sometimes and he gives me a cigarette and we have a chat. It's great seeing him.'*

When I ask him about other friends he mentions Alice. 'Alice is the one who painted Charlie. I had problems with her over the years. I didn't have anything to do with her after October 2012.' This was due to politics. 'I kept falling out with her. She kept ringing me up after midnight and I was half asleep.' Stephen has a beautiful painting she made of Charlie on his wall. The painting is unframed and blu-tacked on. To me it is one of life's hidden gems.

*Reading this back, I ask Stephen 'Can you leave it to me in your will?' He tells me just to take it off the wall when he's dead.*

Stephen occasionally strikes up friendships with some of the carers and when they leave, a few keep contact, dropping in from time to time and sending him greeting cards. Tomas is one of them, 'a wonderful man.'

## *MYSELF*

I'm not sure where to place my relationship with Stephen. At the beginning it could have been described as 'pastoral.' Over the years it shifted into something that I find hard to describe. Stephen is incapable of being anything other than himself, insists on regular contact and for someone who is delusional has the extraordinary ability to strip me of all comforting delusions I have about myself. Perhaps that in the end is the sign of a true friend.

Deciding to write this book changed my relationship with Stephen and changed me. The decision to write it came in the middle of a tumultuous year: 2012.

# Chapter 13

## Walking into the dark: a book begins

*"Write what should not be forgotten."*

Isobel Allende

*Stephen comments, 'Some people at St B's mental hospital said*
*I'd soon be forgotten about.'*
*I respond with angry stubbornness, 'You won't be.'*
*'I won't be?'*
*'No.'*

During 2012 Stephen penned at least nine poems. I found a couple of rare ones from January 2012 that were entirely positive. Here is one of them:

*the Family of Magpies*

> The captivating, enthralling family of Magpies
> vivaciously and gregariously push and shove,
> perched so opaquely and intrinsically
> on that ever-protruding branch above.
> Indeed, this is a most phenomenal scene,
> a scene reminiscent only of LOVE.'

On 13th February he wrote a poem about *The stresses and torments of this life* and introduced the idea of the phoenix:

> 'Those agonising days, so cruel, so insincere.
> I, like a phoenix shall rise from the past,
> and indeed, contemporary reality,
> which I must seemingly endure.'

By 25th February, he took the idea of the phoenix but returned to nature in this extract from a poem entitled

*The Beauties of Early Spring:*

> 'Ah the incandescent effervescence
> of this late February day,
> the intricate delicacy of spring daffodils,
> hope of a rejuvenated season
> rising like a palpitating phoenix
> among such despondency and gloom.'

What is it that makes a person decide to write a poem? Or a book? The poet Padraig O'Tuama, Stephen and I had all agreed that we wrote poetry 'to survive' but what is the trigger? What combination of external and internal factors stew together long enough and what is the catalyst that sets it off? In 2012, after 12 years of knowing Stephen, I asked Stephen if I could write this book. Why?

A lot of factors came together in 2012. In July 2011, I'd left the part-time job at the primary school in order to write and create more drama and then at the end of 2011 I'd taken an eight-week mindfulness course in order to 'fall awake' to my life.

2012 arrived and proved to be not a good year for my family and friends.

*Stephen muses: 'The weather was very bad… a very bad summer.'*

In early February, my mother-in-law, whose health had deteriorated rapidly in the previous six months, died quietly in hospital. Then Carol, Stephen's old primary school teacher, rang and told me she had cancer. She insisted it couldn't be too bad as her daughter had taken her to France and she'd been up dancing till 3am. She was 83 years old.

Shortly after this, the partner of my younger brother was hit by a lorry as she was crossing the road to take her young children to school and her leg was utterly crushed. My brother rang me a few hours later and the world changed shape.

About a month later, the husband of a close friend died from a brain tumour which had returned after nine years. He was 45 years old.

Something cracked inside me. As I sat in hospital next to my sister-in-law, a white sheet covering one leg and a space where the other one should have been, the Christian package telling me this was all part of God's plan would no longer hold. It had been one of my ways to avoid feeling pain, but now it collapsed in pieces. There was nothing else to do except feel this suffering and be with others in it. If God was anywhere, then God was in this mess weeping beside my friend, my sister-in-law, Stephen.

For Stephen, the early spring optimism had evaporated and in May he said flatly to me, 'My life has been a complete and total waste of time.' He may have said it to me before but that moment struck me like a physical blow. This was how he experienced his life.

It was at that moment that I decided I was going to write his story and show him that this was not true. I wanted him to know his life mattered. Perhaps then I might discover that mine mattered too.

But what is it that gives our lives value?

*Stephen answers: 'A sense of achievement, that's what gives your life value. I haven't achieved much. I've achieved some good things, yes, but now I'm heading towards death. I won't make any sense of my life.' I nod, but I don't agree.*

Stephen agreed to having the book written because he wanted me to record the abuse he'd suffered, but he was also terrified of being sued. As a result, we agreed that he would remain anonymous.

Agreeing to write a book is one thing, having an idea of how to do it is quite another. I found inspiration in *Stuart,*

*A Life Backwards* by Alexander Masters, a fabulous book about a 'thief, hostage-taker, psycho and street raconteur.' The character of Stuart came out of the page and punched me in the face. Here was someone unknown whose story was important, difficult and funny. Then I read Kate Clanchy's wonderful *Antigona and Me*, unravelling Antigona's story as a Kosovan refugee who'd escaped to the UK, but also relating with raw honesty and humour the ensuing friendship between her and Kate. Something began stewing. I knew Kate from our children's secondary school, when we'd campaigned to stop it turning into an Academy (we lost). I found the courage to suggest a drink and then ask if she'd consider mentoring me for this book. She didn't say no.

The summer passed and in early September, Stephen and I went to Carol's for the first formal recording for this book. By then Carol was fragile and forgetting things. It is the only recording I have of her. Six weeks later I visited Stephen on his own.

### A Meal Out

I arrive at about 12.30 on a Saturday with my recorder to find Stephen beaming at me.

'I have £25. Maybe we could go to the pub for lunch?'

Stephen smiling and ready to spend money? This is a complete turn up for the books. Also, I've NEVER been to a public place for lunch with Stephen. I realise we'll need to get a move on if he wants to eat. There's only one problem with this: you can't 'get a move on' with Stephen.

First, Stephen has to have at least one cigarette and a coffee, then go to the toilet. After that, I have to bring him his moneybox from its secret place. The key is on a string round his neck, so I need to get that off him, open the moneybox, agree the sum required, lock and hide the moneybox and replace the key. I help Stephen put on outdoor wear, and he turns all the plugs off, checks the doors, the windows, his bag. I put Charlie on a lead while Stephen checks everything again, tells me repeatedly to stop rushing him and finally we arrive at the door of the flat. Locking the inner and outer door will take several minutes and I have to stand and wait while he inspects each lock and pushes the door repeatedly. He cannot begin this process until I'm there and it will take a minimum of 45 minutes. Every time. Any sign of impatience will slow the process.

'I don't like it. People are always in a rush.'

'I'm not in a rush, Stephen.'

We go through a few rounds of 'Yes, you are'… 'No, I'm not' until he feels satisfied.

Finally, we head out of the door, me holding onto Stephen and Charlie and Stephen's bag. Now we discover it's been raining.

'I'm going to fall over; I'm going to fall over' x10

'No, you're not, no, you're not' x 10

Negotiating the car is another detailed process. Stephen finds it difficult getting into the front seat with his useless arm and stiffening legs. Our old Ford Galaxy is roomy enough, but still awkward. Once installed, I have to reach across him and put his safety belt on for him, then re-assure him that Charlie is safe, before we can finally head off.

For those of us who are reasonably healthy and mobile, this procedure would be done with almost no thought in a couple of minutes.

On this day, we drive to a beauty spot near the pub. It's been drizzling, but it clears and the valley comes out clean and strong in the light with that peculiar beauty of a day when the grey is receding, there is no sun but the fields and curves of the hills stand out in sharp contrast against the dark grey clouds. Driving through this lifts me, nourishes me. We arrive at our destination and I walk round to the passenger side to help Stephen out of the car. He's nervous,

'I'm going to fall over; I'm going to fall over!'

'No, you're not, no you're not.' Then I add more usefully, 'Hold onto me.'

He holds on to me and begins to relax, 'Maybe I won't fall over, maybe I won't.'

We manage a short walk with me holding Stephen's hand, a first, I think. In the other I have Charlie's lead, which is very short. I can't let Charlie off the lead because he's blind, so I end up half-dragging him along, embarrassed about how odd the three of us look. After the walk, we leave Charlie in the car (windows opened, of course) and make an attempt on the pub steps:

'I can't do steps. I can't do them in the rain.'

We walk the long way around. It's a big pub, the sort where they show you to a table. I'm thankful we're taken to a quiet corner. We order food, get a drink and then we wait. Stephen sits stiffly, emanating tension which sets me on edge. I try to ease the atmosphere with a time-worn social inanity,

'It's lovely here isn't it?'

'I don't want to talk.'

We sit quietly, while I attempt to look relaxed. His grim silence turns into a low repeated mutter. 'This isn't good enough, other people have their food!' I make mollifying noises, but then someone walks over and takes a spare chair from our table.

'They should have asked!'

I'd prefer physical pain to an embarrassing public scene any day. I suggest he goes out for a cigarette.

'I can't cope. I'm hungry.'

I've just decided to say assertively, 'let's go' when the food arrives and Stephen's mood immediately lifts. He puts a napkin in his collar while I cut up his fish for him. He copes well, eating with one hand. The waitress returns to ask if we're enjoying the food and he's full of praise. My soup is horrible and the bread hard, but in true British fashion, I tell her it's lovely.

Stephen eats silently. He doesn't do social eating. It's either eating or talking. We finish off with coffee and a pudding, by which time he's thanking everyone in earshot profusely. If anything, this is more embarrassing.

We make our way out of the building, passing a man standing outside smoking. Stephen asks him: 'May I smoke?' He replies, 'You can do what you like, mate!' Stephen lights up; the bloke finishes his fag and ambles off while I watch the afternoon light fading.

Whenever Stephen smokes outdoors he never leaves the fag-end on the ground. He is certain it is illegal and definitively immoral. He will spend several minutes grinding it under his heel, then pick it up to inspect it and ensure that it's no longer burning and finally he puts it in his pocket and takes it home. With this process completed, we then make our way back to the car.

On the way home, buoyed by the success of this trip, Stephen wants to know when we can go again. This has been Stephen's first visit to an eatery of any sort in years and negotiating all that social interaction has been a herculean task for him. By taking him there, I've had a taste of what 'going to a pub' means for Stephen. No wonder he was thanking everyone in earshot at the end of the meal, he'd just passed the finishing line!

Back at the flat we manage to do some recording before I head for home, stinking of smoke and exhausted from the emotional wear of being in public with Stephen but we've got somewhere!

~

Although I'd planned to meet up every six weeks or so, I didn't visit Stephen again until March 2013. However, I did begin taking notes on phone calls which was easy, as Stephen didn't like me interrupting him and I rarely got a look-in. Here is a smattering from those first few months:

'I've written a poem you'd might like to hear sometime. It's quite a striking poignant poem.'

'Life is a struggle… unbearable without Mandy, longing for eternal peace'

'I don't believe that faith is something evangelicals say we have to work with, and if we step out of line then we'll burn.

I think they're wrong, faith is a gift.'

'I had a good night in bed last night, all tucked up with a hot water bottle, saying goodnight to all the teddies.'

As for me, my mid-life crisis was still in full flow. As well as constantly feeling that my life had been a waste of time and that I should have had a career (teaching, social work, anything) there was the issue of the church.

*My Diary Entry, October 2012*

'It's like something has massively shifted out of the way and now I can see – with horrible clarity – that I have been part and party to so much sexist attitude so much of my life. And that I did not see it.'

On 21st November 2012 the Church of England voted on whether to allow women to be bishops. The vote failed.

*My Diary Entry, November 2012*

'I have belonged to this church all my life and I now feel excluded, not welcomed, not belonging anymore.'

Yet still, I remained in the church, helping run the children's work, an alternative monthly service in the community hall and various Christmas dramas.

After Christmas Stephen asked about visiting Carol and reminded me again in February. I rang her number repeatedly over several days but got no answer. Finally, a young person answered and when I asked for Carol there was a pause and then: 'She's dead. Shall I get my mum?'

Blankness and then an instruction issued from an automated service in my brain: 'Yes please.' Even frail with cancer, Carol had pulsed with life. How could she be dead? Five years later my chest still compresses – if I could just sit one more time in her presence. The funeral was fixed for the following week.

I'd arranged to see Stephen that coming Saturday, but now I also agreed to take him on the Monday to the funeral. He was very quiet when I visited, muttering repeated mantras:

'I wish I thought about other people more, I wish I thought about other people more.'

Which then shifted into:

'I'm very grateful, I can't thank you enough, I'm very grateful, I can't thank you enough,'

And

'I'm sorry if I've inconvenienced you, I'm sorry if I've inconvenienced you.'

I'd brought some disposable E-cigarettes and managed to show Stephen how to work these as his mantra changed to:

'These final years, this final furlong…'

finishing with the refrain, 'You will come again, won't you? You will come again?'

After hearing me say 'yes' four times, he was satisfied.

At the time it didn't register with me that this repetition was a sign of distress.

### Carol's Funeral

On the day of her funeral, it is snowing heavily and the ground is frozen solid.

*'I nearly fell, March 2013.'*

I drive the hundred-odd miles to Stephen, hoping no roads

are closed and leaving plenty of time for the ritual of getting him out of the flat.

As we leave the safety of his home, Stephen is terrified of falling but grimly determined. We attend the funeral, twenty miles away at an Anglican church. I find the service deeply moving but Stephen struggles. He's twitchy, muttering and impatient. Afterwards he wants to go to the burial, which involves walking down a long narrow, frozen path. It takes forever. Stephen grips me awkwardly and we move at Zimmer frame speed as mourners keep edging past us as politely as possible. To complete the picture, the plot is at the furthest end of the graveyard. Carol was not buried in her boots facing the hill as she'd asked me to arrange ten years earlier. I don't suppose she minds.

Afterwards we make our way back in the same tortuous fashion. Thankfully the wake is a warm friendly affair in the church hall and Carol's children remember Stephen and welcome him.

~

Compared to her family and friends, I hardly knew Carol and yet I cannot begin to express how precious Carol's life has been to me and how much I miss her. She simply shone. Perhaps it is because I felt so immensely valued whenever I was with her. Is there a greater gift?

*Stephen adds: 'She knew me so well. I knew her so well. You didn't, I did. Susie, you can be remarkably insensitive sometimes and sometimes you can be remarkably sensitive. It depends.'*

For Stephen this was a deep, deep loss. She had been there for him for over fifty years, always open, accepting, supportive.

She was one of those rare people he had never fallen out with and whom he could ring any time of day or night. Fairy Godmothers are not supposed to die.

Carol had been there for Stephen through the worst of times, and now she was gone. We could no longer visit her for those roast meals and pancakes. Now, when I went to see him, I did it alone; there was just me, Stephen, Charlie and a book I'd promised to write. Carol's humour, company and love were no longer there to buoy us up.

While Stephen agreed that I should write the book, the ride was bumpy. One early recording session was rounded off with: 'You found out what you wanted to find out so that's it. No more.' At other times, he'd become insistent: 'You need to write down about the abuse,' or 'I've never found peace of mind or achieved peace in this life and I never shall. Only in the next life shall I find peace. You can write that down in your book. Make that the fundamental cornerstone.'

Sometimes I'd show up and Stephen didn't want to talk at all, or he'd start to tell me something interesting and then refuse point blank to explain any more. Other times he'd tell me excruciatingly painful events in detail. He would then be miserable but I'd have go home. Later I'd transcribe the recording which would take a long time and put me in a black mood.

I visited Stephen on my own every six weeks or so, arriving on a Saturday around midday and at some point, sometimes, I would ask questions and record the session. We'd take Charlie out and either combine that with lunch somewhere, or I'd bring food or we'd get a take-away. Sometimes Stephen would need to buy something from the shops. After that, I'd record Stephen's story or read what I'd written back to him. My plan was to leave by 5.30pm when the carers arrived. This slipped closer to 7pm over time.

The week before I came, Stephen would ring to confirm I was coming and ascertain exactly what time I was going to arrive. If I was five minutes late, he would ring Tim, assuming I was dead. Tim kept telling me to give Stephen a time which included a decent buffer for me but I never did, despite the fact that the journey took 2 hours and involved the M25. I cannot explain why.

### *Late Again*

On one occasion in June 2013, I arrange to meet up with someone else in Stephen's town before my regular visit to him. The meet-up overruns, so I ring Stephen to say I won't be there till 1pm, which does not impress him. I have not been realistic about that, either, so have to ring again to shift it to 1.30pm and surprisingly he says, 'I will forgive you'. By the third phone call, 'Either you get to me in 15 minutes or forget the whole thing and don't bother to come.'

Later, as we drive through glorious sunshine, with fish and chips steaming on the back seat, he intones: 'Everything's gone wrong, I just want to be dead.' I feel both angry that he's not grateful and guilty that my lateness has caused his low mood. Then he tells me about a distressing phone call the day before which has triggered an old trauma. Moments like these keep waking me up, reminding me that inside Stephen are deep fissures of pain, wounds that don't heal. My failures are minor irritants in comparison.

What had happened was this: Stephen still regularly visited

the halfway house he used to live in back in 2001, but a member of staff had rung to tell him that C*, one of the men involved in breaking his leg, was now working there. The halfway house was not far from Stephen's flat.

'I'm never going there again.'

The only good news for Stephen is that C* has had a bout of cancer. He starts ranting that C* should go to hell. Finally, when he takes a breath, I interrupt to say I don't believe in hell, other than hell on earth. I'm not sure how he'll take it but he's genuinely interested in this new idea. 'So, C* will simply turn to dust?' He turns this over in his mind and concludes this is satisfactory. We then twist around a corner and past a field with cows in. Stephen informs me they are symbols of goodness and salvation and all animals go to heaven. That is that.

~

I'm not sure when I ditched 'hell' as a belief. It felt like the inevitable outcome of unpicking the Christian package. Once I actually looked at this dogma, it became ridiculous.

By my October 2013 visit I was still turning up late, this time 20 minutes and I rang him en route to let him know. He was disappointed in me. I felt bad about it and it took a long time for me to recognise that this lateness might be in part because I knew I was walking into a dark and painful place and was therefore not in a hurry to get there. At the time I didn't consciously recognise the depths of his pain or its effect on me and I didn't show myself much compassion. After all, as he frequently reminded me, his suffering was much greater than mine. Even now, recalling these events and writing these words brings back the sense of heaviness and weight, thick with failure.

For those first two years, I didn't try and write any Chapters, I simply collected information. Through 2013 I was also putting together a play on the life of C. S. Lewis to be performed in our church in the Autumn to mark fifty years since he'd died. Tim had suggested a 30-minute two-hander but it became a two-hour drama with a cast of 26, exploring Lewis' complex and at times tragic life, through the lens of the Narnia tales and requiring a host of creatures including lions, dragons and sword fights down the church aisle. It was a wonderful, joyful community event.

Then in November, I visited Stephen and I marked the recording 'V IMP'. Not only did Stephen describe in detail the terrible events of his leg being broken, and other abuses, he also, for the very first time told me about the violence he'd meted out on others. That was a very long day.

In January 2014 I went out for a dog walk and chatted to a retired social worker.

*My Diary Entry, January 2014*

'Zig tells me that Stephen can't just be autistic with a personality disorder. He wouldn't get sectioned for that.'

I felt a total idiot.

Around the same time Stephen had been ringing me, upset about a weekly injection that he had at the local surgery, which I'd never asked him about. Shortly after the dog walk chat, I went to visit Stephen.

Susie Stead

*Diagnosis*

On the day, as I enter the flat, Stephen is already in full flow
about the weekly injection. 'I'm going to take it to court. I
want a Prima Facie for them to do it here.' I've no idea what
he's talking about, but finally work out that it means forcing
the surgery to give him the injection at home. He doesn't
want to have to walk there when it's wet or icy outside as he's
terrified of falling. Finally, I ask:

'What is the injection for, Stephen?'

He mutters under his breath, 'Susie, I can't help you, sorry.'

'But what's it called?' There's a brief silence and then,

'Clopixol.'

'What's it for?'

'To make me feel better.'

'Stephen, what is your diagnosis?'

'I thought you knew.'

'No.'

'Oh well, you find out.'

'Can't you tell me?'

'I don't know.'

'Yes, you do know!'

He speaks fast and low, 'Schizophrenia with autistic features.'
He lights a cigarette.

~

Schizophrenia. No wonder he didn't want to tell me. I'd
known Stephen 14 years and it had never occurred to me
that he might have schizophrenia. At this point I didn't

243

know much about it, just imbibed views and phrases: 'split personality,' 'psychotic', 'not in touch with reality', 'dangerous.' The only person I'd previously known with that diagnosis had been so withdrawn it was almost impossible to communicate with him. This didn't match with Stephen. It also made no difference to how I felt about him or about writing the book.

Shortly after this I finally met up with Kate Clanchy around the large wooden table in her kitchen and she simply and terrifyingly said 'pitch me your idea.' As a result, she agreed to mentor me, suggested a structure and advised me to go on an Arvon Writers' course to get started. It seemed that this book genuinely could happen.

In May 2014 I spent a glorious week at Arvon, led by Alexander Masters and Pauline Black. By the end of it, I'd written two drafts of my first Chapter.

I thought it would all be over by Christmas.

As usual, I had no idea.

# Chapter 14

## Charlie

## King of all Dogs

*'He comes first, he comes first,
before anybody. He means more to me than everybody else
put together.'*

Stephen - October 2014

Stephen and I had a disagreement once, when he stated that my dog Zozzi was more important than my family. Didn't I agree? A dog more important than my family? I felt insulted but managed to say drily, 'You're entitled to your opinion.' This wasn't enough for him.

'Do you agree?'

'No, I don't agree.'

'Do you agree?

I tried to reply evenly, 'No, I don't agree. My children and Tim are far more important to me than my dog. You are more important to me than my dog.'

'Surely not? Surely not! No! The dog is more important.'

We couldn't meet on this subject because in my world, a dog was a pet, a nice extra. In Stephen's world his dog was the single most important reason why he stayed alive and found the strength to cope.

*'That's right.'*

~

'I met Charlie at my wife's house, Monday 18th February 2002. He's so very special.' From that moment Charlie gave his allegiance to Stephen. Charlie was a Yorkipoo, a cross between a Yorkshire Terrier and a Miniature Poodle. Most of the time, he looked like a small, animated, untidy, grey rug.

From the first time I met him in 2002, I was told he was 11 years old. He stayed 11 for the next 8 years. Whatever mood Stephen was in, Charlie was always happy, dancing around, asking for balls to be thrown for him, delighted at any chance to go out.

Charlie stayed with us on two occasions; in December 2005 and the summer of 2006. During his stays, we discovered that Charlie was friendly but fiercely independent, howling if he didn't have free rein of the house and ignoring food that didn't suit him. If he didn't want you to stroke him or pick him up, he'd bite you. They were not serious bites, but they hurt. He bit all of us and some of the neighbour's kids. None of the kids ever held it against Charlie.

> 'I'm sorry he bit you, but he was so special to me. He never once bit me, not once. He was so kind to me. He licked me. It was a really wonderful thing. All I can do is apologise.'

After Mandy died in 2008, Charlie came to live with Stephen in the flat. Stephen took him out for a walk in the park every day but there were 'incidents', as Charlie would sometimes growl or snap at other dogs and upset their owners, and this put Stephen on edge. Eventually this became too stressful so he gave up and the by-now rather elderly Charlie would potter in the garden.

By the end of 2012, Charlie had gone blind. In June 2013 we went out to our usual beauty spot but Stephen wouldn't let me take him off the lead and it felt like pulling along a stuffed toy. On the way home, Stephen updated me on Charlie's age. He was now nearly 18 years old.

'He hasn't got long to go. I'm bracing myself for it. I'm preparing myself for the worst.'

'It's hard.'

'It is hard. After Charlie's gone, I hope that I'll pass away.'

Back at the flat Charlie was no longer able to negotiate his way up the step onto the grass in the garden. That summer

(2013) Stephen and I were sitting out and I suggested putting Charlie on the grass but Stephen was adamant Charlie should be free to go where he wanted. 'He's a free agent, he comes and goes. Entirely up to him. He's so special.'

It seemed to me that Stephen linked Charlie's right to freedom with his own.

Charlie was an additional burden for any carers but for once Stephen had nothing bad to say about them: 'They're very good with the dog. He's always friendly and kind. He's so special, he's so special. The carers love him so. I love him so. He's a lovely dog.'

When Stephen talked about Charlie it was the only time, he was in danger of being mushy and mawkish.

I am impressed with those carers. Charlie was not part of their job and the time they were given was always too tight. They didn't complain, even when he became incontinent and they had to clear up his wee and poo on a regular basis. There were those Stephen didn't like, but some were pure gold. They put up with poor hygiene, smoky atmosphere, a very particular and paranoid Stephen who might (and did) accuse them of stealing, and a doubly incontinent dog. All this on very poor wages.

I bow to them.

By autumn 2013, Charlie's incontinence was becoming a major problem. It helped that there was no carpet in the flat, but Charlie wandered freely, leaving messes everywhere. Taxi drivers didn't want him in the car which made trips to the PDSA (Vet Charity) difficult. Eventually we agreed that I should bring a carrier for car travel and Zozzi's old puppy cage for the flat. Stephen would only countenance restricting Charlie's freedom at night, but it was something.

## Pub Outing

A year after our inaugural visit to a pub, I arrive to take Stephen and Charlie out. We're now veterans. We've discovered a nicer, smaller pub in the intervening time and we go there first, leaving Charlie in the carrier, in the car with the window open.

Each visit out for a meal is a huge event, filled with embarrassment, pleasure, frustration and fear; and that's just from my point of view. By now Stephen is losing confidence in walking and despite holding his arm I still have to encourage him to go up even one step.

I can't do it.

Yes, you can.

I can't do it.

Yes, you can.

Maybe I can.

After we finish the meal, we get up to leave. Stephen is in front of me as we walk through a narrow gap between two tables but then he stops. A dog is lying on the floor, blocking his way. Stephen simply stands and waits politely as he doesn't see why he should have priority over the dog. It's up to me to ask the owners to move their pet.

Eventually we get out and visit our local beauty spot for a short walk. Now, as well as being dragged along, Charlie starts making a very strange noise which Stephen claims is sneezing. I feel accusing stares, so I pick up Charlie and make a big fuss of him.

On the way home, Stephen complains that his benefits have been cut because he's got too much money in his savings account. I suggest he spends the money and enjoy himself but this sets him off, 'After Charlie dies, I just want to die and be in eternal bliss with Mandy'. I point out that he is solidly alive at the moment, so why not do something enjoyable? Eventually, after he's satisfied that I understand he will NEVER be happy in this life, he stuns me by saying that he'd like to go to France. Not a trip to the cinema or a new sofa; a trip to France.

I've just expended huge amounts of energy taking him out to a local pub and a brief totter in the open and yet I find myself suggesting that a day trip to France could work. Fortunately, his carer arrives at this point, but Stephen does not forget this conversation and as a precursor to France, starts asking about a summer visit to my house the following year.

~

Autumn became Christmas, became New Year 2014. In January I wrote in my diary:

*'New Year Resolutions*

* Stop whingeing about my life and get on with it!
* Start pushing boulders up hills and build some muscle.
* Stop eating so much!'

Following this up, I got in touch with a local charity who'd gained some funding to run activities for the 'Time To Change Movement', whose main focus is to challenge the stigma of mental illness. I offered my services and signed up as a volunteer. As a result, I was given some training and later in the year took part in different activities which challenged me profoundly and helped me in my engagement with Stephen. There was a lot to learn:

## My Diary Entry, February 2014

'Today Stephen keeps ringing and I feel pissed off with him. I feel a hypocrite. The thing about Stephen is that you have to be 'present'. You can't just fob him off. He calls out for warmth and care and I haven't got any today. I feel cold, tense and shrivelled.'

Unlike me, Charlie didn't need any training, Charlie was always present, always accepting of Stephen. No wonder Stephen loved Charlie more than people. A dog is always 'present' and pleased to see their owner. Also, a dog doesn't judge you.

In early March, Stephen rang in a state. He'd been watching the televised memorial service held for Nelson Mandela at Westminster Abbey when the woman leading the prayers asked that we forgive others like Nelson Mandela did and said that if we don't, 'God will not forgive us.' Looking for comfort, Stephen had rung an elderly member of his old URC church, whom he considered a moderate Christian. She unequivocally told him that he would be damned to hell if he didn't forgive the people who had hurt or abused him. It was in the Bible.

Stephen was beside himself. He'd decided to break all contact with the URC lady to protect his own health. He kept repeating, 'You don't blame me, do you?' and I kept replying, 'No, I don't'. I added that most people in that Westminster congregation couldn't have done what Nelson Mandela did. Over the course of the phone call, Stephen went from, 'I can't forgive' to 'Even if I could, I wouldn't want to' to 'If they asked me for forgiveness, I'd give it'. Wow.

What was I to do with 'forgiveness'? This religious demanding of it only added further burdens to someone who was already deeply hurt. And what about justice?

Charlie couldn't bring Stephen justice, but he could accept him exactly as he was, sit in his lap and lick his face.

Forgiveness, Justice, and then what about Equality? On May 1st I found myself, as part of the 'Time To Change' Campaign, on a soap box in Oxford performing a two-minute drama with a friend called Alice. I was the 'straight one', telling everyone earnestly that we must 'help these poor souls' while my partner responded, 'It's not us and them! Just Us. Mental health is about US! Maybe today you're well. But next year you might not be.'

Off the soapbox, I had always agreed intellectually with Alice but at a deeper level the prejudice had remained. When I'd first met Stephen, I'd regarded him as a 'poor soul' in need of help. Now I was being profoundly challenged. Not us and them, just Us. It felt terrifying to consider that I too could fall apart and end up on a psychiatric ward. Maybe it is this terror that provokes and sustains the stigma. It's safer to think that only certain 'types' fall apart, Them and never Us. People who are 'different', who have a 'defect', rather than people like me. And if they are not like me then I can believe their suffering is less, their needs are less and they can be treated less equally; after all, they are 'mentally ill.'

Thankfully, Charlie did not see a 'defective' or 'mentally ill' person when he saw Stephen. Charlie saw someone who loved him.

The Time to Change campaign was doing its work on me. By mid-May I made contact with Stephen's Care Coordinator, Judith, and for the first time I made requests on his behalf. This was the beginning of my engagement with the 'system'. I'd never previously engaged with any health professional beyond the carers I met on a Saturday. I had no idea how significant this was going to be for Stephen and for Charlie.

Meantime there was the 'grand visit' to our house, planned for Saturday 7th June. The week before, Stephen was briefly upset when he realised he'd miss the final of 'Britain's got Talent' but recovered and then rang me to say that Charlie had gone 'crazy' the previous night, crashing into his cage and running around the house for hours. Would he be alright for the journey? My reassurances didn't wash but the upside was that Stephen decided we'd only stop for a toilet break on the way, so as not to leave Charlie for too long.

## Stephen and Charlie visit my home

On the day, despite Stephen's doom-laden predictions, the weather is beautiful. I have stayed nearby the previous night, and arrive promptly at his flat at 9.15am.

'I'm not ready yet, Susie.'

At least Charlie is pleased to see me. I pay attention to my breath for a couple of minutes (mindfulness practice), and remind myself that this day is for Stephen. Then I become distracted by the number of cigarette boxes piled up on the table next to him. I assume they're empty, but when I pick them up, every one of them has at least one cigarette in. I count 15 packets. The e-cigarettes are lost somewhere on the table, having become an interesting extra rather than a healthier replacement. I ask Stephen why he doesn't finish a packet of cigarettes and then throw it away?

'You're not like me.'

Forty-five minutes later we leave. A further three hours on, we arrive in Oxford, having coped with the nightmare that is the motorway service station in mid-summer. My low moment is having to lurk at the entrance to the men's toilet, waiting for him. Throughout the journey Charlie is completely calm.

That afternoon we briefly visit the church, where we meet a few parishioners and Stephen tells them loudly that he has learning difficulties and has been abused in mental hospital. Everyone nods kindly. We then settle in our spacious and beautiful vicarage garden with Charlie, a peaceful diminutive body on the grass next to our large black sheep of a dog, Zozzi.

Sadly, it is not easy being in a beautiful setting when your mind is in hell. Stephen looks at ease, sat under the parasol but it is not so. He mutters quietly,

'I keep hearing voices Susie. It's because of lack of sleep. I keep hearing voices, Susie. But I need to excrete, Susie, I'm dreadfully sorry.'

Later sitting in the sun, he suddenly panics, 'I'm burning!' When I go into the house to get suntan lotion, he explodes with impatience, before apologising profusely and then shifting to the refrain, 'I'm inferior'.

What must it be like, to be inside his head?

We negotiate these peaks and troughs, manage the return journey and he declares the day a success. When I get back home, I write: 'Feeling fragile, been in Stephen's company for over 12 hours solid.'

~

Over the next few weeks, whenever Stephen rang, he would tell me what a wonderful time he and Charlie had had. On one occasion: 'You'll never know how happy Charlie was that day, that day when he saw Zozzi. You'll never know. He's told me, he's told me.' I laugh awkwardly and he explains, 'In dog language.'

I try and engage, 'Dog owners know what's in the heart of their dog, eh?'

'A nasty carer would have said, "Don't be so stupid, how can your dog talk?"'

I realise how little room Stephen is given for playful imagination. He's always 'delusional'. I feel glad I went with him this time.

While Charlie was a vital ingredient in Stephen's life, letting an incontinent dog wander free inside his flat was a recipe for disaster. Just before my next visit Stephen slipped in the hallway on Charlie's wee. He called the paramedics, who wanted to take him to hospital as they thought he'd cracked a bone in his finger. 'I refused to go.' As I started to argue over the wisdom of this, he shut it down with: 'It's my decision Susie. It's my life.'

Quite right.

Through July and August my tentative contact with his care coordinator, Judith appeared to bear fruit. She began to sort out the issue of the depot injection – basically a long-lasting dose of anti-psychotic medicine, which cuts the risk of someone deciding to stop taking it, or forgetting. She also helped him buy a rather splendid leather reclining chair. This was unprecedented as Stephen never spent this sort of money on himself. Maybe he did listen to me?

I'll change that. Maybe he did listen to me sometimes. Over that same summer I became increasingly irritated at him complaining about lack of sleep whilst consuming vast quantities of instant coffee all day and through the night. When I suggested he try de-caff, it was a brick wall; no discussion, no reflection, just 'No'.

It was his life.

Stephen had the flat, Charlie and the garden and a summer to enjoy them. His best time was in the garden with Charlie pottering in and out between house and patio. In August he wrote a poem entitled 'Dusk in the Garden':

> As the myriads of birds so harmoniously
> blend in with the serenity and sanctity
> of this picturesque summer's eve,
> So, a comforting atmosphere develops,
> A magnificent sense of bliss,
> Which in my opinion can only be discovered in my garden,
> A great and truly special garden,
> a rich and effervescent beauty.

## ONE CAN INDEED SURELY BELIEVE.

From September, a storm began to brew. Because he was considered 'difficult', Stephen had gone through most of the local care agencies and now one of the last ones was withdrawing its care, giving him two weeks' notice. He left me a cascade of phone messages, terrified and desperate:

'Please. Ring. Me. Back. As. Soon. As. Possible. This. Is. A. Major. Crisis. Take Care. Stephen.'

'I'm sorry I've rung you so many times, I'm sorry I've rung you so many times…'

On 10th September I emailed Judith, incensed that the care agency could drop Stephen with only a fortnight's notice. Judith responded to say they were only contractually obliged to give 24 hours' notice. A day's notice to stop vital care to a vulnerable human being? Let that sink in.

Then, ten days before the care was due to be withdrawn, and with no replacement in sight, Judith emailed to ask if I could persuade Stephen to agree to a 'period of respite in a local residential placement' and place Charlie with Cinnamon Trust. This would give her time to find another care agency and get the flat deep-cleaned. Cinnamon Trust is a charity that provides 'foster care' for the animals of people who are elderly or terminally ill, but at the time, all I heard was 'dog's home.'

My first reaction was, 'Put Charlie in a dog's home? Put Charlie in a dog's home!' I was enraged; yes, this was a neat solution but not only was Charlie now 19 years old and blind, he was Stephen's life-line. Stephen would never trust him to strangers and what if Charlie died there?

'Ineffectual Woman' went into the cupboard and angry 'Privileged White Woman' emerged. The same day, in an accent the Queen would have been proud of, I rang the care agency to make a formal complaint. I then emailed Judith pointing out that her plan did not take into account Charlie's age and state of health or the distress this would cause both Charlie and Stephen. I added that I was not willing to raise this with Stephen and that he would never agree to it. She did not reply.

Within days Stephen let me know the care had been extended until Judith could find a suitable alternative. What an indictment on our society; it is not the needs of the vulnerable but the voice of the privileged that gets heard, over and over again.

A new care agency was found and at first it went well. Then in November the RSPCA appeared on Stephen's doorstep. 'One of the carers tipped them off, told them Charlie had been falling over and bumping into things. It's pretty obvious he's blind and he can't help it. They had no right to do that.'

Fortunately, nothing came of this but it was obvious that Charlie could not live much longer. Stephen told me repeatedly that once this happened, he wished to follow, passing away, out in the garden, listening to the birds. It was always 'after Charlie's passed away'.

Throughout this autumn period while the care home drama was playing out for Stephen, I was involved in church, ran drama sessions to engage people with mental health concerns (part of the Time to Change campaign), spent a high-octane couple of weekends filming a short film I'd written and got myself entangled with a community Advent project, which involved organising musicians, dancers and singers, to perform for 15 minutes outside different local shops every day from the 1st December to Christmas Eve. Perhaps this is why, when Stephen's solicitor contacted me in December (on Stephen's behalf) to ask if I would be the executor of his will, I didn't ask Stephen any questions. I just said 'yes' and plunged back into the whirlpool that was my life.

However, something must have been bothering me because when I visited on 3rd January 2015, I decided to take a rough inventory of all the pills in his front room while he was in the toilet. There were at least 15 sealed or half-opened packets of paracetamol, boxes and boxes of ibroprufen, and in a large cardboard box on the side, sheaves of blister packs, each with a day's worth of medication. There were bottles of iron pills scattered around and various boxes of medication including Haloperidol and Carbamazepine (both of which relieve the symptoms of schizophrenia).

There were enough pills here for Stephen to kill himself at least 20 times over. During that visit, while I was recording, we talked a lot about suicide: his sister, his grandmother and my grandmother. Then I mentioned Mandy and how lovely she was and Stephen responded:

'Special, special. Charlie and I are going to be with her, in a better world. I believe in Heaven but not in Hell. That's fair enough isn't it?'

'Yeah.'

'Why should I believe in hell? Why should people have to burn because they won't forgive or they've taken their life?'

No warning bells went off in my head. After all he'd said

something similar so many times before. His misery ('you wouldn't want to be in my shoes, Susie') was a constant background feature like Classic FM, or Charlie's claws clacking up and down the hallway.

I was confident that Stephen would never try to take his own life while Charlie was alive but what would happen after he died?

In mid-January, Judith, Stephen's care coordinator told him on a visit that he should think about having Charlie put down. He rang me, beside himself with fury and distress. Charlie was still eating and drinking well so I couldn't see why Judith had to bring this up.

I don't know what happened or who he'd talked with after that upset with Judith, but at the end of January Stephen rang sounding lighter than he had for a long time. We talked about football (he'd been watching Match of Day), other interests and the pleasure of sitting in the garden listening to the birds. He paused and then, 'It's very sad that Charlie is going to die but he's had a good life.' I waited for him to carry on, 'I don't HAVE to die after Charlie dies. I could live. I have interests.' The enormity of this shift took my breath away. The phrase 'I could live,' pulsated in the air like the first flight of a fledgling. It was possible.

I have no idea how close Stephen came to taking his life. I only know that relief washed through me when he spoke those words.

Earlier in January, the Department of Health & Social Care published its 2015 revised Code of Practice to show 'professionals how to carry out their responsibilities under the Mental Health Care Act 1983 and provide high quality and safe care.' It came out with 5 new 'Guiding Principles.' Point 2 was about to become significant:

'*Empowerment & Involvement.* Patients should be involved in decisions about their care and the views of families, carers and others, if appropriate, should be fully considered when taking decisions. Where decisions are taken which are contradictory to views expressed, professionals should explain the reasons for this.'

In February, Tim and I were away on a writing week. During that week, I received two extraordinary calls.

The first was from a friend who rang to say she was going to Hong Kong in May to visit her son. Would I come? I'd wanted to return to make peace with my past but after the call, I just kept repeating, 'I can't possibly do that' while Tim kept responding, 'Why not?'

Two days later, my mobile rang again but the number was not recognised and there was a moment of choice. It was my birthday, Wednesday 25th February. It was 3.25pm. I chose to answer.

~

It's Judith, Stephen's care coordinator. She tells me that Stephen, with the help of his support worker has taken Charlie to the PDSA and they've said Charlie needs to be put down. He's refused and they have no legal power to force him. This is happening now.

Judith informs me that once the carer has brought Stephen and Charlie home, she'll ring the RSPCA who will remove Charlie and have put him down. The RSPCA have the legal power to do so.

What about guiding principle number two? She's not sounding me out, she specifically says she's only ringing to inform me. And what about guiding principle number three: 'Respect & dignity - for patients, families, carers and friends.'

I react instantly, 'Please, that's awful! Wouldn't it be possible to let Charlie die at home with Stephen?' She explains carefully that Charlie can't walk and he's compacted, ('can't pass faeces'). Charlie could stay alive for some time in pain. I'm begging now, 'Can't you give Stephen some time? Just one night? To get over the shock?' I'm babbling desperately, 'People need time.' Judith sighs and says she'll find out. This is a senior social-worker. I am dumbfounded.

At 4pm Judith rings me back. Stephen has agreed to have Charlie put down if he comes home for one night. Then Judith will take Charlie to the PDSA tomorrow and is on strict instructions to bring the body back. I ring Stephen but I get no answer. On Thursday 26th February he leaves a message, distressed, repeating himself and stuttering:

'Susie it's Stephen. I'm sorry to disturb you. I hope you had a lovely birthday yesterday. Charlie is being put down today at half past four. Please ring me back.'

I ring him back. The neighbours have been kind, a box had been found for 'the remains' and they will bury Charlie in the garden the following day. Stephen rings later, distraught. The Care Coordinator and Support Worker brought 'the remains' back in the cage but 'they didn't get them out, I don't know what to do.' It is the evening carer who eventually sorts Charlie's body. He's 'kind,' putting Charlie's body in a box and finding a cover for it.

~

After 19½ years, Charlie finally died and was buried in Stephen's garden. There is a small wooden cross there which someone must have made for Stephen. Stephen had stayed alive for Charlie. I'm also quite sure that Charlie stayed alive for Stephen.

Charlie had arrived in Stephen's life with Mandy, Stephen's beautiful princess. He had stayed to comfort Stephen for another seven years after she died. Perhaps Charlie was Stephen's guardian spirit or something like the 'daemon' in Philip Pullman's fantasy trilogy, 'His Dark Materials'. In those books, the 'daemon' was an animal attached to a person for life, both protecting them and revealing aspects of the person's inner self. Charlie did all that.

Carol, his fairy godmother had anchored him, Mandy his beautiful princess, had saved him. Charlie, his faithful guardian spirit had watched over him.

Now they were all gone. Where now?

# Chapter 15

## This Being Human

## Weather on the Underground

The tube is full.
The grey upright pensioner,
Reviewing the advertisements
That's me.
Silently
I sit,
Hands folded – body still.

The hurricane within
Continues unabated
Shaking, shattering
Sheering, breaking.

The shell holds.
No fragment escapes
To challenge the shapes
Of your reality.

Tell me
What's the weather like in you?

*By Susie Stead*

Being human can be as untidy and as unpredictable as the weather, especially the weather in England. Whether we like it or not, our lives are always provisional, always transitional, always a work in progress. This book, for instance was not finished by Christmas 2014 as I'd naively imagined, nor did I complete it during Stephen's lifetime with the upbeat ending

I had in mind. As a result, these final Chapters have been written without the benefit of his comments on the text.

Having tasted his responses through the book, I invite you therefore to imagine what he might say.

~

By the 1st March 2015, Stephen is alone in his flat. My first visit after Charlie's death takes place on 7th March.

As I enter Stephen's front room, I see an array of condolence cards on his main table. I comment, 'It's very quiet. Normally his paws are pattering along the floor.' We sit in silence and Stephen agrees, 'So quiet. So strange and eerie.' He hasn't even put the radio on.

We drive to our usual beauty spot to remember Charlie and it all feels very solemn. After we get back, I make some coffee and bring grapes to Stephen as requested. I then ask if I can have some. 'Susie, Susie, Susie…' He pauses to consider, then pronounces, 'Not more than six. No more than six grapes.' I enjoy the moment.

Stephen now asks me to put the radio on and farce commences. I switch it on but nothing happens. He says, 'Do you want to put the plug down? There's two switches there.' I look all over the radio. 'By the TV, Susie'. Now I'm completely confused. 'Stephen, do you want the TV or the radio on?'

'Leave my radio alone!'

'What do you want?'

'Put the switches down!'

'What switches? Something around here?' I'm still looking

on the radio.

Stephen gives up, 'Hopeless. It's absolutely hopeless, Susie.' He gets up as I start laughing. He adds, 'I thought you had a degree.' I'm telling him I have an MA when I finally see what he's doing, 'Oh, the switches! You mean at the plug!' He sits back down, and responds drily to my MA claim, 'It doesn't seem like that to me, Susie.'

It was brain-dead of me but in my defence, I never bother with plug switches at home, so I forget about them. Stephen turns every one of them off every time he leaves the flat.

Before I leave, I step into the garden to see the little wooden cross marking the place where Charlie is buried.

~

Stephen was not happy that he'd been forced to put Charlie down. While his first refusal had managed to buy time, he didn't like being given an ultimatum 'You have 24 hours or we call the RSPCA (none of us questioned how the RSPCA might actually have handled it). Whenever he started to complain on the phone to me, I'd remind him that Charlie was old and ill and he wouldn't have wanted Charlie to suffer.

Now I realise this wasn't the point. This was Stephen's dog, whom he'd loved for over 13 years. From his point of view these professionals neither respected this bond nor trusted him to make a decision in Charlie's best interests. All he needed was some time and space to cling to Charlie and then some gentle encouragement to let Charlie go. Instead of respect and trust, he was given an ultimatum. This is not a small matter. This is how people are demeaned.

Yet when I look at the professionals, most of whom are

dedicated people, I can almost see them wanting to shake me and shout, 'In what universe do I have this sort of time, Susie?'

Fortunately for Stephen he had friends and neighbours who were supportive and Charlie's death also brought loving messages from his family. I found a letter from his mother, dated 11th March 2015, 'I was sad to hear about Charlie… you will have lost a little friend and companion and may find you are rather lonely.' She offered to get him another dog if and when he felt ready and finished by saying, 'I am thinking of you Stephen and wishing I could help. Love, love always, from your Mum.'

As for me, it's been a standing joke in our family that I can only manage sympathy towards others for a maximum of 48 hours. While I'd like to have reported that I was a constant source of comfort and care to Stephen over those first weeks, I cannot. My sympathy waned a week after visiting Stephen, when he began a run of phone calls, sometimes several in a day.

On 16th March, Stephen rang and talked at length before I said I had to go. It was at this point that he finally told me the ground-breaking news that his brother had rung and had also put his mother on the phone. He sounded so happy and his brother had promised to keep in contact. He then ruined it for me by saying pompously, 'See, it was worth it. Sometimes I'm more important than other matters.' I put the phone down, crawling with irritation.

Then there was the on-going issue of Tomas, one of Stephen's ex-carers, who visited Stephen occasionally. Stephen loved these visits but Tomas never rang nor answered phone calls, he simply turned up when he could. If Tomas hadn't been for a while, Stephen would ask me to ring him, something I didn't want to do but never said a direct 'no' to.

On 18th March, Stephen rang yet again and I said politely that I'd like him not to ring me so often. He responded angrily that he couldn't help it: he's ill, I sleep well and he doesn't and if he needs to ring me, he needs to ring me.

This immediately pressed my buttons.

I squeaked tensely that if he kept ringing me so often, I'd stop answering the phone.

This pressed his buttons.

He growled back that he'd had to ring me tonight, to find out if I'd rung Tomas. Had I? He'd asked me twice already that week. When I admitted that I hadn't, he went up a gear; he was disappointed in me, his 60th birthday was coming up and he wanted to see Tomas. I snapped that I'd do it in the next few days, but Stephen went full-throttle, 'Are you going to help me or not? If you don't want to, just tell me and I won't have anything to do with you anymore.'

This extreme response woke me up to how reactive we were both being. I took a breath and then told him that I would help him and repeated this until he was satisfied. When I put down the phone five minutes later, I was still irritated, but I texted Tomas.

Stephen had suffered yet another deep loss and I wish I'd been more sympathetic, more compassionate. Yet, at that time, that's what I was like. Back in December 2014, I'd begun some psychotherapy and by this point it was touching on some excruciatingly painful areas in my life. At the same time, through the spring, I was organising drama in church, youth club, Sunday school and an evening service entitled 'Integrating the Divine Feminine.' I was also putting together, for the first time, a piece of theatre with people with mental health issues, for the Time to Change campaign. Meditation practice just held me together. The light on the horizon was that after a 14-year gap, I would be going to visit Hong Kong. I was hoping to lay some ghosts to rest.

April 3rd 2015 was Stephen's 60th birthday. It was also Good Friday. On Holy Saturday, April 4th I was due to visit Stephen. I cooked a meal, baked a cake and bought a present.

### Celebrating Stephen's 60th

I arrive at midday, ring the bell and wait. Through the glazed glass, I watch his slightly distorted figure emerge, bend down slowly to collect the post and eventually open the door. There is not a flicker of welcome on his face: 'I haven't slept. I haven't slept at all. You wouldn't like to be me, Susie, you wouldn't like to be me'. I've driven for two hours to get here and it's cold on the door step but it's his 60th Birthday. Be nice. 'Hello Stephen! Happy Birthday!'

Inside, Stephen's mood rests on me like a heavy fire blanket as he carries on intoning, 'You wouldn't like to be me'.

'Come on Stephen, would you really want to be <u>me</u>? Would you really swap?'

'Yes. Any day. But it wouldn't be fair on you.'

A vivid, disturbing image of Stephen cross-dressed as me holding Tim's hand flashes in my mind and I look around for distractions: 'Wow, you've got loads of cards!'

'I've got a letter about bowel cancer screening.'

I ask about his presents. His brother sent him trousers and a pair of shoes but he's sure they're too big. I offer him my present and he opens it; a shirt I'd carefully chosen. He takes one look and then, 'I don't like the colour blue'. I put the shirt back in my bag as he apologises and lets me know that yesterday was so lovely, yesterday his brother rang him and Tomas made a surprise visit. He was so happy yesterday. I go to the kitchen and spend as long as possible putting the chicken casserole in the microwave.

When I return, Stephen is monosyllabic so I talk cheerfully at length about Tim and the kids. He makes a real effort to listen and responds, 'Lovely, lovely,' then 'You don't mind opening those cigarettes, do you?' He already has an open packet but apparently those ones give him breathing difficulties and these ones don't. I don't argue. When I tell him I'm going to Hong Kong in May, he becomes alert, 'Nothing will happen to you will it? I'm worried.' Classic FM blares out, thunderously, as he reminds me of the recent murders in Thailand. I re-assure him that Hong Kong is a very safe place and he repeats 'very safe', until satisfied and then, 'Ok. I'll try the trousers on and you make the coffee. Is that alright?' The trousers are too big.

Stephen doesn't wish to go out so we eat the casserole and the chocolate birthday cake I've made him and then we spend time in the garden. Later, his step-daughter and children arrive with their dog and an Easter egg. I watch him gather himself together to be positive while they're there. We narrowly avoid catastrophe when his step-daughter accidentally knocks some washing powder on the floor and he panics that their dog will eat it. She's down on the floor immediately: 'I'm clearing it all up Stephen. Every last bit. The dog won't get harmed, I promise.'

Later when I leave, he insists I ring him to let him know I got home safely. The visit is a low point and the journey home is clouded by his repeated phrases circling in my head: 'You wouldn't like to be me', 'I just want to pass away', 'These final years, this final furlong.'

~

I'd had expectations yet again that Stephen would 'make an effort' to be happy because it was his 60<sup>th</sup> birthday, and also that he should be grateful towards me. Yet why should he? He was having a bad day, he wanted to be happy, but he wasn't.

What I didn't notice till much later was that something was shifting. The weather was changing.

In May 2015, I was on the phone with Stephen when he said: 'I want to enjoy myself'. Like those supersonic jets you don't hear until after they've flown past, the reverberations of this phrase didn't reach me until after I put the phone down. *I want to enjoy myself.* I'd never heard Stephen say that before.

After that he decided to sign up with a local autism charity and two of the staff visited him once a week. He paid for it, £30 a visit. It was the highlight of his week, 'So happy with them. They stand out, a beacon for nice, kind people. They understand autism. Wonderful people. They come every Friday and take me to the café or sit out in the garden. They look after me so well.'

That summer he also paid for a life membership of the National Trust and asked me to take him out on day trips to local sites. It was extraordinary.

I had been reading Andrew Solomon's book *Far from the Tree* in which he explores differences: dwarfism, autism, deafness and others. Solomon discovers amongst all the difficulties, much richness and sweetness in the different groups but, with people who suffer from schizophrenia (and their families), he concludes: 'Their suffering seemed unending, and singularly fruitless,' and 'This disease eliminates a person'. I'd found this description profoundly depressing. Was Stephen just the left over remains of what used to be a person? This did not ring true. There <u>was</u> a person here, who had not been 'eliminated,' and what's more, this person was now actively looking for happiness. A whisper fluttered in my mind, 'Does Stephen really have schizophrenia after all?'

Whatever his diagnosis, what was it that helped Stephen come to this more positive place? Perhaps it was that choice he made, to live after Charlie died? I'd like to think that telling me about his past had helped him.

My visit to Hong Kong that summer helped me to come to terms with my past, returning to the land of my childhood, where my ancestors had been. For me, being part of the ex-patriot British colonial rule in HK meant I was one of the 'bad guys' (Shamefully, the British never gave the Hong Kong Chinese the vote and if you think British colonial rule was good, read up on the opium wars). In beginning to accept that this was how it was, I began also to appreciate what Hong Kong had taught me and how she had formed me. On my trip I was also able to recognise positive elements in my history when I visited a church and a school for Chinese students set up by my grandfather and great uncle, both now Chinese-run.

Returning to England with a greater sense of peace over the past, I now wanted to change my present circumstances, in particular being tied to a tradition-bound, patriarchal church. However, all I could write in my journal was 'I cannot get out.'

The week after I returned, the 6th June, Stephen and I went for our very first trip to a National Trust Property. I booked a wheelchair as he was no longer up to walking more than a few steps.

### National Trust Visit

I arrive promptly outside Stephen's flat at 12.15 as requested. Like a repeating silent movie, through the wavy glass I watch Stephen emerge from his flat door into the hallway, lean down and pick up his post. This time however, he walks slowly back into his flat and shuts the door behind him. Muttering 'what the F...?' I bang on the front door. In slow motion, Stephen returns and opens the door.

From the moment I arrive he is apologising, 'I'm sorry, Susie, I'm very slow', 'Susie, I'm sorry for inconveniencing you'. We go through the usual rituals, but this time he asks me to remove £120 from his money box, a small fortune. Stephen wants to buy some vaporiser cigarettes as well as visit the NT gardens. He was inspired to do this after being recommended them by a friendly biker we met on one of our beauty spot visits. These ones are re-chargeable and re-fillable.

As I stand in the hall waiting while Stephen does his checking, I have a moment of recognising in myself that reluctance to leave, that crossing of the 'threshold'. Finally, we get out and into the car. Stephen hasn't had a good night's sleep. He woke up at 5am with bad rhinitis and breathing difficulties. 'I prayed very strongly to God, but I didn't sleep. God was being awkward.' He so wanted to feel rested for this first visit.

We arrive at 1.45pm. It's a classically beautiful, English summer day, cool, with white fluffy clouds decorating the sky. Once we've negotiated the entrance, seated Stephen in the wheelchair and established where to hang his bag and stick, I push him out into glorious sunshine and almost immediately notice the difference a wheelchair makes. It's harder work physically but the stress falls off me. People adopt the attitude, 'be kind to disabled person' instead of 'be careful of mad person.' At the café, there is no awkwardness cutting up his food, he's 'disabled'.

He eats his lunch, baked potato with sausages in a fennel sauce, and when I offer, he also eats half of mine, meatballs with cabbage and mash. The coffee is difficult. I bring it back as requested, half-filled with cold water but the mug is rather full. I place the mug in the correct space for his left hand to reach it. He sits up, prepares. I tense. His hand closes round the mug. He takes a breath. I'm holding mine. Then in one movement he collects the mug, brings it to his mouth, it starts to spill over, it's going to go... no it isn't. He's done it. He drinks about half the coffee in one take. The danger is over.

Now we negotiate the toilets. He's not happy because I've

reported that the ladies has a fan drier. He's not a fan of fan driers. I take him to the door, apply the brakes, put the foot pedals up and help him put his feet on the ground. With a bit of push he's on his feet. He totters into the men's toilets.

At 3pm we head off into the gardens and nature does her work on us. I see a beautiful redwood tree and draw attention to it. Stephen is so taken by it that he bursts into song. The image imprints permanently in my mind:

Stephen, wheelchair bound
Singing.
That moment like a freed bird.

There are people around but this time neither of us care.

'Susie, people will think I'm mad but I *am* mad so it doesn't matter.' We both laugh and he carries on singing. I put this memory amongst my treasures.

I choose gentle slopes that don't challenge my wheelchair skills and we find a secluded spot where he feels safe to smoke. This time I do the honours: stamping the cigarette out, picking up the fag end and giving it to him to put in his pocket. We have a good moment sitting in the sunshine. Later, after an ice cream we head back, but he still wants to get his vaporiser cigarettes. My easeful mood leaves as I realise how tight the timing is going to be but I still can't rush Stephen.

We arrive after 5.30pm but the shop's still open with a friendly woman and a little dog jumping up and down. She listens carefully, finds Stephen the simplest and easiest vaporiser, treats him respectfully and gives him a good deal on the package. Her shop was supposed to shut at 5.30 but we don't leave until 6pm. Another treasure.

Back at the flat, Stephen is tired and grumpy and the carer is late. He is late because this is the 19th call of his day.

We repeat the visit in July and one of my highlights comes when we're sitting on a bench in the sunshine and Stephen chattily begins: 'God probably won't throw me into the cauldron'. Later he gives me advice: 'Don't mess with angels, angels always get the better of you.'

~

It was during this summer of 2015 that we began discussing getting Stephen a passport, so that he could go to France. After telling me sadly, 'It's impossible Susie,' he contacted his care coordinator to look into it. Nothing happened.

During August while we were away Stephen left a variety of messages:

'I received forms for voting in the referendum and they said something about £1000 fine and also six months in prison. I'm worried sick about it.'

'I feel terrible about New Zealand – power cuts.'

'It'd be nice to know that Aidan [my son] got back safely from Thailand. There are terrible murders there.'

In September, we visited another National Trust Property. The sky was blue, the temperature mellow and some of the trees were beginning to change colour. I found the place spine-tingling. Stephen's mood, as ever, ebbed and flowed. Back at his flat, we spent time recording events from his life and then he began talking about his family. He cannot get hold of his mother. He hopes that his brother will ring him if his mother is dead. The pain in his voice rises as he tells me that he's lost his sister's address and can't send her any cards. 'Susie, it's not my fault!' I go home feeling angry with his siblings for not making more effort to stay in touch, but a memory echoes in my mind of Carol telling me they should not be responsible for him. She knew the family and I didn't. Still, I was angry with what I perceived to be failure in others. My turn at failure was, yet again, just around the corner.

Stephen was looking forward to my visit on Saturday 10th October. On Monday 5th October, my eldest son, Peter rang from Birmingham feeling very unwell. I collected him and by Wednesday he was in hospital, diagnosed with tonsillitis and glandular fever. Tim was taking a funeral on the Saturday so told me to cancel Stephen's visit but I didn't. Why didn't I?

After two days in hospital, Peter came home on the Friday night in a dreadful state. On the Saturday morning, I rang Stephen and he answered the phone with:

'You are coming, aren't you?'

I was not direct, 'Peter is very unwell.'

'You are coming, aren't you?'

'Peter is very unwell.'

'You're not coming?'

STILL, I was not direct. I explained and added, 'He was struggling to breathe last night. I was sitting with him between two am and four. You understand that.' Stephen said he would pray for Peter but added, 'You know how disappointed I am? You know, you know.' He wished I hadn't rung, he felt let down by me, angry that I'd left it so late to let him know. Now he had a whole day set apart with nothing in it.

As someone with autism, Stephen needed clear and direct communication. I was habitually indirect, demanding an emotional empathic response which he couldn't interpret. It would take me some time to recognise how deeply ingrained my responses were and then begin to address them. At the time I just felt dreadful without fully understanding why.

Stephen, having said his piece, didn't refer to it again, except to clarify that in future I MUST ring on the Friday if I wasn't coming. A few days later he left a message, 'I do hope Peter has made a recovery and he's getting better.' He did.

With the autumn came the care agency issues. Yet again, one of the agencies did not wish to carry on (there were always at least two) and Judith had to find a replacement. From the point of view of the care agencies, Stephen was 'difficult'. He constantly rang the offices complaining about the level of care and would lose his temper, hurling insults and occasionally threatening to sue them. In one letter they wrote, 'On Tuesday 24th you called the office nine times in total. Each time you were offered a chance to speak to the Manager but each time you chose to put the phone down.'

From Stephen's point of view, especially being autistic, he needed regularity and reliability and he was not getting this; for example, 'the carer didn't apply deodorant, the kettle wasn't refilled, the rubbish wasn't done properly.' He became particularly upset when his favourite carers failed to show up or were replaced at the last minute with a stranger. The battle was on-going so I never understood why the issue always came up in the autumn. It may have been when the care contract was reviewed.

Another care storm brewed a couple days after we'd been out on a National Trust jaunt. 'A major crisis has blown up for me,' Stephen told me on the telephone. 'I'll cut to the chase. My Home Care. I've been told they're not allowed to tuck my chair in anymore when I eat my meal. I found it a heck of a struggle this evening with my evening meal.' Usually, Stephen would sit in the chair and then a carer would push the chair closer so his legs were under the table. 'I'm afraid I rang up and called them lying scum. I'm frightened of the consequences. Please do help me. I should have talked to you more on Saturday. I think I wanted to enjoy the day more. I didn't want to talk about it.'

Another first. Stephen had wanted to enjoy his day out and not have to talk about his problems. Unfortunately, the difficulty with the chair rumbled on for some time.

Another on-going issue was the lack of continuity of carers which meant they didn't become familiar with Stephen's particular requirements. This applied especially to maintenance of his vaporisers. While I tried to make sure he got refills, the vaporisers themselves often ended up uncharged, dried-up or broken. As well as care problems, there were plenty of other concerns: a ladder leaning too close to Charlie's grave, benefit reviews, itchy skin, sleepless nights, mice infestations, the list went on...

At the end of one of these phone calls, he said 'Susie, I want to be well.' I wrote this down in my notes in capital letters, 'I WANT TO BE WELL'.

On Sunday 30th November, he left me six messages within

15 minutes. His tone moved from sarky, 'Thanks a bunch for ringing me and not ringing back,' to miserable, 'Have you no feelings for me? I've not got a friend left in the world,' to despairing, 'I'm seriously contemplating ending my life at this moment.' On the next call, he sang slowly into the phone from the Simon & Garfunkel song 'Bridge over Troubled Water'. A final call brought the message: 'Don't worry Susie, I won't take my life. 100% guaranteed. Do take care.' During this time, I'd taken the dog out for a walk.

Life was hard but he kept coming back for more. In December, in the midst of informing me about his bath chair getting serviced, a visit from the incontinence nurse and that he 'invariably' heard voices, he also told me how wonderful it was to speak with me and threw in some exciting news. 'You know I'm going to get a hamster?'

We also discussed getting a passport and then he said, 'I spoke to my care coordinator and I suggested psychotherapy. You've got to go to Moorhaven Hospital– they provide transport. It's in a group.' Stephen was actually willing to go to the hospital for the group. Sadly, as far as I know, it never happened.

In another phone conversation he was delighted because he'd had his pulse taken and 'She said I have the pulse of a race horse. And very good blood pressure. My pulse and blood pressure are trying to be nice and comfort me.' He then added: 'Looks like I'll be around for a while yet, maybe 10 to 12 years, even 15 or 20 years. I accept that. This is my final furlong.'

On the other end of the phone, I was smiling. Over the last few years his mantra had been, 'I don't want to live long, no more than five years, maybe seven years, eight years'. Now he was considering 15-20!

And neither of us knew he would have less than three.

# Chapter 16

## Passport

*'If I had a passport, I'd have been in the South of France*
*years ago'*
*'You'd prefer to be in France?'*
*'Je préfére.'*

Conversation in March 2015

The word 'passport', as well as meaning the official document we use to move between countries, can also mean an authorisation to move somewhere or to pass a barrier. Stephen needed an official document to get him to France. I needed a passport out of the church.

Back in 2013 after telling me repeatedly that he'd never be happy in this life, even if he did go to France, Stephen had mentioned: 'Tomas and I are planning to go on a weekend by ferry boat or Eurostar tunnel. I'm never going by aeroplane.'

Tomas was not only willing to take Stephen and look after him but he'd said he'd pay for his own travel and keep. Aware that Stephen would not recognise the need to reciprocate this generous act, I made the suggestion that he buy Tomas a meal, to which Stephen responded cheerily, 'Buy him a meal, buy him a meal, wouldn't that be so wonderful?' I reminded him how Mandy would be telling him to be generous and he chuckled, 'She was so special. She was so special.'

Tomas had thought Stephen could obtain a European ID card for travel but the UK does not issue these. Stephen needed a passport and it turned out he'd never had one (how he got to France in earlier years I do not know). Helping him obtain one was never going to be a priority for his psychiatric support team, so after a flurry of interest the subject went quiet. After Charlie died, Stephen mentioned it again and finally in the autumn I took up the baton. By then the idea had morphed into a day trip involving Tomas and myself. I liked Tomas, whom I found very steady, with a good sense of humour. I imagined that between us we could manage Stephen's mood dips, enjoy good food and have an adventure.

Getting a passport sounded simple for someone who was

born in the UK and had lived here all his life. All we needed was a completed application form and a photo and then ask for 'check & send' at the post office. As usual I was on 'the outside' making assumptions with the confidence of an able-bodied member of the middle classes.

On Sunday 13th December 2015 I went to visit Stephen with the application form and a plan to get his photo taken at the local Co-op photo booth. Unusually it was a Sunday, as I had a dress rehearsal for an outdoor promenade nativity play on the Saturday. This was someone else's idea that I was supporting after fifteen years of producing my own nativity plays (modern takes with songs and pantomime). Letting someone else run the show cut one of the threads tying me to the land of church.

### A Sunday Visit

The visit begins well. I bring a stew, arrive on time and when I get there, Stephen is smiling and pleased to see me. His hair is neat and has been well cut and he has a rather cool black jacket on which goes with his hair. He's way too thin and his khaki trousers are so big they ruckle where they're drawn in with a belt.

We sit in comfortable companionship while he smokes some cigarettes and tells me about his sleeplessness and his worries about having his benefits cut because he has too much in savings. Then I microwave my stew, put his apron on him, help him sit down, push his chair in and rest his bad arm on the table. I join him and we eat together in silence with Classic FM keeping us company.

Then the 'weather' changes. One of my sons rings in a

distressed state so I leave Stephen eating and take the phone out to the garden. Shortly afterwards I hear Stephen shouting and go back into the front room, still on the phone. He's grumpy now.

'How long are you going to be?'

'It's my son and he's very upset.' I still have not learned to be direct.

'At least he gets some sleep. I haven't had any sleep and I suffered hell in my life. I've got rhinitis and breathing difficulties and…'

Ice forms in my veins. I tell Stephen coldly that I'll be a few minutes and go to the kitchen and back into the world of my son.

The next thing I'm aware of is Stephen approaching me and growling. 'That's enough!' If Stephen could identify facial emotions, he'd get the fuck out of my space. I blank him, walk into the garden and gently bring the call to a close. When I return to the sitting room, I'm in no mood to back down. Stephen complains that the phone call has ruined the day. I retort that it's just interrupted his lunch. I tell him I feel angry and he tells me he can't help it, he's autistic. Nobody understands autistic people. He can't help it. He hasn't had any sleep. He is also angry.

Stephen wants more food so in silence I bring some, lay it out, put his apron on him and sit him down. My brain reminds me that Stephen only sees me every few weeks and he does not want interruptions. My brain affirms that Stephen is autistic but all my feelings of compassion are in deep freeze.

Sitting there at the table Stephen tells me, 'In my younger

days when I got angry, I was violent'. Is he trying to threaten me? Stephen carries on, 'That carer, Liam, when I said that to him, he said that was a "veiled threat".' I say that I agree with Liam, which has Stephen almost spitting with fury. 'No it isn't! Of course, it isn't!'

I explain evenly, 'When you mention being violent, right after you've said that you're angry with me, that's what it sounds like. A threat.' For the first time in 15 years, Stephen shouts at me. He is sitting less than two feet away and his face contorts. His shouting is more of a scratchy rasp, and he tires quickly. I say nothing and he gives up and finishes his food while Classic FM plays a gentle piece.

When he speaks again, he tells me that if I decide to leave because of this and don't come back then he will never trust anyone again. He won't let the carers in, he won't let anyone in. He will shut himself off from everyone. He repeats this several times. I begin to defrost and my anger seeps away. I reassure him that I'm not going to do that: 'I've known you 15 years. If I was going to leave, I'd have done it before.' It takes time for him to accept that I'm not planning on disappearing forever. We manage a thoughtful conversation where we both try to understand each other and the atmosphere calms. We have had a real and equal exchange.

At this point, it fully sinks in. This relationship with Stephen is not going to end. I could never abandon him. For the first time, I tell him that as far as I'm concerned, he's 'family' and that while he will annoy me and I will annoy him, I will not leave. He laughs, 'I'm not family!' He suggests that he could be a good friend maybe, but not family? I say that he can decide what he is to me. He replies, 'Well if you say I'm family, then I am.' He's pleased.

After that he apologies. All the time. He feels terrible. He feels ashamed. He's so sorry. He apologises until I leave at least three hours later.

Now, finally, we can go out to get the passport photo. We manage the journey out of the house into the car fairly smoothly, but we have to park opposite the Co-op, pay for the car parking and wait while Sunday traffic passes before making the agonisingly slow walk across the road. At this point the time is 3.45pm and the shops close at 4pm. I become over-cheerful to cover my frustration and Stephen is fed-up and muttering as we approach the photo booth at the back of the shop; it's small, awkward to get into and the seat is far too low. We haven't time to faff around so I give it a few brisk twists and hope that's enough. Stephen sits down and I attempt to direct him so his face matches the oval area shown on the screen opposite him. By now he wants to go home. We get the photos and walk out by 3.55pm. Success!

~

Recalling this day, I'm still impressed with how both of us negotiated our different areas of darkness.

The following week, the outdoor promenade nativity went ahead, supported by a number of local people and complete with live sheep and goats. We expected around 60 to 80 people to turn up. It was a perfect, crisp, starlit, December evening and three hundred people arrived. We were gobsmacked.

On Christmas Eve I joined our community Advent project 'Big Sing' outside the local Co-op food store (yes, we did it again) but for the first time that I could remember, I chose not to go to Midnight Mass. Another thread was cut.

In the warmth of his home, Stephen watched the Advent Songs of Praise and then on Christmas Day went as usual to the lunch put on by the Methodist Church (blessings upon them).

During the holidays, he rang me with some positive notes amidst the less-positive:

'Tomas came on Tuesday and we had a wonderful time and I had a wonderful time on Thursday with my support worker and had a lovely meal at the Italian café.'

'I think some of the pain I get could be from too much frowning and not enough smiling. "Dad's Army" is on tonight and I intend to laugh my head off. Half an hour completely lost in comedy.'

'I woke up completely saturated from night-time incontinence. Got up at quarter to three and I tried to go back to sleep.'

'I lost my faith two or three times but it came back. Watching "Songs of Praise" last Sunday, it really did uplift me.'

'I hope you can stomach me.'

In the New Year of 2016, I took the passport application to my local post office. It had recently moved from a warm brick Victorian building into the white, strip-lighted vacuousness of a supermarket. The queue was the same, as were the staff, one of whom was a delightful man who enjoyed bantering with his customers. He was in his forties, dark eyes glinting with life, forever smiling.

### The Post Office

After the usual wait in the queue, Delightful Man (DM) is serving me from behind his glass barrier. We wish each other Happy New Year as I pass the documents across and ask for the 'check & send.' DM looks at the forms, looks at me:

'I can't pass this photo.'

I panic, 'Why, what's wrong?'

'The stubble for starters,' he chuckles. 'And there's the small matter of the gender.'

I respond too earnestly 'It's for a friend, who has mental and physical disabilities.'

He hands me back the documents. 'I still can't pass it.'

'Why not?'

The banter is over. 'His neck is covered and his eyes are not absolutely central.'

I gather the documents up silently as DM assures me I won't have to pay again, just bring the correct photos.

I gear myself up for round two.

### Photobooth – Round Two

On March 19th, I visit Stephen, determined to be upbeat, but the prospect of squeezing him into the photo booth a second time and achieving a perfect passport photo with 'absolutely central' eyes, brings back the image of Sisyphus, endlessly pushing his boulder up the hill.

I arrive, stand outside in the freezing cold and watch Stephen's shadow loom on the other side of the bubble-glassed front door and then disappear as he picks up the post. And does it again. I practice mindful breathing.

When he finally opens the door, he's looking cheerful and relatively ready to go but then I notice his black jacket and with 'perfect photo' still in mind, find myself focussing on a small button of Weetabix welded onto his breast pocket, and then another and then, 'Stephen that jacket is too stained. You need to take it off and get it washed.' He agrees immediately. We find another which looks much fresher. The carers do wash his clothes regularly but the words 'stain removal' and 'soaking' belong to another world. Stuffing clothes in a washing machine and hanging them up afterwards is the limit within the squeezed time-frame appointed to them.

After the usual rituals we're ready to leave. For the first time, Stephen is willing to leave his bag behind. It is usually slung awkwardly across his chest, heavy with bronze coins and bulked out by half-filled cigarette packets, tissues and old receipts. He decides, 'Less trouble for you, less trouble for me.' Maybe this boulder is going to just roll up that hill.

In a repeat performance, we drive to the Co-op and park opposite. I reluctantly pay £1 parking and ease Stephen out of the car. We wait for some time before it's clear enough to walk across the road at Stephen's pace. Inside the Co-op, the photo booth is out of order. The boulder slips.

Stephen suggests the railway station, but by the time we're back at the car he's fully incensed at the failure of the Co-op and the trials of life and he doesn't want a passport anymore. I ignore him, drive to the station and nip out to briefly check the phone booths. There are two and one is large, hurrah! I've got energy to push that boulder just a little further up the hill.

We park again and I moan about paying more parking fees. Stephen says miserably, 'It's not my fault'. When I assure him that I never thought it was his fault, he cheers up enormously and laughs, 'At least that's one thing that isn't!' We wait to cross the road in the freezing cold and Stephen observes that cars should wait for pedestrians. I couldn't agree more! Why should a person wait out in the rain for the occupant in the warm dry car to pass?

We make it to the photobooth. Stephen claims he's 5ft 8 but he's now so bowed he's about my height (5ft 4), so I sit in the booth to adjust the seat to my height. Whatever I do appears to make no difference whatsoever. The boulder totters. Stephen then sits in the booth and attempts to make sure his face fills the outlined oval on the screen and his eyes are level with the dotted line. He's concentrating hard on the image when I reach in, trying to physically align his head. He starts shouting, 'I can't do it! I can't do it! I'm not a machine!' I look around anxiously, but the concourse is empty. Stephen shrieks, 'I can't do it Susie!'

But he can. And he does.

We inspect the photo. Because of the damage to his shoulder, one comes up much higher than the other. I obsess about this and decide to spend another fiver on another photo 'just in case'. I nag him to adjust his shoulders. He shouts again, 'Susie, I can't! I'm disabled.' Still no-one comes to arrest me. We get another photo. Not bad. That boulder is well up the hill. Now I just have to get it past the post office.

We make our slow progress back to the car. It's now 2.30pm. It has taken two hours to get a passport photo and we haven't yet had lunch. We head for a pub we know. When we get there it's nearly 3pm and the front area is almost empty right by an open fire. I go to the bar to order. The young barman is completing another order and has just filled half a pint with froth. We both admire this while the other staff member ignores me and answers the phone instead. I judge her silently.

When I return other people have come in and proceed to sit near us. What's the matter with them? Who eats lunch at 3pm? Stephen tenses, and says what I'm thinking, 'Why can't people just leave us alone?' The food arrives. It's beautiful. Roast lamb with a colourful array of vegetables. I shift the table closer to Stephen, put a napkin on him and cut up his food. He's looking at the bloke on the other table with a familiar paranoid expression and speaks just too loudly for my comfort.

'People shouldn't listen to other people's conversation!'

'Nobody's interested in your conversation, Stephen! They have their own lives to think about.'

He raises his voice and I cringe. 'I can't help it if I'm disabled. It's because of the abuse, all the abuse I've suffered.'

I try to distract him by telling him about my brother's recent successes on television. He tells me to be quiet while he eats, but afterwards in a loud voice, recounts what I've said for the benefit of the bloke nearby. 'That's fantastic Susie that your BROTHER is doing so well on TELEVISION. YOUR BROTHER... who PRODUCES TV programmes. And you say he's just gone to AUSTRALIA?" I look out of the window and catch a glimpse of blue sky.

By the time we make it back to the flat and Stephen's settled with coffee and fag, I've got less than 30 minutes to read Chapters of the book to Stephen before the next carer comes. He gets fed up with me asking him to repeat himself:

'I don't like talking when people can't hear.'

'I can't hear because Classic FM is playing loudly in my ear! You won't let me turn it down. Can I turn it down?'

'No. It's not my fault.'

'I'm not saying it's your fault. Only that IF you want me to hear what you say then I will have to turn down the music.'

Pause, then heavily, 'Ok. Turn it down.'

That was 'The Day of the Passport Photo'. 19th March 2016

~

The following week was the week leading up to Easter Sunday, called Holy Week in the Church's calendar. I've always found this time special, especially the final three days, called the 'Triduum'. The Maundy Thursday evening service recalls the last evening Jesus spent with his disciples and in church people are invited to have a foot washed by the priest in memory of what Jesus did and to remind us that following him means being willing to lay aside power and position to care for one another. After this, the altar is stripped of all finery and a silent vigil is kept until midnight. On Good Friday, many churches keep a three-hour vigil in the church to mark the time Jesus hung on the cross before he died. Holy Saturday is quiet and often there is a service late that night and also on the Sunday morning, to celebrate Jesus rising from the dead. Usually, I'm at all of these.

This year my diary informed me: 'Didn't go on Maundy

Thursday, didn't go to Easter Sunday morning service.' Then 'How hard it is to prise oneself from that which one has fixed to – I need alternative actions.' Not long after this, I signed up to train to teach mindfulness.

On Holy Saturday, Stephen rang and amongst the usual wide range of issues he said, 'I was happy in the garden yesterday. I experienced a spiritual experience, felt God comforting me.' Hearing him say that felt like a warm hug. He was not the only one who felt comforted.

After Easter I rang Stephen with a couple of questions for his passport: where were his father and mother born? He was instantly agitated. 'I don't know, it's not my fault.' He carried on for some time. He didn't want me to make a guess, 'In case they sue me'. Stephen then proceeded to tell me about the current issues in his life, but still fixated on the passport, I wasn't listening to anything he was saying. After a few minutes, I realised his tone had become particularly emphatic:

'You must never tell anyone! Or I'll never talk to you again.'

'I won't tell anyone.' That's for sure.

'You won't?

'I won't.'

'Do you think the government is listening in?' Now he's worried they've tapped the phones and have the information.

'Of course the government's not listening in!'

Tim, passing by, comments that this might not be a helpful response for paranoia. I change tack:

'The government has NO interest in you. They want to find

out about terrorists. They don't care about you.'

'How sure are you? 80%? 90%?' We barter:

'100%'

'99%?'

'99.9%'

I never did find out what I wasn't supposed to tell anyone.

A few days after this, I returned to the Post Office and lurked about until nobody was in the vicinity and Delightful Man was available.

### *Post Office – Round Two*

The opening scene is friendly. I put on my warmest persona, and we beam at each other. I remind him of our previous encounter, tell him I've got just one question and then throw several at him. He quips, 'I'll have to charge per question.' I hope he's joking.

We begin with the photo and whether it passes muster. He examines it carefully and gets out a ruler. The shoulders are definitely out of kilter but Stephen's eyes, peering out of the picture at us are beautifully level. DM puts his ruler down. The photo has passed the test. First obstacle over.

Now for the question about whether I need full details of his parents' birth places and dates? After all Stephen is over 60. DM thinks this doesn't matter. Hurrah! Scene over.

Except... twist 1:

I mention this is Stephen's first passport.

'That's different. You will need the birth certificates of both parents.'

What?! I blanch. Passport is dead in the water.

But... twist 2:

A more senior woman has been listening in and tells DM,

'That's nonsense, she just needs the birth certificate for the applicant.' Relief.

Then she adds the killer twist 3:

'But he will need to go for an interview. They're asking all first-time applicants to attend an interview in London.'

Blanch 2. I tell them he's mentally ill. She replies, 'Then he'll need someone to go with him.'

I'm emphatic. 'No – he's <u>really</u> mentally ill.'

They stare at me. I smile weakly and walk away.

~

After reading the passport notes again, I established that we needed both his parents' place and date of birth and if we were going to avoid a 30-minute interview in London we would need Stephen's full diagnosis and a supporting letter from a professional. On the 1st April (!), I emailed Judith, his care coordinator asking for this help. She replied positively ('but not yet, I'm very busy') and gave me his diagnosis: 'He suffers from paranoid schizophrenia and Asperger's syndrome.' I imagined the Passport people reading this and began to feel hopeful.

While I waited for her reply, I signed up with a family history website and did some detective work. Stephen reckoned his mother was born somewhere in London on 16th April 1928. The words needle and haystack came to mind but at least she did have an unusual surname. I found the records, scrolled through them and there she was! It was a glorious feeling. His father's details were easier to find and now we were on our way.

Other parts of my life were not working out so wonderfully. On Sunday 15th May, a small group of us put together an evening service at church called 'The Female Face of God.' It went well but I was surprised by the resistance from friends with otherwise liberal views. While telling me that they didn't see God as male and they weren't bothered about pronouns, they still declared it 'unfair' to have a service where all the pronouns about God were female. Two thousand years of calling God 'He', but when we call God 'She' for one service, suddenly men have become the victims? Anger, hurt and rejection are thin words to describe the pain I felt. The long term and on-going repetitive damage that the male imagery and language inflicted on me and others, seemed incomprehensible to people I thought would understand. Perhaps, in a tiny way, I was having a taste of what it felt like to be Stephen, whose sensitivities had been constantly ignored or denied. The land of church was no longer my home. After over 30 years of service, it was either stay and die or go into exile.

For Stephen, the possibility of travel to France was coming closer. Towards the end of May, after some polite prodding on my part, Judith sent me the requested letter. She laid it on thick with an A4 paper's worth, single spacing. As well as his complex mental and physical health problems, she mentioned his stammer, his lack of vocal clarity due to his failure to wear dentures, his high levels of agitation, and his tendency to 'adopt a default position of verbal irritability, or more frequently, verbal abuse and hostility.' This felt promising; after all who would volunteer to do this interview?

Tim and I were due to go for a week's holiday in Cyprus and I wanted to get the passport sorted before we went but Stephen left a strongly worded message on the answerphone: 'Please don't get my passport until you come back, just in case.' We'd agreed to have the passport sent to me, as he'd had trouble getting to the door in time for special deliveries. Now he was worried our plane would crash. 'How would I possibly get my passport if anything bad happened to either of you? I hope you both have a wonderful time.'

We did have a wonderful time. The day after our return Stephen rang. Below is a soupçon from that conversation:

'Thank goodness nothing went wrong with the plane!'

'I saw the dawn and the birds at 5.30am.'

'The neighbourhood watch came and that went smoothly.'

'I spilt coffee on my genitalia and that upset me.'

'Night before last I had a good night's sleep. Took an extra sleeping tablet. Please don't tell anyone.'

'I was enjoying myself. I was happy.'

'I've bought two pairs of sunglasses.'

On 18th June Stephen and I headed off to one of our now-familiar National Trust properties. Before I left, he signed a letter requesting that the passport (if the application was accepted) be sent to me for ease of delivery.

Two days later, Delightful Man at the post office declared the application sound and sent it off. I felt this deserved a minute's silence but the lengthening and already mildly irate queue behind me suggested otherwise.

On 23rd of June the Referendum was held and on the morning after, our household went into shock. Stephen rang later and shared his response. 'There will be profound and devastating consequences for this. Really, really bad. I went to vote in the rain. It's going to be extremely difficult for all of us: man, woman and child, dog, cat and every animal. I don't think they should have had a Referendum; people shouldn't have been trusted. Country before people. Cameron made a profound mistake. I'm extremely upset.'

My own views are not printable.

In July we heard that Stephen's application for a passport had been successful and he became the proud owner of a dark red 'European Union United Kingdom of Great Britain and Northern Ireland' passport.

Sometimes, just sometimes, that boulder gets near the top of the hill. Now all we had to do was get him to France.

# Chapter 17

## Seeing and Not Seeing

*"And now here is my secret,*
*a very simple secret:*
*It is only with the heart*
*that one can see rightly;*
*what is essential*
*is invisible to the eye."*

Antoine de Saint-Exupéry, The Little Prince

Why is it so difficult at times to 'see'?

At the beginning of September 2016, I visited Stephen and brought his new passport. After he'd checked it over, he asked me to lock it away carefully in his money tin before we went out. Stephen had decided we would go to France once he'd had his cataracts done and could see more clearly.

Over the previous four years, Stephen had occasionally referred to having cataracts but hadn't raised it as a problem until this year. Back in May, I'd given him a book, which Tim had written, called, 'Mindfulness and Christian Spirituality'. He was delighted to have it but rang a few days later, disappointed: 'I've read four pages of Tim's book but my eyesight's beginning to fail. A cataract operation is needed. I turned the light on and put my glasses on and even then I couldn't read it. My eyes have gone. You wouldn't want to be in my shoes.'

I hadn't expected this outcome. Mindfulness is fundamentally about cultivating awareness, 'seeing' more clearly. In trying to read the book, Stephen had become aware of his physical lack of sight. As a result, Stephen went to his regular opticians, had his eyes tested and in August was given an Ophthalmic Referral for bilateral cataracts. It would take the NHS another five months to rumble into action, but it was now on the cards and more importantly Stephen was agreeing to a procedure which would involve at least one dreaded hospital visit.

In fact, over the last year, while I'd been obsessing about his passport, Stephen had been making a number of positive steps. He had of course, constantly re-assured me throughout the same period that he wanted to be dead and in March

2016 had stated 'If Donald Trump becomes president, we leave Europe, Gove dishes out nasty budgets and I'm shunted out of here, the best thing I can do is take my life.' Donald Trump become president, UK leave Europe? Ridiculous!

Despite these dire and in some cases prophetic warnings, Stephen still pushed ahead, looking for ways to enjoy his life more fully. After his support worker Alyssa suggested he needed spiritual care, a mental health chaplain called Peter began to visit. They got on well as Peter was reassuring and non-judgemental.

Stephen also got himself set up with 'meals on wheels' twice a week and begun going out for more meals with people. He went out quite regularly with Alyssa.

In March he'd chosen to start taking anti-depressants to help with the on-going depression and in the same month he mentioned that Julie and Bill from the autism charity were going to help him get some guinea pigs: 'One or two guinea pigs in a pen in the kitchen. Wouldn't that be wonderful Susie? I feel a cautious optimism. There's always hope, isn't there?' This phrase, 'There's always hope isn't there?', was to become a new refrain of his, a definite improvement on 'You wouldn't like to be me.'

By September 2016, despite on-going health and care issues and a spate of horrible nightmares, Stephen had set in place various things to look forward to. Julie and Bill visited him weekly, I took him out monthly, the chaplain, Tomas and one or two others visited from time to time, and we had a plan to go to France.

Shortly after my September monthly visit to Stephen, I began training to teach Mindfulness-Based Cognitive Therapy at the Oxford Mindfulness Centre. Secular mindfulness was developed to help with depression, stress, chronic pain, etc., but in its essence, it is about cultivating awareness with a gentle, compassionate approach. We practice experiencing what is here now, without judgement. We begin to notice our own reactivity: unhelpful patterns of thought and behaviour and often a lot of self-criticism. Self-compassion is essential in allowing us to begin to see and accept what is actually here so that we can then respond with wisdom. Stephen was hopeful that the training would help with my insensitivity.

Fortunately, he had Julie and Bill, and over the last months they'd been helping him with a project close to his heart. It came to fruition on the 10th September. 'I've got some really excellent news for you! We've now got the guinea pigs. On Tuesday I went to the pet shop with Julie. One is whitish with a black tinge at the front and the other is ginger. We're calling them Fred and Ginger. We've got all the stuff sorted. The best cage, best treatment. I've got Julie's telephone number in case of emergency. Carers know exactly what to do.' He wrote a poem to celebrate their arrival:

### *The Arrival of the Guinea Pigs*
September 2016

In amongst this foreboding scene of melancholy,
amidst the pervading sense of turbulent despair,
There comes a rapturous moment of ecstatic bliss,
The Guinea Pigs!

Such innocent creatures in close proximity here,
enable surging rays of illuminating brilliance

to surround this enthralling
and serenely captivating scene.

This is indeed a time of optimistic reflection
in an otherwise dark and sombre era.

The guinea pig cage was put in the kitchen and the various carers were drawn in, 'Eva was here and she's very good with animals. Reef had a guinea pig when he was a child. Ladies from My Home Care came yesterday to see the guinea pigs.' Stephen was upbeat and cheery: 'I mustn't smoke near guinea pigs… The Cigarette lady said she was frightened of the guinea pigs – bit odd don't you think?'

Watching the guinea pigs, sitting in the garden, listening to the birds, these were what gave him delight and soothed him in his difficult times.

Nowadays some GPs are prescribing nature, including bird-watching for chronic and debilitating illnesses. A leaflet by the mental health charity MIND in 2018 recognises the benefits of nature for our mental health and tips include: sitting in your garden, bird-watching and having a pet. Stephen was ahead of them but unfortunately Adult Social Care was not. In October 2016, Stephen (and support worker) made an application to Adult Social Care to make his garden more accessible as he was increasingly finding the steps down and up difficult to manage. They turned it down: 'To be eligible under the Care Act, we must be able to demonstrate that a client is likely to suffer significant harm if they were unable to achieve a specific outcome.'

So, no interest in any significant benefit, then. Even back in 2012 a US report had concluded that access to a garden not only reduced pain and stress and need for medications but it also reduced the cost for 'long-term, assisted living and dementia unit residents.'

Time and again, I notice that what people crave is beauty, nature, music, creativity. Yet it is never on the top of the political list for education or health and certainly not in the budget. Why is it so difficult to 'see' that creative writing, sports, playing guitar or growing flowers is as important as studying history? People endlessly tell me they're not creative but I do not accept this. Either their definition is too narrow, they haven't had the opportunities or their spirit has been crushed.

In Autumn 2016, after two years' delay, the short film a friend and I had put together was ready for the festival circuit. We'd gathered nearly 20 volunteers (we paid the actresses), filmed over two weekends and spent swathes of time and a chunk of our own money to make this. Why? Because it is what feeds the heart.

In October I took Stephen out again to a familiar National Trust garden. The beauty fed us both. I love autumn and yet rarely simply stand there, mouth open at the burning brightness of the leaves.

Now, almost as predictably as the leaves falling, the care providers threatened to remove their provision for Stephen. Amongst the usual difficulties was the issue of the smoky atmosphere in the front room as some carers understandably didn't want to endure passive smoking. Yet there was no effort by management to find a proper solution; Stephen just received a bureaucratic letter telling him not to smoke when a carer was present.

Stephen had a new care coordinator to deal with it this time; Gemma had taken over from Judith. Again, as far as I know, Gemma did not attempt to engage with the care agencies to resolve the difficulties. 'I've seen Gemma. There is no care agency willing to come here. Ghastly impasse. Not one. My Home Care kindly told me they will keep sending carers until another care agency can be found. Care Maxim were horrible to me, implied I'd have to go into care. It's possible. There are only a few carers in my area. Worried sick. Horrendous.' This rumbled on for over a month and got to the point where Stephen was saying, 'If euthanasia were legal, the most humane thing would be to have me put down. I'd have to agree to it.' On 6th November, he told me, 'I've had four or five days, terrible phone calls, worrying about being put into a care home.' In the middle of this his TV went kaput. It was a lifeline for Stephen. Fortunately, Julie and Bill helped him get another.

By the time the trees were bare, another care provider had finally been found but not without adding uncertainty, stress and anxiety to Stephen's life. Even when he had provision, the turnover of carers was high, they would sometimes be late, occasionally not arrive at all and they would always be under time pressure. On 11th November, 'I was keeping the two-minute silence, remembering Mandy and Charlie but the carer had to get on because she had to be bang on time for the next call.'

Stephen also had another on-going issue with his health centre. The weekly depot injection had been finally sorted (Gemma was also a Community Psychiatric Nurse and could give the injection herself) but as a result of his poor eyesight, Stephen was now losing pills and the surgery refused to replace them. They suggested he hold the blister pack or bottle of pills over a white bowl so the pills would fall in there and be easy to see. However, 'Sometimes the brown carbamazepine bounces out. That's my mood stabiliser which I really do need.' Stephen was furious with them: 'I'm not sending them a Christmas card and I'm using their card for lists.' I was enjoying the creativity of his revenge when it struck me that this hated health centre had taken time to send him a Christmas card and it was clearly his practice to send them one too. I'd never received one or sent one to my surgery.

Stephen was looking forward to Christmas:

'On Wednesday, neighbours came with mince pies.'

'I've got the decorations up. I've got three advent calendars.'

'The Methodist church will pick me up on Christmas Day for the lunch and Rose will come on Christmas Eve.'

'Chiropodist came on 22$^{nd}$ with present and card. Julie came on Fri 23$^{rd}$.'

Despite difficulties with his eyesight, he sent his Christmas cards out, with help from his support worker; 'Mandy's mother is going to be a hundred years old next year. It's my duty to get her a special card.' I found myself blurting out, 'But she didn't like you!'

He agreed, 'She never liked me. But it's my duty to turn the other cheek and get her a card.'

On 2$^{nd}$ January 2017, I got a review:

'Christmas Day. The meal was pretty good, plenty of turkey and pudding. Cheese and biscuits got stuck in my throat and there was a huge great scene. Two people looked after me, took me there for the meal and back home afterwards. They were especially kind. The point is they reckon it's not really my fault. I was panicking.'

'Christmas TV was good. 'Coronation Street', 'For The Love Of Dogs', 'Maigret'. I enjoyed Boxing Day but they didn't have any of the films like 'Mary Poppins', they put on rubbish.'

'I got slippers from Rose, gloves from my sister. The wallet from you will be extremely useful.'

'I enjoyed New Year's Eve but horrible feeling in my stomach and lungs after smoking some cigars, Dutch cigars.'

Once the festivities were out the way, Stephen's mood ebbed. On my January visit, the pills issue raised its head again. 'What a miserable sod Dr D can be, says it's dangerous to replace them. It isn't dangerous. Suing them if I become ill.' He did eventually get the pills he needed but the problem of getting them out of the packet hadn't been solved. While there, I attempted to help. I was unused to his A4 sized pieces of card with days of the week and times of the day printed out. In each section there was a blister pack with the correct pills. Even being reasonably dextrous it was difficult to get the pills out; the tiny ones were particularly prone to popping up in the air and disappearing.

The pills issue was then rapidly overtaken by the drama of getting Stephen's cataracts done. This involved going to hospital, a trigger word if ever there was one. The first stop was the pre-operative assessment. He was very anxious and tormented by voices. 'Pray I sleep well on Monday night and cope with pre-op at 3pm. It will be about three hours.'

On the 15th January, the day after the pre-op, 'I lost my head. No CPN [community psychiatric nurse] or support worker with me and the hospital transport failed me going back and I completely lost my head I'm afraid.'

Stephen had a diagnosis of paranoid schizophrenia and autism, he was physically disabled and became hysterical at the very word 'hospital' and no one was designated to take him? I should not, perhaps, have been surprised. In a report by the Kings Fund (Jan 2018) staff repeatedly mentioned high caseloads as a major problem in providing proper care in the community.

Despite being on his own and losing his head, the pre-op did go ahead and Stephen now had a date for the operation in April, another three-month wait.

For Tim and myself the year 2017 had not begun well. Tim had been struggling with prostate issues over the late autumn and it was getting worse. Now, he would sometimes have excruciating pain down one side which could last up to 15 minutes after urinating. The doctor suggested a catheter and issued stronger painkillers which didn't touch the pain. There was something else that did. On one occasion, our son Aidan, now aged 21, noticed Tim emerge from the toilet physically shaking with shock and pain. Instinctively, he hugged his father until the pain subsided. Not only was this deeply comforting for Tim, it reduced the time he was in pain. Aidan made it his habit to do this whenever he saw his Dad head for the toilet.

It is this gift of the heart that sees what is needed and touches us when words and pills cannot.

Over the next few months, Tim carried on as best he could, regularly getting infections and taking bath loads of antibiotics. The possibility of a prostate operation loomed and the fear of cancer, while unlikely, sat in the background.

Stephen, meanwhile, as well as waiting for his operation was waiting for a new door, being hassled on the phone by scam calls, hearing voices, having nightmares, sleeping badly and still regularly losing his pills. As for the care agency that had started in November: 'Care is terrible, I'm always worried they're going to stop the care. Tracy had a right go at me. You know who she is! Care Manager of Independence at Home. They're not happy with the way I respond to care.' Stephen decided he'd get a restraining order put on the Care Manager but fortunately, in my view, the solicitor kept putting the phone down on him when he rang.

He was particularly upset in early February because Tomas hadn't visited for a long time (I had texted) and he concluded he must have gone home to Holland and given up on Stephen. 'It's sad about Tomas not coming. He used to comfort me.' The wistful tone in his voice touched me. He was missing that gift of the heart.

A week later Stephen rang, much relieved, a carer had seen Tomas, he was studying for a Biology A level and would come when he could. 'We can still go on the day trip to France.'

The trip to France now back on the table, Stephen had to get the cataract operation out of the way. As he waited, he imagined the possible ghastly outcomes, 'I could lose the sight in my right eye. I will barricade the house up if they try and put me in care.' Near the end of the phone call: 'In the coming weeks things are going to be hell. You need to pray that I'm able to cope.'

The garden and the guinea pigs kept Stephen going, 'I had a really nice day. I was out in the garden on Tuesday enjoying the sunshine. Absolutely glorious.'

'The guinea pigs are running around. Fred is hogging the water and the food.'

In March, I had a dream about Stephen. He was in bed and I was sitting beside him talking to someone else earnestly. Then I took Stephen's hand and I held his hand in mine and there was a feeling of mutual love and affection I didn't know was there till that moment. It felt good. This was the first time I'd ever dreamt about Stephen.

Before the operation Stephen had his birthday to look forward to. He sounded warm and happy on the phone: 'The big day is getting near, not far away. I'll be 62. Caroline [ex-carer] came to visit me. Lovely conversation. Tomas has been here and I'll be seeing you soon. If the weather's fine I'll be in the garden for my birthday. Autism people will come and see me at lunch time.' There was more good news. The autism people had managed to email Stephen's sister and he was now back in contact with her. This was a huge boost to him.

The cataract operation was due on 25th April. After receiving the letter outlining the procedure, he rang to tell me mournfully that he had no choice but to cancel the operation. He had to have a coffee before getting dressed and the letter said he couldn't eat or drink anything on the morning of the operation. Therefore, the operation was off.

A more insightful person would have recognised his anxiety and been re-assuring. Instead, I got cross. 'Don't be ridiculous, you have to have the operation! There must be a way round this.' He repeated sadly that it simply wasn't possible. I bit my irritated tongue and suggested he have a conversation with his care coordinator to see what could be done.

The on-going training in mindfulness was slowly doing its work. I was becoming aware of how overwhelming I found other people's sorrows and how I would either try and 'sort' them, mentally minimise their pain or emotionally cut out. On Good Friday evening, 14th April, Tim was in so much pain that we rang 111 and were told that if he couldn't urinate in the next 6-8 hours it would become an emergency. Fortunately, he was able to and he made it through the Easter Services but it was a dark time for him and I stayed with him in this darkness.

Having on-going prostate issues himself, Stephen was very sympathetic towards Tim and often offered to pray for him. When Stephen had a prostate crisis his first port of call was the paramedics: 'I had bad PTSD and I was unable to urinate on Saturday night. Paramedics came on Sunday morning in pouring rain and wanted to take me to hospital but I wouldn't go because of the guinea pigs. I was able to urinate while the paramedics were here.'

On another occasion he told me, 'Ambulance guy was very kind. I couldn't urinate at all. He made me Weetabix and stayed with me. He wasn't angry – he said I was just as important as the others.' Another gift of the heart. Every now and then someone 'sees' what is needed.

## *The Cataract Operation*

I visit Stephen on Sunday 23rd April, two days before his operation. His care coordinator has organised it so that Stephen will go into hospital the night before, thus neatly sidestepping the coffee issue.

We manage an afternoon drive, and sit facing an English valley; fields patch out before us and even a tiny English game of cricket. Yellow rape splashes across the scene like careless paint. Before I leave, he makes sure I know exactly what time his operation is and I re-assure him that I'll be praying for him. He is terrified.

Two days pass.

On the Tuesday evening he rings. The operation hasn't happened.

On the Monday night Gemma had accompanied him to hospital and the following day they prepared him for the operation. It was at this point that they mentioned his post-operative needs; drops in his eyes three times a day for two weeks. This had apparently not come up in the pre-op and no-one had been set up to do this, so they cancelled the operation. He'd gone through all that trauma for nothing.

I want to scream. Stephen tells me: 'They apologised to me but I told them that I would not forgive them.'

~

For most of us, sight is of prime importance. It was crucial for Stephen: for his independence, his confidence, his physical and mental well-being. How could something so simple and vital have been overlooked? The hospital had sent a letter about the needs of the operation day, why couldn't they have laid out the follow-up needs in the same letter? Stephen had attended the pre-op alone in a high state of anxiety. Why was his care coordinator, Gemma not there, asking questions, taking notes to ensure that everything would be set up? That's why they have a bloody pre-op. All this effort, all this time, all wasted.

A few days later Stephen rang to say that they'd set it up for August with a pre-op in June. He added 'Trump is pulling out of Climate Change. I don't like the British Public, the British Government or the US government.'

The delay of this vital cataract operation was a huge blow to Stephen. In the weeks after this he reported, 'I'm getting far more nightmares. They are about past abuse at St B's. It seemed so real.' Clear eyed, mentally if not physically, Stephen addressed his future. 'There's going to be a time when I need 24-hour care and they will want me to go into a home and I pray that never happens.'

Death was never far from Stephen's mind. On May 17th Stephen rang me to say, 'It's nine years today since Mandy died. I woke up with desperation when I remembered Mandy passed away. I don't like people who don't believe. It's good to believe. I believe that where Mandy and Charlie are, I'll be there.'

A week later, Stephen rang me on Ascension Day (25th May), which celebrates when Jesus 'was lifted up, and a cloud took him out of their sight'. He had, he said, a problem with Ascension. 'Heaven is a spiritual dimension; you don't ascend into heaven. It's not above the blue! In my perception that's nonsense. It's not five billion light years till you get to heaven.' For Stephen, this was not a philosophical discussion. If he was going there shortly, he needed clarity. I agreed with him completely.

In July, Stephen asked me directly, 'Do you think I'll make it to 70?' That would be another eight years. Stephen had problems with walking, sleeping, seeing, breathing, prostate and bladder control, depression and on-going care. I wasn't sure what the right answer was, so I asked, 'Do you want to?'

'Yes. I don't want to die, Susie.'

Yet again my view had been from the outside in. Yes, Stephen often told me he wanted to be dead, but this was an expression of anguish, not a desire to actually die. Not only did he want to live, he had plans for the following year. 'Tomas came recently and we had a nice chat. He said he was very busy, but we are going to France.' Planning a year ahead, Stephen was already working on the practical details; he would need an early call and I'd need to be at his flat for 5am. On the other end of the phone I blanched, but agreed.

Tim and I were also planning for the future. In between bouts of infection, Tim was looking to find an innovative church setting where community, creativity and spirituality could flourish, where people of any faith or philosophy could gather. By now I'd mostly extracted myself from church responsibilities, was finishing my mindfulness training and was up for something new myself. In order to move forwards, Tim needed to sort the prostate problems out, and it was finally agreed that he'd need an operation in August. Stephen was kind, 'I'm very sorry for Tim's operation. I'll pray for you all and if you can please pray for me that I sleep well and don't get nightmares.'

While Tim's operation went ahead, Stephen was not so lucky. 'They won't do the cataract operation because of my COPD, an x-ray on my lungs showed chronic obstructive pulmonary disease. I've got no idea when I will have my op.' This was not good news but my mind was on Tim's operation. Like Stephen, I worried about all the worst possible complications: incontinence, erectile dysfunction, cancer.

I took Tim to the hospital the day before his op was due and watched him walk slowly away through the double doors. On the day, dread heavy, I waited; his operation was due at 2pm. Stephen rang at midday, 'I know Tim's got an operation but he's got the luxury of an operation which I don't have.' I wanted to shout at him, but I also understood, so I said nothing. Later when I got back from visiting Tim at 9pm, the phone was ringing. I thought it would be my mother, but it was Stephen again, upset and angry that I hadn't let him know how the operation had gone and 'worried sick'. At the time, he pissed me off, but I also recognised that he cared about Tim and was genuinely upset.

What I didn't recognise was that my behaviour towards him was much the same: concern coming out as irritation. In the midst of warm days and beautiful sunshine, Stephen told me his failing eyesight meant he'd stopped going out into the garden unless there was someone there to help him manage the steps. This meant he'd only get out on a Friday afternoon if it wasn't raining. I absolutely hated this thought and got frustrated with him, refusing to accept that his eyesight was so bad that he couldn't manage a few steps, and nagging at him to 'just try.' He was adamant, though. 'It's no use, Susie.'

Tim's operation was successful, although we still had to wait to hear if there was any cancer. I was also hopeful for Stephen. He now had another new care coordinator, an energetic man called Paul, the first one to actively get in touch with me and Julie [from the autistic society] to find out our views. He was also visiting Stephen weekly as he was a CPN and could administer Stephen's depot injection. He looked promising.

Unfortunately, Stephen did not agree.

# Chapter 18

## The Capacity to Choose

*'People have the right to make decisions that others might regard as unwise or eccentric.'*

Mental Capacity Act 2005, principle 3

Paul, the new care coordinator, bounced tigger-like into Stephen's life in July 2017. Stephen found him 'overwhelming' but Julie and I were full of hope. By 1$^{st}$ September, Paul was in full gear, sending an email to the council with a list of requirements for upgrading Stephen's home, including a deep clean and crucially a ramp from the back door, including a handrail. Julie was over the moon: 'It will change Stephen's life.' I was delighted but Stephen was circumspect. 'Paul's intimidating me about the house. He's good about the garden.'

The autumn began well for Tim and I. Tim was making a good recovery and the short film my friend Andy and I had made had been nominated by a number of festivals. A high point came when it won the audience award at a London festival in September.

Over those first two weeks in September, in the midst of the usual mix of news and 'if you were in my shoes…' from Stephen, there was a lot of unusual positivity. He seemed to be getting on well with his carers and enjoying a run of good nights, sleeping well, without nightmares. It was obvious when he had slept well, because his whole tone and demeanour became lighter. The autism charity had relayed an email to Stephen from his sister and Tomas had visited, too. 'We had a nice chat. Our first visit will be France, then Belgium. Would be lovely wouldn't it?' In one phone call, he unexpectedly said, 'I need to seize these good moments while I can.'

On the 15$^{th}$ September I heard from Paul with regard to the council:

*Email from Paul, 15 September 2017*

'The council are currently refusing to pay for any of the items I listed except for a deep clean – I intend to appeal this... I continue to do my best to move things forward for Stephen...'

Remarkably, Stephen had agreed to the deep clean. Then, on the same day, Paul set in motion something that raised the hairs on the back of my neck. He rang to explain that he was planning to do a test on Stephen to check his mental capacity to make decisions. Paul was specifically looking into whether or not Stephen had capacity to understand and make an informed decision about whether it was best for him to stay in his flat or not. Paul said this process would take several weeks and went on to explain why he was doing it. The very idea of taking Stephen's freedom from him triggered me and I was no longer on receive.

*My Diary Entry, September 2017*

'Having a melt-down over the issues of 'capacity'. I feel frightened, powerless and weepy. My son says this institution is there to help Stephen but all I see is a huge power machine which wants the neatest solutions and has no interest in individuals. Institutions crush you.'

My own background haunted me. A child in a boarding school has no power and is forced to comply. In my view, boarding schools are very effective in creating obedient citizens. I couldn't even park on a double yellow line when Stephen would have benefitted from it.

To his credit, Paul was making a major effort to be transparent with us, but when he spoke to Stephen about the issue of capacity, the conversation did not go well. On my next visit I found Stephen unsurprisingly distressed. In the following week, Paul spent some time reassuring Stephen.

On 25th September, I made an anxious phone call to Zig, my retired social worker dog-walking companion and asked about the mental capacity test. He explained calmly that four questions would be asked of Stephen. If the answers to one or more of these was 'no' then this meant he didn't have capacity and could forcibly be removed from his home. The four questions were:

* Can he understand information?
* Can he retain information?
* Can he weigh up information?
* Can he make a decision and communicate that decision?

I was confident Stephen could do all four of those and my friend said he would be safe. He did however find it strange that Paul was going to take several weeks over this, when these questions could be answered in 10 minutes. After going over emails and phone calls from Paul I emailed Zig:

*Email to Zig, 26 September*

'I'm very concerned that this CPN (Paul) has said I shouldn't go ahead with changes to the garden until the conclusion of his mental capacity assessment… He mentioned twice to me that capacity might be called into question if there were an 'impairment of brain or mind.' Who decides that? I feel Paul has an agenda. He wants this man tidied away and looked after 'properly' and he has not understood that this is the last thing Stephen would ever want.'

My friend replied, suggesting I ask why this was being done and also request an AMHP (Approved Mental Health Professional) to do the assessment, adding that the assessment was not a process that took time. It just consisted of one interview. He finished by saying something I found vitally important:

'Remember, people have the right to choose where and how they live even in the shittiest conditions with severe health problems.'

I emailed Paul immediately and while I was able to ask why he was doing the assessment, I didn't ask for an AMHP to do it instead of him. I found it too difficult to make this direct challenge to Paul's authority. Paul replied to my email on the same day and I could almost hear his tired exasperation.

*Email from Paul, 26 September*

'As I had hoped that I had explained properly to you on the telephone, I am carrying out the Mental Capacity Assessment because I may/we may be about to carry out a piece of work to sustain Stephen in his property, and I want to be able to account for and document my decision-making process, as well as be certain that I am/we are doing the right thing in the eyes of the law in order to sustain him in his home.'

This made sense rationally, but emotionally it didn't touch me. I listened to my 'reason'. Carol would have told me to listen to my heart. I was grateful that Stephen at least was feeling confident and reassured: 'I know what is best for me... I've got capacity and Paul thinks I've got capacity, but he needs to do a review.'

The decluttering of Stephen's house was a major autumnal project. Stephen went hot and cold over this. He spoke to Rose, his step-daughter, 'she thinks I will benefit from it greatly.' When I went to visit, I would go through a pile of papers and explain each one and he would decide whether to throw or file it. Once the de-cluttering had been completed, the plan was for me to bring some containers for his belongings. Julie would then look after the guinea pigs, while on the appointed day I would take Stephen out as the deep clean took place. We were looking at early December to accomplish this.

As Stephen braced himself, other more profound questions were being raised. October 13th 2017 was a significant day for Stephen and also for Tim and me.

In the autumn of 2017, Tim and I had been in the present church for 10 years and on October 13th we went away for a few days to reflect on our future; it was pivotal. At the end of this time we considered not just leaving this particular parish, but leaving the church.

Also, on October 13th Paul sent a long document relating to the capacity assessment. He wanted us to read it and comment and said it would take six weeks for him to complete the assessment (24th November). The document posed a real threat to Stephen's future, making crystal clear where Paul's preferences lay. In it, Paul raised various different concerns and for every one of them, he suggested that 'alternative accommodation' could be the answer, providing a smoke-free, clean and care-filled environment. I politely emailed back pointing out that Paul had not mentioned what could be done to support Stephen in staying in his home and offering my own suggestions:

*Stephen – What would you need to do if you want to stay?*

* *SMOKING:* A clear plan to reduce or stop. You would need to use e-cigarettes as a main source, not an extra.

* *CLEANING:* Pay for a regular cleaner and allow them to clean.

* *CARE AGENCY:* Agree a maximum number of times that you can telephone them in a day.

* *CARERS:* An A4 laminated list of jobs because carers keep changing.

* *GARDEN:* Pay for changes in the garden, and sort this with Susie and Julie.

I also pointed out that the care agencies had failed to provide appropriately trained carers and that Paul had not mentioned the downsides of Stephen being put in a care home: 'You mention his PTSD nightmares, but these revolve around his experience of abuse from staff while under the 'care' of the institution. Going into supportive accommodation or even the expectation of it, may make his PTSD much worse and I would worry about a collapse of his mental health as a result. I do not have faith in under-trained staff being able to offer him an appropriate level of care.'

Paul replied the next day: 'Thanks for your email. I think you make some valid points around the balance of the document.'

Julie emailed, agreeing with me, and Stephen's support worker, Alyssa was succinct: 'From my perspective, I believe that moving Stephen to supported housing would be detrimental for his Mental Wellbeing.' This felt heartening.

Meanwhile Tim and I came to the end of our week away. What about our future? On that last day, sitting around a kitchen table in a cottage in the Cotswolds we thought we'd try on 'the idea' of leaving the church institution. It felt good. Both of us were now trained to teach mindfulness so could earn some money through this, but we needed to check our finances as we'd have to buy a house. As we got up to leave Tim's phone went. It was the hospital, phoning to give him the results of the biopsy.

I waited outside. When he eventually walked out and joined me, we stood there in stillness facing a small square of English garden. His biopsy had come back clear. There was no cancer. We were free to go and live; free to make unwise and eccentric decisions; free to leave the institution.

After that, the experience became in some ways, surreal. It was as if we'd been walking into a headwind for years and just agreed to turn around. Our finances were better than we thought, the first house Tim looked at was made for us and the flat that we'd kept over the years sold within four days of being put on the market at the full asking price.

By the 13th November, one month after we arrived at that cottage in the Cotswolds, we had in principle sold our flat and bought a house.

*My Diary Entry, 15 November*

'Going down a rabbit hole, becoming tiny and then huge. Reality shifting in great waves and nothing is certain. It's wonderfully exciting and terrifying and overwhelming and glorious. The whole thing could fall apart… but I don't have to put up with a church that doesn't add up to me. I don't have to put up with a church at all.'

As I readied myself to leave one institution, the struggle to keep Stephen out of another was about to get serious. As far as I was concerned, Stephen had full capacity to choose and he wanted to stay in his beloved home. This is how it played out.

At the end of October, Paul set up a big interdisciplinary meeting to be held on 15$^{th}$ December to discuss plans for Stephen's future, to which I was invited. Paul wanted Stephen to be there, but he was reluctant.

Through the autumn, Stephen plugged on with intermittent nightmares and variable care. His morning care had been reduced from 90 minutes to 75 minutes and he'd lost his temper with the manager, James. Shortly afterwards came the threat to withdraw care. Managers seemed incapable of working out how to limit Stephen's calls or engage with him as a human being (unlike the autism charity). To them, Stephen was the problem, not the care agency structures. This time it was the agency with the statutory obligations that was threatening to walk away. Paul reassured Stephen that they weren't permitted to leave Stephen so vulnerable and would be forced to wait until Paul found a suitable alternative. Unable to recognise the effect it might have on a key figure in authority, Stephen lost no time ringing the already irate manager, James, to rub his responsibilities in his face.

While the 2005 mental capacity act outlines the mental requirements needed to make decisions, other factors need to be in place to allow a person to actually act on them, for instance: finance, health, the support of others. Tim and I had these and were able to make the decision to leave the Church, even though it would affect his pension. Stephen was on far rockier ground as his health was poor, he couldn't afford private care and his choice to stay depended on the support and goodwill of a wide range of groups and people. If they withdrew support, it didn't matter how good his mental capacity was. Stephen was in a Catch 22 situation. He relied on care agencies with tight budgets, constant staff shortages, no time and a lot of boxes to tick, yet his autism meant he reacted angrily to uncertainty, last-minute changes and anyone in a rush. The most essential quality and the true key to Stephen was kindness.

'Daniel [carer] has improved. Nicer and kinder. A teddy bear got misplaced but we found it at the back of the bed. He's wonderful.'

'Peter [chaplain] is very kind. Peter assured me, once you've passed away, you find peace.'

The autism people were always kind. They understood, as Julie wrote in one email, that 'above all Stephen responds to warmth, patience and consistency. He also respects boundaries when he understands the reasons why.'

If they weren't kind, but bureaucratic, rushed and impatient, then Stephen would 'cut up rough' with them, which made the situation worse and put him at risk. At one point he rang the health centre so many times that they refused to take any calls from him and a carer had to ring on his behalf. Stephen didn't trust them, so when in November he confessed to me that he'd been taking more than the recommended dose of paracetamol, he refused to get in touch with them in case they had him sectioned. It took a considerable amount of dodging and diving before I established: 'Three times, you might have taken three, and not two?'

'And once I may have taken four, in the last week or two.'

He was worried about damage to his liver, but concluded that his liver was not his priority. 'The worst things are going into care and being sectioned.'

The big question was, would Paul prove himself to be 'kind', or not? He was due to report back on his Capacity Assessment by 24th November, but the date came and went and we heard nothing.

Ten days before the deep clean, Stephen rang me: 'I've got some really good news. Paul was looking into two new care agencies and one of them has contacted me. Private care agency. Wouldn't it be great if we had a new care agency?'

I agreed it was wonderful.

The day of the deep clean loomed, Monday 4th December. We were going to be in each other's company for at least eight hours and we needed a plan. Stephen wanted to visit an historic town, a decent drive from his flat. I suggested we have lunch there and then head north to visit a friend of mine whom Stephen knew and liked. We'd have tea with him and be back in the flat by 5pm.

On Saturday 2nd December, Stephen rang to report that the new private care agency wouldn't take him unless he gave up smoking. They'd given him six weeks to stop. This was huge.

On Sunday 3rd December I headed over to stay with a friend who lived near Stephen. Even though the day out would be difficult, I was glad to leave the parish for a couple of days as I was dreading an imminent local meeting about the planned extension to the church. Planning permission had been granted but we still had to wait for permission from church authorities. Now, for some reason, we had to have a public meeting so that locals could hurl verbal abuse at Tim. I felt I had to go, but the prospect made me feel physically sick.

On the Sunday I dropped in on Stephen briefly before heading over to my friend's house. Stephen was in a terrible state, feeling suicidal, his eyes sparking with fear. He had no idea how he was going to give up smoking. I kept trying to reassure him; Paul would have to set up a plan, it would be ok.

### *The Deep Clean*

Monday 4th December – I arrive at 8.40am and Paul turns up shortly afterwards, followed by the cleaners. Stephen now has a wheelchair which I put in the back of the car. Then Stephen insists that I collect four different socks from his drawers to shove in his pockets so his keys won't fall out. Finally, after he asks loudly, 'Can we trust them not to steal my stuff?', we leave.

The historic town Stephen wants to visit is a 90-minute drive from his flat. That is if you don't stop. First, we have to buy a nasal inhaler stick which can only be bought from Boots. Then we stop so he can check his keys and then, of course, Stephen needs the toilet. I eventually find a pub: we park, I walk to the back door and am told the pub is closed. Fortunately, the bloke who tells me this allows Stephen to use the toilet, which involves me helping him out of the car, walking very slowly down the path through the garden into the building, then waiting, reversing the journey, propping him up against the car and helping him light his cigarette, because I won't let him smoke in the car. He's not happy with me. I can't remember why I insisted on this rule, but I probably had some idea of helping him cut down.

We finally get going again and drive two miles before he insists on stopping again, this time because he can't find his keys. I park in a layby, get out of the car, walk around to his side, open the door and find the keys. By now I'm in a shit mood. My timing for the day is truly screwed.

Eventually we get to the town, admire the architecture, push Stephen's wheelchair over cobbled stones and find a friendly 'ye olde' café. While we're eating lunch, Paul rings me, sounding slightly desperate. He has a plan to get Stephen to move over to vaporiser cigarettes today. Literally, come home, throw all the cigarette packs out and just smoke vaporisers from now on. I tell Paul politely that I can't speak now but that I can't see this working - and finish the call.

I don't mention this to Stephen. Stephen is feeling ok now with a coffee, some toast and jam. The people in the café are kind. Afterwards we have a peaceful moment outside, surrounded by historical buildings.

The drive to my friend Steve's place is fraught. I'm using a sat nav on my phone which confuses me and we get lost. Stephen becomes more and more agitated and upset and I compensate by being overly positive and cheerful. When we get there, it's an oasis. Steve is warm and welcoming and very, very, kind. After a hot toastie, coffee and cake, Stephen visibly relaxes. So do I.

The trip home is unproblematic but Stephen becomes quieter and more morose as we get nearer. When we get in, the flat feels alien, stripped back and with the smell of cleaning fluids hanging in the air. It doesn't feel good leaving Stephen there and I wait until the carer arrives before heading back.

~

The next few days were strange and manic. It took three days to find out what was behind Paul's phone call at the café, but first came the dreaded church buildings meeting. The locals were not 'kind', not even close.

Then on the Thursday, Julie emailed Paul, copying me in. Stephen had rung her that afternoon to say that his care package was being stopped the following Monday, in four days' time. I sat there in shock realising that Paul must have known on the Monday when he rang me. The new care agency refused to start until Stephen had stopped smoking, so what was going to happen? Julie wrote, 'Stephen has today threatened that if he is left with no care from Monday then he will be forced to take his own life. I said I would need to inform you of this as part of my duty of care.' She made the suggestion that in the short term his redundant bedroom could become a no-smoking dining room and Stephen could agree only to smoke in his front room which carers would not have to enter. She added, 'Can we look at this as a reasonable plan, rather than the threat of care being withdrawn? I think this is actually illegal, as Stephen is entitled to care in his own home.'

Paul replied, 'There is a legal obligation to provide a care package: that is my understanding. However, there is no legal obligation to provide this in someone's home and it can be offered in another setting.'

Paul ignored Julie's suggestion and James, the care manager had his revenge. James only allowed a few extra days in order for Stephen to be allocated a temporary care home. It was check mate. Not kind.

Forget capacity, and all our worries about it. Stephen was screwed by a system which simply didn't include the possibility of kindness when things became challenging.

Stephen couldn't survive without care and he knew it. On Saturday 9th December, he rang. 'They're ending their care package on Sunday 17th. I've got to give up smoking by then. I've got to acquire superhuman strength to do it. You have to pray intensely all the time. A long time - not like you usually do.' He then shared more bad news: 'By Monday 18th I'll be in temporary care. Jane, the manager of the private care agency will come on 20th to see the flat is smoke-free and [even if it is] they won't start for another two to three weeks to get all the carers ready. It is very unkind.'

Stephen was accepting that he would have to be in temporary care for a few weeks over Christmas and New Year. He re-assured me he wasn't planning to barricade up the house, but he also said, 'You always say it won't happen, Susie, you're wrong. There will be a catastrophe. I'm terrified of everything in this situation. I feel desperate and suicidal. I don't know if God can help me.'

Only one thing reassured Stephen. 'The council have told me I'm safe. I won't lose my flat which is so wonderful. Sometimes I can bring myself to feel cheerful.'

On Sunday 10<sup>th</sup> December, the day after this phone call, Tim announced in church that we were leaving. Thick snow lay everywhere, so few people were present and none of them seemed very surprised. For me it was beginning to feel very real.

Over the next few days, reality was also hitting Stephen and he became increasingly upset and angry. 'Paul lied to me about the care. He said I couldn't be left without care and then I get this. He said he got the wrong information. There needs to be an inquiry into this as to why. I'm going to go through unbelievable hell. I want to be in my home. I always have been and next year it will be back to normal.'

Then there was the huge issue of smoking. He told me, 'I've just about stopped smoking lit cigarettes, I'm smoking e-cigarettes' but then the care home told him they wouldn't let him smoke the e-cigarettes in the home either, because 'they set off the alarms.'

By that stage, Paul and I had had more than one tense exchange of views. On the subject of smoking, Paul didn't think Stephen was committed to giving up and I didn't think Paul or any of the other professionals involved had done anything constructive to help Stephen.

The most difficult exchange was a phone conversation we had about 'what was best' for Stephen. Paul's capacity assessment had never appeared, probably (my interpretation) because it would have suggested Stephen didn't need to go into a home. On the phone, Paul came across loud and clear that he knew what was best for Stephen and that Stephen should have been moved to a care home long ago. With white hot anger knifing me, I replied as evenly as possible that Stephen should be allowed to make decisions about his life even if they didn't seem to be the 'the best' ones as far as Paul was concerned. I also thought his desire to put Stephen in a home was 'convenient' for him, rather than the best option for Stephen. With a distinct edge in his voice, he politely disagreed. The conversation was jagged and dangerous.

Friday 15th December was approaching, the date for the big interdisciplinary meeting to discuss Stephen's future. Julie and I had been increasingly in contact with one another, both worried for Stephen. We agreed some items for the agenda and the first one was: 'Is there an agenda to remove Stephen from his home permanently?'

By now, we were both feeling out-manoeuvred.

The day before the meeting I got a stomach bug which laid me out and prevented me from attending but I knew Julie would raise the issues. In the event Julie felt the meeting achieved very little, Paul was simply trying to tick boxes and move on.

On 17th December, Julie collected the guinea pigs and on 18th December, Paul emailed round to say, 'Just to let you know that Stephen has been moved safely and seemed OK when I left him there at 2pm this afternoon.'

Tick.

And from Stephen's view? I rang him on 30th December and his first words were, 'Things are diabolical here. I had bad depression last night.' The changes had thrown him. Nothing was where it should be, they didn't have a commode which he needed and he had to go outside in the freezing cold to smoke. On 30th December he told me he'd managed without a lit cigarette for three or four days and was smoking an e-cigarette, would I buy him some more? The only good thing was the food. Julie, Rose and Tomas had been to visit and he persuaded Julie to check on his flat because he'd become very worried that he'd left the heating on (he had). The 30th of December, Stephen told me, was Mandy's 65th birthday.

Just before he rang off, he asked: 'Pray that I get to go home.'

# Chapter 19

## Waiting

It was now January 1st 2018. Over the last three months, Stephen's life had been up-ended. My life has also been up-ended but of my own choice.

And there was something else.

As well as being Stephen's care coordinator, Paul was a community psychiatric nurse and from July until December 2017 he'd had considerable contact with Stephen. At the end of November during a phone call with me, he made this statement:

'I don't think Stephen has schizophrenia. I think he's autistic.'

The implications of this did not hit me till much later. Was it possible that Stephen's psychotic episodes were not linked with schizophrenia? If Paul's view was correct, then what did that imply about Stephen's 25 years on psychiatric wards? Or the 40 years of taking heavy duty anti-psychotic drugs?

Right now, Stephen had more immediate problems. He'd gone from living on his own for just under a decade, to residing in an alien environment surrounded by people and noise. This wouldn't have been an easy transition for anyone, but for an autistic person this was a nightmarish overload. Added to this were traumatic memories of being abused 'in care.' In the midst of all this, he was expected to give up a 30-year smoking habit before being allowed home.

Christmas came and went in the new home. Stephen could only sit and wait for this nightmare to be over, waiting to go home.

Waiting, waiting, waiting.

Tim and I were also waiting: waiting for the people who were currently renting our flat to leave, waiting to exchange on the flat and the house we were buying, waiting to complete, waiting for that final church service in April.

Waiting, waiting.

Then, on Thursday, 4th January, 17 days after Paul delivered him to the home, Stephen had a fall. He fell in the home and when the paramedics arrived, he fell again and was taken to A&E but the care home didn't contact me or Rose. Julie rang me on the Friday because she'd gone to visit him and was told that he was in hospital. When she got there, he was still in A&E on a respirator, with the diagnosis of a chest infection. His face was badly bruised and he was emaciated. His first question was about the guinea pigs and once he knew they were fine, he told Julie he was worried sick about not getting back into his flat.

Julie was bewildered by the lack of care. Nothing had been put in place to help Stephen give up smoking, and the staff had been wheeling him outside in the freezing cold to smoke.

I rang Tomas who was angry and frustrated that the care agency had failed to keep Stephen in his flat, 'Agencies are dreadful. If someone is difficult, they just pull out, no proper care.' I wanted some hope, so I mentioned the possibility of Stephen getting to France. Tomas thought a day trip might be doable with both of us, but he was concerned about Stephen's mobility and pointed out that if he stayed in bed in hospital for any length of time, his muscles would waste.

There was still hope.

On Saturday 6th January I woke at 5.30 am, worrying about Stephen dying in a hospital surrounded by strangers. On Tuesday 9th January, Rose rang to let me know that Stephen had now been diagnosed with a bowel obstruction and pneumonia. He needed an operation and as his next-of-kin, she'd been asked if he'd want to be resuscitated and she'd said yes.

We arranged to meet at the hospital the following evening after the operation. Meanwhile Julie rang, further distressed by what she described as a strange phone call from Paul, in which he appeared to be justifying his actions, claiming that Stephen's needs had been growing too serious to be provided for at home. When Julie challenged this, pointing out that Stephen had only had care twice daily for a total of two hours, Paul said he'd done all he could do to help Stephen and at the end, asked if she'd been happy with the call.

Tick.

After the phone call I thought about the fact that Stephen had agreed to go to the care home. Yes, he was pushed, but he was Stephen, he could have refused. Uncharacteristically, just before he went into the home, he told me: 'At least I will be warm and safe over Christmas.'

Warm and safe – precisely what he wasn't.

This assumption of 'safety', which most of us feel is the key reason for anyone to go into a care home, needs challenging. An NHS Scotland pamphlet on managing falls in care homes states: 'Older people living in care homes are three times more likely to fall than older people living in their own homes.' Contributory factors mentioned by the report included physical inactivity and unfamiliar surroundings.

As a direct result of being put in a care home for his own good, Stephen had contracted a chest infection and had fallen. Now, he had pneumonia and a blocked bowel and in this state, he was having an operation.

### Hospital Visit – 10th January

On the Wednesday, I arrive at the hospital about 4.30pm and walk the NHS maze to find the Acute Medical Unit.

Stephen is on an open ward of about eight beds. He's asleep and I stand at the foot of his bed, taking in this setting: hospital smells and noises, Stephen's wasted face propped up by pillows, the oxygen tube hooked to his nose, another tube affixed to his left arm. In the cubicle to his right, a man sits in a chair, peacefully reading a newspaper. To Stephen's left, a man lies barely breathing, an anxious woman holding his hand. Opposite Stephen, an elderly woman is telling jokes to visiting family members.

I move to Stephen's side, gently speaking his name. It takes him a few moments to open his eyes and focus.

'Will you stay with me?'

'Yes.'

'Am I going to die? I'm frightened I'm going to die.'

I speak firmly, only half-believing this,

'You're not going to die. Despite having pneumonia, you've survived an operation. You're going to be ok.'

I tell him that Rose had said he wanted to be resuscitated. 'Yes, I want to live.' Looking at him lying there, this feels more painful than if he'd said he'd had enough.

He tells me that he can't use his normally good arm because the hospital staff have abused it. I try to explain that they've put a tube in to help him, but he isn't interested. He asks for water and then asks me to wipe his mouth as some froth is emerging. I do what he asks, but my stomach heaves. This process repeats itself several times and I keep heaving, hoping I won't actually vomit.

When he asks for a hot water bottle the charge nurse is adamant, hot water bottles and microwavable hotties are banned due to the danger of patients burning themselves. No alternative is offered so I request an extra blanket. At this point the nurse wakes up. 'Ah yes, he had his depot injection this morning. It's probably made him feel cold.' He finds a blanket for Stephen.

Stephen now asks me to rub his itchy eyes for him. I've got a cold and have been concerned about passing on bugs to him, so I've been cleaning my hands with anti-bacterial spray every few minutes. I spray my hands yet again and then poke his eyes; it's not pleasant. Fortunately this doesn't last long and then he asks me to hold his hand and we sit companionably together for a few minutes before I'm instructed to tickle his left elbow.

'Tickle?'

'Tickle.'

I sit in the available upright chair and for five minutes I just tickle his left elbow and arm. He seems to like that.

We don't talk much. The loudest he gets is when he asks after my 'famous' brother and chuckles when I report that I saw him on Christmas Day.

We watch people. A couple of young hospital orderlies energetically wheel in an empty trolley bed, park it behind a curtained bed diagonally opposite and say a little too loudly to the charge nurse, 'She's going to be difficult to slide on to this.' The charge nurse disappears, returning rapidly with a mat, the curtains are drawn back and the patient concerned is moved efficiently onto the trolley. She slides well. They prop her up with pillows and I catch a glimpse of her eyes before they wheel her off.

How does so much fear get conveyed through the eyes?

An hour and a half later, I'm flagging. The family members have left the elderly lady who now has an oxygen mask on; the patient next door is still breathing and another visitor is there; the bloke to the left of Stephen remains in his chair, now looking at a crossword puzzle.

By now Stephen has recovered from his first terror and returns to more familiar phrases like 'You wouldn't like to be me' but I notice he doesn't say the one that goes, 'If you were me, you'd wish you were dead'. Rose finally arrives at 6pm, hurrah! She brings warmth and calm, chats about her children and shows us photos of her dog and the recent litter of puppies. The food comes, but Stephen is insistent he needs his pills first and when the nurse brings them, she has to name each one before he agrees to swallow them. He hasn't given up yet.

As I feed Stephen chopped up sausage, mash and carrots, Rose encourages Stephen to move as soon as he feels able, but in his view, 'It's not possible'. Then, 'I'd like to live another five years if God will let me. If God thinks I deserve it.'

After a brief diversion on the subject of getting what you deserve, Rose leaves us about 7pm and I tell Stephen I also need to go, but he wants me to stay till 7.30pm. He's still hungry, so I buy an assortment of food from the hospital shop including a muffin, which is a mistake. I spend a good five minutes trying to clear the crumbs off the bed. Before I leave, I take Stephen's hand, 'Stephen, you do know that I care about you, don't you?'

'Drive carefully.'

~

That was the 10th of January.

On the 21st of January for the only time in my life, I was invited to preach a sermon in church. The Bible text was from the wedding at Cana, the story in John's Gospel, where Jesus turns water into wine at a local wedding. It is a fabulous story, in which, according to the gospel writer, Jesus produces somewhere between 120 to 180 gallons of fine wine. For me, the central message of this story is this:

'God does not want people to survive on the minimum, bread and water. God wants people to have fullness of life: rich social interaction, meaningful lives with joy and beauty, music, art, community. God wants us all to discover that fullness and then share it wildly and abundantly with others.'

That pretty much sums up what drives me in life.

A week after this, on the 28th of January, I visited Stephen again. I couldn't bring Stephen 'fullness of life' but at least I could be there.

### Second Hospital Visit

Stephen is now in a side room on his own. He looks weather-beaten with his unkempt grey and black flecked beard contrasting with the sharp white sheets. His face has more colour and his eyes are brighter.

'Hello Susie, can you get me a yoghurt?'

I get one and feed him.

'Thank you. It's hell here, hell, hell, hell.'

It's quiet in the room and he looks clean and comfortable in the bed with lots of pillows propping him up. I want to tease him that if this is 'Hell', he's doing well but I know by now, this is just the view from the outside; nice clean sheets, nice clean Stephen. The worst horror movies are like that; everything on the outside looks normal, even pleasant, but the hairs on the back of your neck know otherwise. I don't have to wait long to find out what is going on inside Stephen:

'Will you and Tim come to my funeral?'

'Yes, of course we will.'

'Will you?'

'I'll probably be organising it! Maybe you could think what you'd like to have in it.'

And he starts to sing,

'The King of Love my shepherd is, whose goodness faileth never...'

And I join in with, 'I nothing lack if I am his and he is mine forever.'

'That tune,' he says.

[*Dominus Regit Me*. I don't insert my usual 'she' at this point]

After asking after Tim, he tells me, 'We may be abroad, come and see me if we're not abroad.'

'Where are you going?'

'We might go away for six months: France, Italy, Belgium.'

'Lovely.'

Then he wants another yoghurt and out on the main ward I find a round cheerful nurse with training in mental health who promises me they are trying to get Stephen moving, but he's very reluctant. As we seek out a yoghurt, she good-humouredly tells me: 'Oh yes, we get on fine now. At one point, Stephen told me he was going to stab me and I pointed out that if he stabbed me, I wouldn't be able to feed him and he said "fair point".'

She gives me a form to fill in, to help staff know more about Stephen's needs. A Chinese nurse passing by overhears his name, smiles and says tenderly: 'Oh, my lovely Stephen.' By the time I get back Stephen is shouting for me, where have I been? He doesn't like the form and after briefly engaging with it, he whispers to me: 'I don't like it that they're listening to us talking.' I make the mistake of asking if he is hearing voices, to which he responds by shouting over and over, 'Are you calling me a liar?' The nurse appears, asking if everything's alright. Stephen goes thin-lipped and silent as I say something asinine like, 'He was just a bit upset.' After she leaves, I start fussing about setting up TV or radio for him and he growls, 'I shall make a scene and they will ask you to go.'

'Am I annoying you?'

'Yes.'

'I will stop.'

We sit in silence and gradually Stephen recovers and says, 'I'm still talking to myself.'

'It must be tiring.'

'It is.'

After about an hour and a half, he asks me to leave and I notice a sense of disappointment, the flatness of it. I'm not used to him wanting me to go. As I gather my things, he says, 'I'm sorry I can't help you.'

'You don't have to help me. I'm here to comfort you. You don't have to do anything for me.'

As I walk down the hospital corridors, I feel that he picked up on my need to be affirmed, which was why he said, 'I can't help you.' Friends who've been in hospital have told me how sometimes visitors are exhausting because they want reassurance. Stephen's words forced me to recognise this in myself.

~

At the end of January, Paul (who was still 'lead practitioner') put me in touch with the hospital social worker Liz, who was supposed to be finding accommodation for Stephen. On the phone she seemed kind, but nothing happened.

Waiting, waiting, waiting.

By the 10th February Stephen had been in hospital for over a month. Tomas and others had visited him and Tim and I came over. Stephen was delighted to see Tim, but distressed and desperate to get out of hospital. What must it be like to lie there day in, day out, at times turned, prodded, fed and cleaned with precious few distractions from the bile of the negative voices?

Waiting, waiting, waiting.

The sale of our flat became bumpy. Unexpected issues arose and the potential buyers were 'considering' them. In the midst of this I sat in meditation and allowed myself to be with the obsession over the situation and the money. What came up was that relationships matter more. Something eased.

Waiting, waiting.

On Tuesday 6th March, the exchange went through. I stood in the garden in sunshine, feeling a lightness. Stephen, however, was still in hospital, two months after being admitted. Eventually Liz the social worker got back to me. She'd been seconded somewhere else for two weeks, so nothing had been done. Just as Tomas had feared, Stephen's muscles had wasted, spending so much time in bed and now he was not walking at all.

Liz finally found a care home for Stephen, but it was an hour's drive from his home and out of area and he did not want to go there. She'd completed an assessment and concluded that Stephen did not have capacity which infuriated me, but she did recognise it would be better if he agreed to go, and asked me to persuade him.

On 11th March, I sat with Stephen in that hospital feeling shit. I told him that he was between a rock and a hard place. He'd been in hospital for more than two months now, and he was desperate to get out. I suggested that he agree to the home Liz suggested with the proviso that she acknowledged this as temporary and recorded his wish to be moved back nearer his home and the people who supported him, as soon as possible.

The move went ahead. On 14th March, Paul emailed us with

the cheery heading, 'Stephen moving on to pastures new'. He wrote, 'It is a nursing home with staff trained in mental health. This, I hope, will mean that he gets more understanding and patience with regard to how he communicates with others.'

After ten weeks in hospital, Stephen was finally transferred to Brook Care Home on 19th March 2018. That date was five weeks before our final church service, two weeks before Stephen's birthday and four days before we were due to complete on the sale of our flat and purchase of the house.

Waiting, waiting, waiting.

I spent the morning of Friday 23rd March pacing up and down, reading on-line horror stories of house sales that had fallen through at the last minute. At 11.45am the text came through, the sale was completed. Later we drank Prosecco in the garden of our new house and felt totally overwhelmed.

Waiting.

On 3rd April, Stephen's 63rd birthday, I rang him at the care home. I could hear people in the background shouting and wailing. Stephen begged me to get him out of there. He'd arrived with almost nothing; his DAB radio, his bag, his wallet, his cards and most of his clothes were all still back at the previous care home. Rose and Tomas weren't able to visit because of the distance, but finally after about a month, Julie managed the two-hour round trip to see him. She was not happy with the place and didn't feel anyone had made efforts to get Stephen more mobile.

The day after she visited, 17th April, Paul sent an email to tell us he was going to transfer Stephen's care over to the new health authority, permanently.

Tick.

This was a total betrayal of Stephen. He would be shifted out of area against his wishes, lose his home and be resident in an unsuitable home, miles away from his support network. Rage simply exploded in me. I still feel it now. I wanted to grab this man, Paul, dig my nails into his arms and demand that he did the fucking job he was supposed to do, to care properly for this vulnerable human being, not tick a fucking box.

Fifteen minutes later I replied: 'I object strongly to you passing Stephen out of area. I cannot think of anything worse than leaving Stephen where he is. He knows no-one there and there is no support for him outside the home.'

Julie also weighed in, 'Please send me the details of your senior to correspond with as unfortunately I feel you have lost sight of what would be best for Stephen.'

Paul had not visited or spoken with Stephen since he took him to the first care home in December. His view of this present care home relied entirely on its own PR.

Tick.

'Privileged White Woman' appeared again, truly white with rage, and rang the mental health care team, voice shaking. No, I did not want to speak with Paul, I wanted the senior manager. The receptionist promised that the team leader, Mr Weston, would ring back. Meanwhile I emailed him, attaching a four-page document outlining point by point, the serious failings of his care team and demanding that Stephen's wishes be listened to. Julie also contacted Mr Weston and Rose fully supported us. Paul had said there were no care home places near Stephen's home 'within the budget.' We wanted the budget reviewed.

Mr Weston rang me back on Thursday 19th April and within ten days Paul had visited the home and it had been agreed that Stephen would be brought back into area.

In my view, Paul was a good man, swallowed whole by what a psychiatrist friend of mine calls 'the piranhas' of the NHS; the management structure grafted forcibly from the business world onto a profession that was fundamentally about caring for people, not making profits or beating off competitors. Decent, compassionate individuals have ended up browbeaten by 'targets' and 'outcomes' and, unsurprisingly, lost sight of their true purpose.

Three days later, we left another institution that I believe has forgotten its fundamental purpose: the Church. By 'fundamental purpose', I mean showing unconditional love to those on the edges of society. Everything else is just rules for the membership of a club.

On Saturday 21st April I wrote:

> Tomorrow is the last
> day of the last life.
> Tomorrow closes a door
> that may never open
> and opens a door
> I hope will never shut.

On Sunday 22nd April, we had our last service in church. The church was full and it was a good leaving. The following week we moved out and on May 1st, we celebrated May Day in Oxford as the beginning of this new life.

On the same day, a door opened for Stephen. As a result of the complaints to Mr Weston, a new social worker, Ben, visited Stephen, assessed him and found that he did have mental capacity. Ben rang me on 2nd of May and it was the most wonderful relief to hear the news and also to speak with someone who agreed that autonomy was of fundamental importance to Stephen. Ben noted that some people do want institutional care, but this wasn't true for Stephen. It was particularly heartening to hear him say that social care was still a needs-driven service, not a budget-driven one and that there was still a possibility that Stephen could be given a place with a live-in carer and maybe, just maybe, if the flat could be adjusted, he could go back there. The first step was to move him to a care home that was back in area and we'd go from there.

Stephen was pleased to hear the news and especially that there was still a chance he could go home, but every day in the present home was nightmarish for him. I finally managed to visit him on the 13th May after he'd been there nearly two months.

### *Care Home Visit 13th May*

I stand in the small entrance lobby as tinny vile music plays. The posters are all telling me what a great place this is, but that doesn't extend to anyone coming to the door when I ring. To the right is a door marked 'Manager' but it's Sunday and the door is locked. Finally, after I've rung the bell three times, I see an assistant through the glass door and wave manically at her. She's in her twenties, with a friendly face, long hair and multiple-coloured extensions and she's pushing an elderly woman with wild white hair, in a wheelchair. She opens the door for me and then has to stop the elderly lady from escaping.

I'm led down corridors to another door which must be opened for me and into a very large room with windows down the right-hand side and people standing, sitting, slumping at various intervals. The air is stale with the smell of unwashed bodies in a warm room.

I see Stephen in his wheelchair and greet him, but he looks at me guardedly. I have to 'register' which means walking to the far end of the room, where there's an open-style office space occupied by a kind-faced man and a tired-looking woman. They don't smile, just take my details. I walk back the length of the room to where Stephen is parked and suggest we go out, which pleases him. Now I have to get permission from the staff, and then obtain suntan lotion. I return once again to Stephen and begin applying the suntan lotion. I become aware of residents gathering around, the atmosphere charged. Nobody says anything except Stephen, who gives me brief instructions: behind the ears, the back of the neck, the tops of the ears. I write later:

> Like famished ghosts
> They stand and watch
> As I cream each crevice
> And curve on Stephen's face
> And neck and arms.
> Vicariously they share this intimacy
> This tenderness,
> Their hunger palpable in the silence.

The intensity of this shakes me. I want to get out of there but when I ask the kind-faced man for help to get Stephen in the car, he looks surprised. Don't I know that he needs a hoist now? Stephen hasn't stood up on his own since he arrived.

He suggests I push Stephen to the beach, a ten-minute walk. I begin to wheel Stephen to the door before realising that I have to go back to the desk to ask if someone can let me out. This lack of any pro-active help from the staff is draining. The tired woman reluctantly gets to her feet and crosses the room, gently batting away the tall scrawny man standing jerkily by the door, like a race horse waiting for the gates to open.

We get out finally and it's breezy, so I put my blue hoodie on Stephen to keep him warm. As we head for the beach, my first feelings are of elation: cool May weather, blue skies, trees in their fresh leaves. Stephen has been encouraged by Ben's visit and keeps repeating that I must help him get back into his flat. Unfortunately, he's back on ordinary lit cigarettes, but I don't mention this. The view at the beach is peaceful and we get ice cream. Then the wind builds, Stephen's mood drops and we head back.

Stephen has been ranting about the staff, but as we approach the home, he hunches into himself. He doesn't want to give me back my hoodie so I let him keep it. Before I leave, I set up a radio in his room, so he can listen to Classic FM.

~

Throughout May and June, back in Oxford, I taught mindfulness, unpacked boxes, got used to the new home, rang Stephen and spent long stretches of time sitting in the garden watching frog life in our little pond. Just as we were finding freedom and new choices, Stephen was losing his at a pace. He had lived on his own, albeit with carers morning and evening, for nine years and now in this care home there was no privacy whatsoever, no self-agency and precious little respect. On the phone, he told me staff would pet his hair without asking, demand that he stop repeating himself, and 'When they change me, they take my pad off and very brutally make me stand up. I'm in terrible discomfort. They say, "We'll let you fall to the floor."'

This home claimed the following: 'Brook Home is also able to offer dedicated specialist care for those with nursing Mental Health/Dementia needs.'

Stephen found other residents intimidating: 'There's a man who threatens me, enormous great man.' In the middle of a phone call with me, he interrupts: 'A woman is standing over threatening me. She's being taken away by a member of staff.' He wasn't sleeping well, 'I'm terrified of this lady called June. She picks things up and you never know whether she's going to plonk them down on your head.'

I started to become more worried when he became delusional, this seemed to be a sure sign of extreme distress:

'I'm bringing action against staff and a member of "Not The Nine O'clock news." Wherever I go they say they know all about me. They continually use ESP.'

He told me repeatedly that he was going to be transferred to Rampton, the high security mental hospital in Northamptonshire.

On one of the phone calls Stephen told me about an abusive

incident and was insistent that I make a formal complaint to the management, so I did, naming the staff involved and copying in Paul:

***Email to Brook House Manager, 27 May***

'Stephen has asked me raise with you a serious incident which needs attention. He said two staff came to change him first thing in the morning and he urinated by mistake while they were in the middle of changing him. They became angry, told him he'd done it deliberately and slapped him. He was petrified. He wants this issue addressed.'

The manager replied in management-speak: 'I will respond to your concerns in line with our company policy and will write to you within 28 days with the findings of my investigation' (she never did). On the same day, she contacted Paul to issue an eviction notice on Stephen because of 'his increasing behavioural issues which place staff and other residents at risk of allegations.' When I challenged her, she denied point blank that there was any connection between Stephen's complaint and the subsequent notice of eviction. The notice of eviction was in fact a blessing, as it meant Paul now had to get his butt in gear and move Stephen. Paul also finally discovered that three bags of Stephen's belongings were still at his first care home.

*Visit 12ᵗʰ June*

On the 12ᵗʰ June I visit Stephen again. On the wall outside, in big, friendly letters is the vomit-inducing, '*They are not residents in our care home, we are carers supporting them in their home.*'

I've emailed the centre manager but have received no reply. I feel I should speak with her but when I find her, she's very sorry but she can't stop to talk, she's busy. I don't want to talk to her either.

This time Stephen is outside in the sun, sporting a mottled green sun hat and he gives me a warm smile. We return to the beach, the tide is out and the long spread of browns, blues and greys shimmers. There is a glorious strip of blue which I want to point out. Then I remember Stephen has cataracts.

We get ice creams and I hear about the care – or the absence of it.

'They keep me waiting, always saying "wait a minute, wait a minute"'.

'You never were very patient.'

'No. Karla said she has no time for self-pity and I should stop it. That was cruel.'

'I thought they were trained to care for people with mental illness.'

'Susie, they are over-worked, underpaid, and under-trained.'

We sit together in silence amidst the bare beauty of the shore and distant sea. When I tell him we need to leave now, he says quietly, 'Give me a minute.' Then earnestly, 'I will overcome, I will overcome, but I don't know how.'

I'm equally earnest back. 'You will overcome. You've got a lot of strength and stubbornness. I value how you've always stubbornly remained exactly who you are.'

He smiles, 'All these years, I kept my individuality.'

'Yes, you were bloody-minded!'

He laughs with pleasure but as we head off, his head sinks.

Outside the home, 'I don't want to go in.' I wait until he nods. Fortunately, when we do get in, a carer greets him warmly and tells him that a staff member he likes is on duty today. I kiss Stephen's forehead goodbye and then hunt out my blue hoodie before driving home.

~

Ten days later Paul finally found a care home close to Stephen's home town and took him to see it. This was not a day too soon as Stephen's phone calls in the intervening period were getting more and more fixated on Rampton, which in my view related to his need for safety.

'The Rampton staff are outside. They won't let them in. I'm frightened that something is going to happen to me tonight, similar to what happened to Princess Diana. They're going to say that I had a nasty accident and my life could be taken.'

'They've been telling my mother that she's a prostitute, under their breaths, the ESP I have. You don't really care, you're happy in Oxford.'

In another call he said, 'The Rampton staff are out there in the large digger. They're going to smash their way in.'

Fortunately, Stephen approved of the new home. He was going to be moved on 12th July and this time the manager had agreed that Julie would deliver some training on autism to the staff and in particular how best to support Stephen. Wow. It appears not all care homes are the same.

Thankfully, the move went ahead smoothly but it was yet

another change for Stephen. At first he worried that staff were intending to kill him by giving him an overdose with his weekly depot injection. Julie agreed to come over every Friday to ensure that he felt safe.

### New Care Home Visit – 26th July

Two weeks after his move, I visit with our dog Zozzi and Stephen's first words are, 'It's a terrible place.' We're sitting on a pleasant patio, evening sunshine bathing us and a staff member has just brought us some coffee. Zozzi rests quietly at our feet. After a few minutes, Stephen relaxes, 'It's not so bad here.' We ask the staff for a lighter for his cigarette, but they're too busy, so I take his cigarette to light it from my car lighter. This process is repeated every 20 minutes over the next two-and-a-half hours.

We sit together watching people come and go, occasionally chatting. Julie has been and they had 'a lovely time.' There's a lavender bush nearby and when I discover Stephen likes lavender, I break off a bit and put it under his nose.

Stephen is struggling with the voices in his head. I attempt to say something helpful, but he asks me to stop and we sit in silence for a long time, interrupted every 20 minutes by another cigarette lighting mission. He struggles with his voices while I struggle with boredom and irritation at having to repeatedly walk back and forth from the car.

The sunset does its work on us and finally I say, 'Thank you Stephen. It's good sitting here,' meaning, thank you for the space to sit in silence together, to watch the sky change colour, to be present, to be here. Stephen replies simply, 'Thank you for keeping me company.'

By 9.45pm, it's almost dark and a staff member comes to wheel Stephen back in. I send him everyone's love; he sends it back and I give him a last hug. Zozzi and I watch as the staff member reverses him back through the doors.

~

That was the last time I saw him alive.

# Chapter 20

Endings

On the 5th August, ten days after I visited Stephen, he caught a chest infection. The staff called a doctor but Stephen refused to be examined. Eventually the doctor was persuaded to prescribe some antibiotics and by Saturday 11th, Stephen was feeling a bit better and even told the manager of the home that he was enjoying the small fete the home had put on. On Sunday though, he was feeling groggy.

Tim and I had been away, off-grid, since 1st August and knew nothing of what had happened. We got back on the Saturday and on Sunday I knew I needed to ring Stephen but I didn't want to. I kept putting it off, feeling a mix of guilt and irritation. I finally sat with this and began to realise why; I'd been in a chilled holiday mood and now I'd have to listen to him telling me at length how miserable he was. As I recognised this, I felt compassion rise, both for myself and Stephen. Now I wanted to ring him.

It was just after 7pm on the Sunday evening. One of the staff answered and took the phone to Stephen but reported back that he was feeling too groggy to speak with me. I asked him to send Stephen my love and say that I'd ring in a couple of days. The staff member assured me he'd do this and I finished the call.

### Monday 13th August 2018

On the Monday an unrecognised number rings me at 8.30am and I don't answer it, I'm writing. At 11am Julie rings, asks me to sit down and speaks, her voice breaking, 'Stephen died yesterday. The care home tried to ring you this morning and I said I'd get in touch with you.'

I'm holding the mobile phone to my ear, looking through

the window at our long thin garden, the low brown buildings of the Warneford Mental hospital behind it and the huge beech trees that mark the border, filling the sky.

Julie is talking, she is telling me something. I remember some of it. They found Stephen dead this morning and I think he must have died in the night and thoughts swirl around me. I am unable to take this in. Julie is angry, angry that it came to this, angry at all the failings that led to this. I admit to a sense of relief and so does she. After the call, I go into Tim's study and we sit together, holding hands for a few minutes.

After that I start to make the necessary phone calls. I begin by ringing the office where Stephen's brother works. He comes on the phone and this is the first time I've ever spoken to him. It's awkward and it feels like he doesn't know how to respond; after all I'm a stranger to him. He says that of course Stephen was ill and I say yes but it was very sudden. I tell him that I'm sorry for his loss and sorry to have to tell him. I have no idea what is going on in his mind. Before ending the call, he gives me a personal email to keep him in the loop.

Now I ring the care home and discover from the manager, Claire, that Stephen died on Sunday evening. They checked on him at 8.30pm (an hour and a half after I called) and he was ok and then they came back to check on him around 8.50pm and he was dead. She tells me he didn't suffer but all I can think is, 'How do you know?' Twenty minutes is a long time if you're struggling for breath.

I ring Rose. She is shocked but she has a house full of kids. She will help in whatever way she can.

I ring Tomas and leave a message.

~

Two days later, on the Wednesday the post mortem took place and the coroner rang me. As the executor of Stephen's will I was down as the person sorting out his death and funeral. Rose was happy for me to deal with this.

The coroner was not how I imagined a coroner to be: formal, cold, bureaucratic, male. Instead she was warm and kind. She told me that he had died of ischaemic heart disease compounded by a chest infection. She told me that he would not have suffered, it would have been as if the lights went out. This comforted me enormously.

Later that day I went swimming and sat in the cubicle afterwards and cried. A day or so later I wrote:

> 'I feel odd crying. I'm sad – they talk about waves of sadness but it feels more like weights of sadness descending on my chest, squeezing the chest cavity.
>
> I want to talk to Stephen.
>
> I asked Jesus, God, source of life to send me a dream to let me know that Stephen is okay and of course I didn't dream that dream. I want to speak to Stephen to know that he's ok and I can't. To say I'm sorry for so much hardness and lack of understanding. I'm sorry.
>
> Stephen is dead and I can't show him the copy of the book that I will publish about his life.
>
> There is a heavy suffocating cushion pressing into my chest.'

Days passed and things got sorted. It was exhausting

continually telling people that Stephen was dead,

Stephen is dead,

Stephen is dead.

The Water Board had sent Stephen a final warning so I rang them. My voice cracked as I told the man on the phone, yet again that Stephen was dead. He was kind: 'You need to go and get a cup of tea love, before you ring anyone else.'

I rang Stephen's brother again in case he wanted to say anything at the funeral. He agreed to read a poem and also remarked that Stephen was one of the first 'eco-warriors.' I liked that.

Tim and I drove the two hours to register his death and see the funeral directors. I took a bag to deliver to the funeral directors with a suit that I'd bought for Stephen. We met up with Rose and Julie at the funeral parlour, and agreed between the four of us how best to remember Stephen. Stephen had left enough money to pay for his funeral so there were no financial worries. Together we chose a bamboo coffin and a natural flower arrangement. Julie came up with some French music and I promised to bring a couple of Stephen's poems which we would read. It was a warm and precious meeting. After that visit I wrote:

'In our love, however little, we create a web
that breaks a person's fall.'

At some point along these days, it had finally dawned on me that I loved Stephen. It feels strange writing it down even now. Not a romantic love but a something else love. A fierce, loyal, angry love. The sort of love you have for family.

### *The day of the Funeral*

The day of the funeral arrives. Tim and I are the only ones who want to see Stephen's body, so we drive down early. We arrive, park and go into the funeral parlour. It's a pleasant room, with gentle wallpaper, careful lighting and a white curtain at the end. Stephen rests in the middle, in his bamboo coffin. We're silent and respectful and I go to look at him first. It both does and doesn't look like Stephen, but I'm glad to see his body – it feels important. I can see the top half of him and the jacket I bought. The bottom half of him is wrapped in white material. There's something there under the jacket. I look closer and then, out loud, 'That's where it is – that's my blue hoodie!' I'd been looking all over for it. It's the same blue zip-up hoodie I'd lent Stephen when we'd walked to the beach back in May. I know I'd got it back, so how did it end up here, on Stephen's body? Then it dawns on me that I left it in the bag with the suit when I was out shopping. The funeral directors must have assumed this was also for Stephen.

Tim laughs and says it would be wrong for Stephen to be dressed just in a suit. I feel a warmth and gladness that he's taking something of mine with him.

Stephen stipulated that he wanted to be buried as close to Mandy as possible and I've found a place for him in the same cemetery. The funeral is due to take place in the cemetery chapel. No-one wanted a religious ceremony and Rose and Julie are pleased that Tim has agreed to lead the proceedings.

It's a beautiful sunny day. Stephen's brother and his nephew are there, Stephen's step-daughter and her family, his stepson, Julie and Bill from the autism society, Judith his ex-care coordinator and various carers and staff. And there, stepping out of the Citroen C1, are my three children come to honour him. I want to cry.

The hearse arrives and as the staff are manoeuvring the coffin out, I turn to see a man on a bicycle weaving his way towards us with several enormous sunflowers sticking out of his front basket. It's Tomas.

We all enter the chapel and take our places. Stephen's fairy godmother, Carol, is leaning against the altar, her eyes crinkled up in a smile. She waves. His wife and wild woman, Mandy sits in the pew behind her children and wraps her arms around them, weeping. Charlie, his guardian angel barks from the door. They've come to take him home.

When it's my turn to give the eulogy, I stand at the lectern looking out at this precious array of people. I finish by saying:

'When he was low Stephen would say to me, "There is always hope, isn't there? There is always hope" and I would say, "Yes, Stephen there is always hope." *Au revoir* Stephen. May you rest in peace.'

Stephen, we did sing "The King of Love my Shepherd is."

And Stephen,

We will not forget you.

# Epilogue

*October 2020*

It is now over two years since Stephen died. After his death I couldn't write anything for six months. Then in December 2019, I was truly stunned to win the Impress Prize for new writers and that pushed me on to finally finish the draft on his death day 12th August 2020.

After Stephen died, I had to sort out his will and organise a headstone for the grave. The money in his account paid for all the expenses and left a small legacy for his step-daughter and son. He also gave money to the Red Cross and PDSA. I cried the day that Rose rang me and gifted me money from the legacy she'd received.

When I began writing this book, I had no idea.

No idea it would take this long.

No idea what would happen.

No idea how much Stephen would come to mean to me nor how much he would teach me.

He taught me about being with brokenness and darkness, he taught me about being real and honest, he taught me about friendship and faithfulness, he taught me how to be human.

Perhaps most of all...

He said his life was a waste of time but he lived it as if every particle of it mattered.

## With Gratitude and Thanks

My first thanks go to Stephen who trusted me with his story.

I will always be grateful to Kate Clanchy who mentored me and without whose encouragement, I would have given up.

Thanks to the Arvon Foundation and to Alexander Masters and Pauline Black for the writing week in which I wrote the first Chapter.

I am deeply indebted to Impress Books for awarding me the Impress Prize for 2019. Also to Jeff Collyer, the publisher whose patience and quiet skill has supported me throughout the publishing process.

Thank you to the many others who have also accompanied me:

Rachel Lawston for your friendly, collaborative approach to the book cover and for the gorgeous colours and textures that emerged.

e.k.mosley, for your wonderful illustrations and for the philosophical zoom conversations which accompanied our discussions.

Matthew Baylis whose rigorous copy edit helped give the text much greater clarity. Also thank you for your exclamations (ha!), additional comments and vital praise.

Abbie Joyce and Ella Wilson for helping with marketing, Caroline Guillet for typesetting and others who helped birth this book.

Finally, I want to thank Tim who has spent years repeatedly telling me I'm a writer, sometimes with love and sometimes with irritated frustration. He read the first full draft, inspired me to greater creativity and regularly appeared with tea, tears in his eyes, reminding me this book was very, very, good.

# References

## Chapter 1

P.12: First recorded in 1838 in A. E. Bray's *Traditions of Devonshire – Wikipedia*

P.16: Bonnie Evans – The Foundations of Autism: The Law Concerning Psychotic, Schizophrenic, and Autistic Children in 1950s and 1960s Britain, http://www.ncbi.nlm.nih.gov/pmc/articles/PMC4196690/

P.17: ibid

P.20: The Bible – Luke Chapter 10 verses 25-37

P.24: Joanne Greenberg – book: 1964, film: 1977, 'I never promised you a rose garden' by (pen name: Hannah Green)

## Chapter 2

P.32: Alastair G. Cardno and Michael J. Owen, Genetic Relationships Between Schizophrenia, Bipolar Disorder, and Schizoaffective Disorder https://www.ncbi.nlm.nih.gov/pmc/articles/PMC3984527 published 24.2.2014 – accessed December 2020

P.36: https://www.nhs.uk/conditions/autism/signs/children/ – accessed December 2020

P.36: https://www.autism.org.uk/about/what-is.aspx – accessed December 2020

P.36: Deborah Hyde article in the Guardian, 6th March 2018

P.38: 1955 Underwood Report Chapter IV part 117 taken from http://www.educationengland.org.uk/documents/underwood/

index.html

P.39: https://en.wikipedia.org/wiki/Refrigerator_mother_theory – accessed December 2020

P.39: Underwood Report Chapter IV part 119 – taken from http://www.educationengland.org.uk/documents/underwood/index.html

P.39: https://en.wikipedia.org/wiki/Benjamin_Spock – accessed December 2020

P.40: https://www.autism.org.uk/advice-and-guidance/what-is-autism/the-causes-of-autism – accessed December 2020

## Chapter 3

P.60: Bonnie Evans - Foundations of Autism, http://www.ncbi.nlm.nih.gov/pmc/articles/PMC4196690/ – accessed December 2020

P.65: https://www.psychologytoday.com/blog/evolution-the-self/201307/why-we-all-need-fairy-godmother – posted 24th July 2013

## Chapter 4

P.77: https://en.wikipedia.org/wiki/Mainline_steam_trains_in_Great_Britain – accessed December 2020

P.81: Hansard, William Compton Carr, 18 May 1960 – taken from Bonnie Evans, The Metamorphosis of Autism: A History of Child Development in Britain, https://www.ncbi.nlm.nih.gov/books/NBK436840/

P.81: NA/ED50/969: Special Education Sub-committee Report, 28 January 1963, p. 1. Taken from Bonnie Evans, https://www.ncbi.nlm.nih.gov/books/NBK436840/

P.82: http://www.legislation.gov.uk/ukpga/1970/44/enacted -

point 26

P.83: https://iancommunity.org/cs/autism/dsm_iv_criteria – accessed December 2020

P.83: https://www.autism.org.uk/advice-and-guidance/what-is-autism/asperger-syndrome – accessed August 2020

P.89: https://www.autism.org.uk/advice-and-guidance/what-is-autism – accessed December   2020

## Chapter 5

P.101: Enoch Powell quote from Water Tower Speech – http://studymore.org.uk/xpowell.htm

P.101: ibid

P.102: https://www.bmj.com/content/bmj/337/bmj.a1837.full.pdf – page 2

## Chapter 6

P.108: Anthony Clare 'Psychiatry in Dissent' (1976) – page 389

P.109: https://www.medicines.org.uk/emc/files/pil.4558.pdf

P.119: Anthony Clare, Psychiatry in Dissent (1976) – page 391

## Chapter 7

P.128: https://citeseerx.ist.psu.edu/viewdocdownload?doi=10.1.1.366.882&rep=rep1&type=pdf – page 2

P.135: https://farleigh-court.co.uk/history.php

P.136: http://editorial.health.org.uk/theme/national-scandals-regarding-care-mental-handicap-hospitals

P.140: 2006 'The reliability of diagnosis revisited' https://www.ncbi.nlm.nih.gov/pmc/articles/PMC2990547

P.140: Rosenhan, 'On being sane in insane places.' Originally

published in *Science*, New Series, Vol. 179, No. 4070.
(Jan. 19, 1973), pp. 250-258. https://www.oulu.fi/sites/
default/files/content/AOH%20Terveen%C3%A4%20
ep%C3%A4terveiss%C3%A4%20paikoissa.pdf – page 12,
accessed December 2020

## Chapter 8

P.163: 1983 Mental Health Act – Part VIII section 117 (1) 'It
shall be the duty of the District Health Authority and of the local
social services authority to provide, in co-operation with relevant
voluntary agencies, after-care services

P.163: The History of Mental Health Services in Modern
England: Practitioner Memories and the Direction of Future
Research https://www.ncbi.nlm.nih.gov/pmc/articles/
PMC4595954/#fnr62

P.164: (2015, July 22nd). *Case study 1: Deinstitutionalisation in
UK mental health services.* Retrieved December 2020, from
https://www.kingsfund.org.uk: https://www.kingsfund.org.uk/
publications/making-change-possible/mental-health-services

P.165: https://www.kingsfund.org.uk/sites/default/files/field/
field_publication_file/independent-audit-nhs-under-labour-
1997%E2%80%932005-sunday-times-march-2005.pdf – page
54

## Chapter 9

P.182: https://www.mind.org.uk/media-a/4380/report-for-
frontline-staff.pdf

P.185: *Wikipedia*

P.186: https://www.kingsfund.org.uk/sites/default/files/
puremadness.pdf

P.186: Ibid

Chapter 10

P.195: Section 3, part 1 of the Public Order Act 1986

P.201: https://openaccess.city.ac.uk/id/eprint/7236/

P.201: https://www.kcl.ac.uk/ioppn/depts/hspr/archive/mhn/projects/lockedfinal.pdf

P.201: https://www.nursingtimes.net/archive/self-harm-and-violence-towards-nursing-staff-more-likely-in-locked-up-mental-health-patients-08-12-2008/

P.202: https://www.ncbi.nlm.nih.gov/pmc/articles/PMC4595954/#fnr62

P.202: https://www.ncbi.nlm.nih.gov/pmc/articles/PMC4599636/

Chapter 13

P.250: Isobel Allende in Zinsser, William, editor. *Paths of Resistance the Art and Craft of the Political Novel*. Boston: Houghton Mifflin, 1989 – Pages 41-45

P.252: Jon Kabat-Zinn phrase

Chapter 14

P.290: https://assets.publishing.service.gov.uk/government/uploads/system/uploads/attachment_data/file/435512/MHA_Code_of_Practice.PDF p22 – 5 guiding principles:

1.  Least restrictive option and maximise independence
2.  Empowerment & Involvement. Patients should be involved in decisions about their care and the views of families, carers and others, if appropriate, should be fully considered when taking decisions. Where decisions are taken which are

contradictory to views expressed, professionals should explain the reasons for this.

3.  Respect & dignity – for patients, families, carers and friends
4.  Purpose and Effectiveness
5.  Making fair and efficient decisions

P.294: https://www.scholastic.com/teachers/videos/teaching-content/philip-pullman-interview-pullman-his-inspiration-daemons-his-dark-materials-series/

## Chapter 17

P.341: https://www.theguardian.com/uk-news/2018/oct/05/scottish-gps-nhs-begin-prescribing-rambling-birdwatching

P.341: https://www.mind.org.uk/media-a/2931/nature-and-mental-health-2018.pdf

P.342: https://www.ncbi.nlm.nih.gov/pmc/articles/PMC3372556/

P.347: https://www.kingsfund.org.uk/publications/funding-staffing-mental-health-providers – impact on staff

P.354: The Bible – Acts Chapter 1 verses 6 to 9

## Chapter 18

P.357: https://www.scie.org.uk/mca/introduction/mental-capacity-act-2005-at-a-glance

## Chapter 19

P.381: https://www.laterlifetraining.co.uk/wp-content/uploads/2011/07/Falls-and-fractures-guidance-care-homes-interactive-V3.pdf – page 2

P.400: BBC 2 comedy show that ran from 1979 to 1982

# About the author

Susie is an award-winning writer with an MA in Dramatic Writing. She has been writing and creating drama in community settings since 2000. She wrote her first drama sketch in the same year she met Stephen.

*Stephen from the Inside Out* is her first published book and it won the 2019 Impress prize for new writers. Both in writing and in life, Susie finds herself drawn to the very different landscapes that people inhabit and their felt reality of life within community and society. She has spent time working and volunteering amongst and alongside people with various and often wildly different backgrounds to her own. Many of these have challenged her beliefs and attitudes (sometimes very painfully) and enriched her life immeasurably. Stephen was one of those who did that for her. In spades.

At the present moment, Susie lives in East Oxford in a small intentional community of three humans and two dogs. She can be contacted through her website www.susiestead.com and is interested in engaging with groups who would like to read and discuss the issues raised in this book.

Photograph taken by Mel Cunningham – https://www.vivaciousmelphotography.com/